Ireland [1913]

By **Richard Arnold Bermann**

Ireland [1913]

By **Richard Arnold Bermann**

TRANSLATED AND EDITED BY

Leesa Wheatley and Florian Krobb

CORK **cup** UNIVERSITY PRESS

First published in 2021 by
Cork University Press
Boole Library
University College Cork
Cork
T12 ND89
Ireland

Library of Congress Control Number: 2020945084
Distribution in the USA: Longleaf Services, Chapel Hill, NC, USA

British Library Cataloguing in Publication Data
A CIP record for this book is available from the British Library.

ISBN: 978-1-78205-435-1

Printed by BZ Graf in Poland.
Print origination & design by Carrigboy Typesetting Services
www.carrigboy.com

COVER IMAGES – Esplanade, Bray, County Wicklow, Eason Photographic Collection,
Reproduction rights owned by National Library of Ireland.

www.corkuniversitypress.com

Contents

Introduction

In 1913, Ireland was anything but a random, idyllic or escapist destination for European travellers. In the German collective perception, it had not yet achieved the status of quaint and unadulterated backwardness that would dominate its image for decades after Heinrich Böll published his *Irisches Tagebuch* [Irish Journal] in 1957 and, to this day, to some extent still determines German tourists' expectations. In 1913, a uniquely Irish situation, including poverty and social deprivation, Catholicism and folklore, were not yet seen as symptoms of self-sufficiency and a quaint identity that had withstood the forces of modernisation and consumerism, but as symptoms of exposure to the dominance of its powerful master and next-door neighbour, as the nearest site of Britain's global reach. Ireland was a political destination, the backyard of the world's greatest power and global cultural force. It was also a troubled, unruly political entity, and in spite of some degree of interest and also of romantic projection, it was home to a population that had remained quite alien to the public of continental Europe.

This very perspective dominates Richard Arnold Bermann's report of his visit in the summer of 1913. As his day job, Bermann wrote for one of Berlin's leading dailies, and indeed a good proportion of the material that eventually went into his book first appeared as a series of seven articles in the *Vossische Zeitung* between 14 July and 16 August 1913 under the pseudonym of 'Merlin'. He had to feed the German reading public topical fare as, in his own assessment, newspaper readers had developed a keen interest in Ireland because of a possible outbreak of hostilities that could ignite the whole continent. The German public wondered if conditions in Ireland might have any impact on the United Kingdom's preparedness to go to war in Europe.

Bermann was skilled in presenting his observations in a light-hearted, sometimes playfully self-deprecating, perceptive and variegated way. In this respect, his writing shows the hallmarks of literary journalism as had become a popular genre during the nineteenth century (Bermann counted Heinrich Heine and Peter Altenberg among his chief influences). His approach is guided by general interest and personal preference; he is not a specialised traveller with, for example, expertise in early Christian monastic culture or Celtic lore. He intersperses his itinerary with historical excursions, essays on literature, ballads, fairy tales, interviews, anecdotes, extracts from standard tourist guidebooks such as the Baedeker he had in his luggage (probably the 4th edition *Grossbritannien: England (ausser London), Wales, Schottland und Irland*, 1906 [Great Britain: England (excluding London), Wales, Scotland and Ireland]) and *Black's Guide to Ireland* (8th edn, 1912). He foregrounds his own narrative voice and creates a distinct persona – that of *flâneur*, cynic, astute political commentator; and he does not hide his literary ambitions when revelling in wordplay and embellishment. In this vein, he attempts to offer an alternative to the information and opinion available in standard sources such as tourist guides and history books – often with a view to correct, expand, contextualise and complement the circulating knowledge with personal experience about Ireland. His devices are often sarcastic and polemic; he is not afraid to exaggerate or to condense complex issues into telling sketches and anecdotes. In a review for the liberal German magazine *März*, Hermann Hesse emphasised the 'Unsentimentalität' [sobriety] of Bermann's approach to mapping what Ernst Weiss, in another review, called 'ein Stück Weltgeschichte' [a piece of world history] (cf. *Bermann alias Höllriegel: Österreicher – Demokrat – Weltbürger*, pp. 29–32 and notes on p. 62).

The context, however, that lent poignancy to the casual appearance of this book has a very serious dimension. The contradictions of Ireland's position inside the British Empire, and in her reaction to the prevailing conditions, interested newspaper readers in the German capital – not least because events there had immense repercussions for the rivalry between the two great powers, the continental and the maritime one, at the height of imperial muscle-flexing. In 1913, as the imperialist conflict between the European alliances reached its pinnacle, the 'Irish question' acquired an unprecedented pertinence and urgency. This is what draws the journalist to Ireland: the desire to understand one piece of the puzzle that is globality in an age of empire, to inspect the backyard of the leading imperial power. While he acknowledges British cultural pre-eminence and relishes poking fun at British cultural idiosyncrasies ('spleens'), he refrains from peddling in cheap polemics against the rival for dominance on the world and European stages, as so many other German commentators did at this time, using every opportunity to revile the inimical cousins (an example is German colonial icon Carl Peters' pamphlet *England und die Engländer*, 2nd edn, 1913). Instead, at every stage of the itinerary he employs a strategy of measuring the present against an accumulated, latent reservoir of cultural knowledge about Ireland, consisting of more or less stereotypical elements such as Catholicism, a Celtic heritage, a history of saints and scholars, a body of unique legends and mythologies, the unruliness of the population combined with mysticism, placidity and some drunken melancholy. The expectation, though, of finding something genuine, unspoilt, elementary, remains tangible throughout the narrative, and is generally disappointed. Often Bermann struggles to reconcile his contradictory perceptions and to accept the signs of modernisation and commodification of Ireland as a destination. His particular umbrage is aimed at the traces of mass tourism prone to erode the serenity of the autochthonous culture where it might still survive, and the blatant exploitation of visitors by entrepreneurial yet intrusive individuals who offer their services as guides or coach drivers. In hindsight, this sketch of Ireland in the summer of 1913 gains significance because it was the last comprehensive one of its kind before the outbreak of the First World War and the last before Ireland's process of gaining autonomy as a Free State culminated in the Anglo-Irish Agreement of December 1921.

For Richard Arnold Bermann, his Irish journey was the first of a string of trips which, over the best part of the next three decades, led him to all four corners of the world and made him into the furthest travelled of the leading journalists of German-speaking central Europe. Indeed, Bermann's big topic, his life's work, was devoted to reporting global scenarios, capturing a globalising culture, and chronicling seminal cultural revolutions throughout the world – a project clearly indebted to his experience of momentous changes not only as regards the First World War, but also as regards technological advances with their impact on lifestyles and every individual's orientation in a world in perpetual transformation. His overriding concern as a travelling journalist was the homogenisation of culture under the auspices of globalisation – and the frictions that this trend generated. His short book on Ireland is imbued with the striking dichotomy between the particular and the global, the distinct and the uniform – and how their interplay produces culture and forges history.

RICHARD ARNOLD BERMANN: TRAVELLING JOURNALIST

For three decades, Richard Arnold Bermann (1883–1939) was one of the leading journalistic writers in German-speaking central Europe, a driven traveller, an icon and chronicler of modernity's fragility and ambivalence. Born in Vienna when his father, an insurance clerk, was stationed there, his family soon moved back to Prague where he received his early education, then back to Vienna where he finished grammar school, then back to Prague where he attended university, and again to Vienna where he graduated with a doctorate in Romance literature in 1906. Bermann subsequently worked for a while in Milan as a tutor before relocating to Berlin to pursue a career in journalism. Some years later, he had established himself as a journalist. Originally mostly writing for the *Berliner Tageblatt*, he soon became known under his pen name Arnold Höllriegel (literally: the latch of / before Hell). Later in his career, he also contributed to some of the leading papers in German-speaking Europe, notably the *Frankfurter Zeitung*, *Prager Tagblatt*, *Vossische Zeitung*, various Viennese papers such as *Der Tag / Der neue Tag*, *Der Friede*, *Die Zeit* and *Die Stunde*, as well as many others. He also started to publish novels and book-size travel reports, most of them based on his extensive tours to the most far-flung destinations.

The trip to Ireland in the summer of 1913 was his first longer journey, the beginning of his frenetic, restless, almost driven travels all around the world. In the twenty-five years before he left Europe for good in 1938, he had visited Palestine, the Middle East and India, Asia and, on a separate trip, the Pacific region, Brazil and the Amazon basin twice, as well as northern and western Africa several times; he had circumnavigated the world and traversed the North American continent from one coast to the other at least twice. In some years he crossed the Atlantic Ocean several times to visit the United States and Canada. All of this was interspersed with journeys within Europe, from the trips he undertook as an accredited war correspondent (member of the 'Kriegspressequartier') to all the regions where Austrian army contingents were engaged, as reporter from the peace negotiations at Saint-Germain, to frequent regular visits to many European capitals, including London. Again, he often visited London several times a year – once simply to attend the European premiere of his friend Charlie Chaplin's film *City Lights* (28 January 1931).

As his Jewish ancestry prevented German editors from employing him after 1933, he relocated to Vienna, or rather, he used Vienna as a base for his continuing adventures. From 1934, Bermann was one of the driving forces behind the American Guild for German Cultural Freedom and the associated German Academy of Arts and Sciences in Exile, for which Sigmund Freud and Thomas Mann served as honorary presidents (until the latter's falling out with the organisation's managing director, Prince Hubertus zu Löwenstein, in 1939). Bermann's connections in the USA assisted fundraising efforts there; he himself headed the Viennese branch of the organisation. In March 1938, shortly after the German annexation of Austria, he had to leave Vienna via Prague and London for the United States, where he arrived in August of that year. He died in September 1939 from a heart attack in Saratoga Springs where he stayed at the artists' colony Yaddo. He had checked himself into this facility ostensibly to recuperate from the strains of his recent endeavours. At the time of death, however, he was frenetically penning his autobiography – which remained uncompleted and was only published in 1998 (*Die Fahrt auf dem Katarakt*).

The most notable aspects of his work concern the new medium of film, Hollywood and popular visual culture. Another focus concerned European engagement in, impact on and relationship with the overseas, both the Americas and the African and Asian global south. Some intriguing film treatments labelled as 'Kinodramen' (never realised and probably created to be read rather than filmed) published in German Expressionist Kurt Pinthus' famous *Kinobuch* (1914), various so-called film novels (i.e. narratives that experiment with filmic methods of story-telling and/or use film, the artistic implications of virtual reality, Hollywood customs and aspects of the industry's specific culture as their subject matter) and several reportage books on the centres and protagonists of the American film industry are testimony to this specifically modern interest in the rising art form of the early twentieth century. One overriding trope here forms the encroachment of fiction into reality, the successive indistinguishability between art and life.

On his travels, he sharply excoriates the globalisation of modern culture, the Europeanisation of the world. In this context he comments on the uniformity of passengers on board cruise ships and visitors in hotel lobbies who embody a global colonial culture that largely adheres to English fashions; he notices the ease of motoring across landscapes that, less than a generation ago, had been largely impenetrable, such as the Nubian Desert and the Canadian Rockies. He associates these trends with his own longing for excitement, for genuine stimulation from the culturally different, for unique and existential experience – as only to be found in the remotest locations. While always maintaining a highly critical and often self-deprecating attitude, as visitor and as reporter he is not immune to the attractions of exoticism, and he occasionally falls into the quintessential exoticist trap of being instrumental in and witness to the disappearance of what is so attractive: the culturally different, the enticing and the intriguing. Without laying claim to being an explorer or professional adventurer himself – he was in fact a rather unfit man – he nonetheless attempted to reach the outer edges of civilisation ('den äussersten Rand der Zivilisation', as he wrote to actress Elisabeth Berger from the Egyptian oasis Kharga on 19 March 1933) so as to investigate the very nature of modern civilisation from this vantage point. His participation in an excursion to find the legendary oasis of Zarzura epitomises the ambivalence of his endeavours: hailed as the penetration of one of the very last white spots on the map of Africa, the project, and his participation in it, was only made possible by the very exemplification of technological progress: the motor car capable of traversing the desert, and aviation for aerial detection of hidden landscapes. The involvement of British adventurers H.G. Penderell and Sir Robert and Lady Clayton in this venture contributed to Bermann's popularity in the English-speaking world. More recently, this trip has been remembered because its initiator and guiding spirit, Bermann's friend the Hungarian adventurer Count László Almásy, was the model for the protagonist in the book and film *The English Patient*.

However, the only one of his books to have been translated into English during his lifetime was his literary biography of the Sudanese prophet Muhammad Achmad, who gained notoriety throughout Europe for crushing Egyptian dominion over the Sudan, defeating several British generals in Egyptian service and establishing an Islamic caliphate that existed for fifteen years. Entitled in German *Die Derwischtrommel* [The Dervish Drum], after the instrument that provided the intoxicating rhythm to the anti-colonial movement's military advance and to the dervishes' monotonous religious recitations, it appeared in English translation with additional illustrations only a few months later as *The Mahdi of Allah* (1932). No less than Winston Churchill, who had served as a young lieutenant in General H.H. Kitchener's army that defeated the Mahdist regime in 1898 and had written about it in *The River War* (1899), contributed a foreword – which, ironically, completely contradicts the tendency of Bermann's work. Not avoiding exoticist undertones in his mourning of the loss of genuine Africanness on the altar of global British coloniality, the Austrian nonetheless attempts to generate sympathy for the African leader and his mission by clearly identifying the social and cultural conditions that gave rise to his movement. In his 'Preface', the British politician in contrast – who by then had held the offices of under-secretary of state for the colonies, head of the Royal Navy, and other posts at the helm of Britain's imperial administration – vehemently defends colonial mastery as fulfilling an inevitable historical destiny.

VISITING IRELAND

In the eighteenth and nineteenth centuries, Ireland was an intriguing destination for European travellers. Their reports forged an image of Ireland among interested circles in German-speaking Europe against which Bermann's account reveals its originality. Two mutually enabling tendencies guided the attention of these visitors. There was, on the one hand, the search for an original, distinct cultural substrate associated with the Celtic and with an early Christian culture that left its impact all over Europe (Julius Rodenberg: *Die Insel der Heiligen: Eine Pilgerfahrt durch Irlands Städte, Dörfer und Ruinen* [The Saintly Island: A pilgrimage through Ireland's cities, villages and ruins; 1860]). On the other hand, there were the political and social upheavals experienced by the island which resonated with German audiences (Bernhard Lesker: *Irlands Leiden und Kämpfe: Mit Berücksichtigung der irischen Landfrage* [Ireland's Struggles and Suffering: With a treatment of the land question; 1881]). In general, German observers struggled to fit Ireland into their systematics of the European cultural, political, social and historical landscape; their assessments often veered uncomfortably between identifying similarity and difference. The exceptionality of Ireland with regard to a history of glory and shame, a culture of myth and mourning, a heritage of ruins and riches, and an ethnicity and language dating back to pre-Roman times, though, became a common trope.

The search for an elusive Celtic culture on the edges of Europe, and more specifically on the fringes of the United Kingdom of Great Britain and Ireland as it became known after the Acts of Union in 1800, received its initial impetus from James Macpherson's publication of epic poems of a fictitious Gaelic bard, Ossian, in the 1760s. The poems were enthusiastically received all across Europe and exerted a great cultural influence on literary movements such as the Storm and Stress and the Romantics in Germany. Ireland was subsequently sought out as the home of an unspoiled cultural substrate that manifested itself in myths and epics, in a rich folklore of heroes and fairy characters. This is particularly evident from the 1820s onwards when Wilhelm and Jakob Grimm's volume *Irische Elfenmärchen* (1826), the translation of Thomas Crofton Croker's collection *Fairy Legends and Traditions of the South of Ireland*, popularised Irish folk culture. Thereafter followed numerous collections of Irish fairy tales and legends in German translation, such as O.L.B. Wolff's *Mythologie der Feen und Elfen: Vom Ursprunge dieses Glaubens bis auf die neusten Zeiten* [Mythologies of Elves and Fairies: From the origins to recent times; 1828], based on Thomas Keightley's *The Fairy Mythology*, and Karl von Killinger's *Erin: Auswahl vorzüglicher irischer Erzählungen* [A Selection of Splendid Irish Tales; 1847]. Thomas Moore's *Irish Melodies* were initially translated into German by Karl von Killinger in *Kleine Gedichte von Byron und Moore* [The Shorter Poems of Byron and Moore; 1829], and were followed by many subsequent translations (1839, 1841, 1870, 1874 and 1875). Moore wrote English lyrics to a number of traditional Irish airs and had a musical collaborator adapt the melodies. Moore's *Melodies* were immensely well received in the German-speaking world. The popularity of such works was rooted in the search for a Celtic cultural mystique and unique literary imagination which was assumed to be alive in Ireland at a time when, in much of Europe, the forces of modernisation, reason and expediency had eradicated the colourful irrationality of ancient pasts.

As anthropological disciplines gained importance, including the study of prehistory and ethnography to explain mankind's origins and diversification, contemporary Irish culture was studied as a living remnant of an ancient Celtic culture and ethnicity. This led to the foundation of Celtic Studies as an academic discipline in Germany by figures such as Franz Bopp (*Über die keltischen Sprachen* [On Celtic Languages; 1839]) and Johann Kaspar Zeuß (*Grammatica Celtica*; 1853), and is reflected in travel accounts from the second half of the nineteenth and early twentieth century (e.g. Hermann Osthoff's *Bilder aus Irland* [Images from Ireland; 1907]). Visitors to Ireland perceived a unique Irish *Volksgeist* and they framed their impressions of the Irish people in terms of the systematics and taxonomies of the emerging discourse on *Völkerpsychologie*. Racialist radicalisations of such thought attributed the alleged, for many, apparent backwardness of present-day Irish culture, manifest in the squalor of living conditions, alcoholism, inertia and political dependency, to the ethnic composition of the majority of the population. This is particularly evident from the middle of the nineteenth century, when authors such as Knut Jungbohn Clement (*Reisen in Irland oder Irland in historischer, statistischer, politischer und socialer Beziehung* [Travels in Ireland or Ireland in relation to historical, statistical, political and social circumstances; 1845]), Johann Georg Kohl (*Reisen in Irland* [Travels in Ireland; 1843]; *Land und Leute der britischen Inseln: Beiträge zur Charakteristik Englands und der Engländer* [The Countries and the People of the British Isles: Articles on the characteristics of England and the English; 1844]), and Arnold von Lasaulx (*Aus Irland: Reiseskizzen und Studien* [Travel Sketches and Studies from Ireland; 1877]) increasingly apply racial criteria in their accounts, including commentary on physiognomics and phrenology.

When more current Irish political phenomena were noted, German commentators lauded movements from Daniel O'Connell's Repeal Association to the Irish Republican Brotherhood, Home Rule and Land Leagues, among others, as emancipatory forces, manifestations of universal struggles for self-determination. The role of Catholicism, oppressed throughout the eighteenth century and thereby becoming the symbol of denied human rights, and during the nineteenth century then increasingly the dominant cultural force and distinguishing feature from the English-Protestant ruling elite, was enmeshed in this ambivalent evaluation of Irish realities, its status equally contested as either a force for autonomy or a source of socio-cultural backwardness.

A second motivation for visiting Ireland was, consequently, the unique and often radical social, political and cultural conditions, including religious divisions, so characteristic of Ireland under British rule. Certain momentous events, such as O'Connell's campaign for Catholic Emancipation and a variety of nationalist and secessionist movements, attracted German curiosity, particularly when they corresponded to German preoccupations such as the Prussian annexation of the traditionally Catholic Rhinelands after the Congress of Vienna in 1815, and concurrent nationalist dynamics in Germany. Jakob Venedey, for example, was one such commentator, whose account *Irland* (1844) was even translated into English and published in the very same year as the German original under the title *Ireland and the Irish during the Repeal Year*. Politically motivated interest in Ireland reached a climax at this time on account of these common points of identification. This is reflected both in terms of the number of Germans who visited and published reports on Ireland as well as the overall number of German publications pertaining to Irish conditions during this time. The Famine, the social conditions thereafter including work-houses and mass emigration, and the various crises, movements and events were also features of Irish reality that were reported widely throughout Europe.

The second half of the nineteenth century, however, witnessed a pronounced drop in the number of travellers to Ireland from the German-speaking lands. From 1871 up until the outbreak of the First World War, interest in Irish conditions often centred on Britain's treatment of Irish Catholics, as this again corresponded to German domestic affairs, namely the *Kulturkampf* under Bismarck's chancellorship. This interest is reflected in numerous publications in journals and newspapers, as well as works such as Alphons Bellesheim's *Geschichte der Katholischen Kirche in Irland von der Einführung des Christenthums bis auf die Gegenwart* [The History of the Catholic Church in Ireland from the Advent of Christianity to the Present Day; 1891] and Joseph Blötzer's *Die Katholikenemanzipation in Großbritannien und Irland: Ein Beitrag zur Geschichte religiöser Toleranz* [Catholic Emancipation in Great Britain and Ireland; 1905]. Meanwhile, in the run-up to and during the First World War and Second World War, interest was again politically motivated. Bermann himself penned two articles for the *Berliner Tageblatt* dealing with the situation in the North and the Home Rule question ('Die Ulster Leute' [The People of Ulster, 22 July 1913] and 'Die Rebellen von Ulster' [The Rebels of Ulster, 31 July 1913]), which largely reflect the content of the present volume, demonstrating that this question very much occupied the German political public's interest. Some commentators espoused hopes of a German–Irish political alliance, claiming affinities between German and Gael in the face of their common enemy. This manifested itself in titles such as *Deutschlands Sieg: Irlands Hoffnung* [German's Victory: Ireland's Hope; Hans Rost, 1915], while during the Second World War portrayals of British treatment of Ireland were utilised as anti-British propaganda in Germany.

Though visitors since the eighteenth century, such as Germany's most famous gentleman traveller of the time, Prince Hermann von Pückler-

Muskau (his book appeared in English as *Tour of a German Prince*; 1831–2), relished the wild natural beauty, picturesque landscapes and unique garden designs in many parts of Ireland, the primary motivation for most visits to Ireland could hardly be described as purely touristic. During the eighteenth, nineteenth and early twentieth centuries virtually all visitors to Ireland came because it was an integral part of a United Kingdom – the country that had developed into the mightiest maritime power of the age – a peripheral and culturally distinct region like Scotland or Wales; not a colony, or a nation in her own right held against her will in dependency of a foreign power. Yet, through their visits, many received an impression of nascent Irish nationhood, and hence reshaped their opinion of the country as merely a quirky appendix to a much larger entity.

In many respects, Bermann is much more astute than many of his predecessors, and much more aware of the nationalist currents and unionist counter-currents, of the cultural significance and political repercussions of religious divisions; he also demonstrates a keener awareness than his predecessors of the history that produced the current situation. The reason for this alertness certainly lies in his journalistic sensitivities, i.e. his attention to the significant detail that encapsulates, and explains, wider contexts. He brings a less specialised focus to his subject than archivalist and 'scientific' travellers on very specific missions, and deliberately dismisses any romantic notion about a place of particular sanctity. He displays considerable knowledge but refuses to disperse it in an academic way. Instead, he incorporates historical excursions into his narrative in deliberately unusual ways, such as a synopsis of Irish history as annotated fairy tale, or the relation of a specifically telling episode in the form of a ballad or popular song. He furthermore uses different genres such as poems, folk tales, legends, plot summaries of plays and novels, accounts of interviews and conversations, sketches and anecdotes of encounters to enliven his report. Bermann does not reveal the sources that he often directly refers to as points of departure for his ruminations. Some of these sources can, however, be reconstructed – and information on them is provided in the notes. Others have not been established. To the titles mentioned above, as possible sources for Bermann, or at least works that shaped an overall contemporary collective knowledge, we have to add Leopold von Ranke's *Englische Geschichte, vornehmlich im sechzehnten und siebzehnten Jahrhundert* (1859–69) [English History, Chiefly of the Sixteenth and Seventeenth Centuries], Robert Hassencamp's

Irland in der Zeit von 1660–1760 (1883) [Ireland in the Period 1660–1760]
and *Geschichte Irlands von der Reformation bis zu seiner Union mit England*
(1886) [The History of Ireland from the Reformation to the Union with
England], Moritz Julius Bonn's two-volume *Die englische Kolonisation in
Irland* (1906) [English Colonisation in Ireland], which looks at the effects
of British colonialism on Ireland from 1169 up to the Famine, Heinrich
Neelmeyer-Vukassowitsch's *Grossbritannien und Irland: Mit besonderer
Berücksichtigung der Kolonien* (1886) [Great Britain and Ireland, Paying
Particular Attention to the Colonies], and also various articles by Reinhold
Pauli in *Preußische Jahrbücher* written between 1861 and 1873.

And finally, Bermann's travel narrative is characterised by his keen,
somewhat embarrassed and coquettishly displayed awareness that he is,
indeed, a tourist, engaged in a round trip with pre-booked accommodation
and transport, and that he follows well-trodden paths. He deliberately
refuses to travel further along the west coast of the island simply because
Thomas Cook promotes the area so extensively. His attempt to rise above
the cliché by satirising his fellow tourists, by pinpointing the encroaching
Americanisation of the beauty spots, by dwelling on insignificant details
such as his difficulty in finding suitable souvenirs to take home from his
sojourn, often borders on the affectatious, but equally often makes for quite
hilarious reading. Bermann wrote for a German audience, he wrote to
establish himself as a journalist of punch and substance, he wrote to prove
a point. In spite of the rhetoric, in spite of some gratuitous posturing, he
conveys a very vivid picture, and his acute sense of bewilderment enables
him to identify paradoxes, to highlight curious details, to give a poignant
flavour of the Ireland of his day and the absurdities of the island's past and
present.

FRAMING IRELAND

Underneath the conversational exterior and a seemingly simple structure –
in that the narrative follows the traveller's itinerary – this volume actually
possesses a very intricate design. This is particularly obvious in Bermann's
method of blending the Irish past, present and prospective future. The
current picture is diverse and contradictory. For the outsider, life in Ireland
seems neither exciting nor progressive at present; land use seems inefficient,
the romantic mystique seems folly as it is based on backwardness, even

misery; and the moaning under the effects of landlordism bespeak not only hardship and heroism, but neglect. Bermann's synopsis of Irish history in the alienating style of an allegorical fable interspersed with laconic commentary achieves a tremendously polemical effect. He inserts the synopsis at exactly the point when the description of his contradictory first impressions of arguably the most attractive and touristy parts of the south-west of Ireland have reached a pinnacle of confusion: the commodification of natural beauty, the inaccessibility or, rather, access as privilege, the dilapidation of cities all meshed into a product for tourists that offends the Austrian's middle-class sensibilities, his sense of justice, his European prerogative of moving freely. He then continues to intersperse his itinerary with further excursions of various kinds into Irish culture and history: a rendition of the life and times of Brian Boru and the Viking invasion of Ireland that re-imagines one of the most glorious victories as a lament of despair of the aged warrior-king (Battle of Clontarf, 1014); a balladesque popular song about the hapless hero Lambert Simnel, who, for a brief moment, became the poster boy for Irish ambitions (coronation, 1587); a tour of the site of the Battle of the Boyne (1690); an ekphrastic rendition of a sentimental play about the hero of Tullow, Father Murphy, whose stance was associated with the Irish Rebellion (1798); an interpretative re-telling of George Bernard Shaw's play *John Bull's Other Island* (premiere, 1904) – all placed at fitting junctures in the course of the book, all highlighting historical moments and conditions of exemplary significance: Ireland as a site of invasion and conquest in the early Middle Ages; as a base of rebellion against the forging of a centralised nation state in Britain in late medieval times under the incoming Tudor dynasty; as an example of the entanglement of Irish affairs in international confessional and dynastical power politics in the age of Absolutism; Irish rebellion in the context of the French Revolution, leading to the abolition of the Ascendancy's self-government and the declaration of the Union (execution of Father Murphy, 1798); and finally recent history and the specific travails of modernisation as captured by the playwright Shaw. Added to this mix are fairy tales and legends, for example one about the Giant's Causeway which is presented as a parable of the enduring relationship between the two islands. Such passages increasingly supersede descriptions of land- and cityscapes which – such as half dilapidated, half opulent Dublin and commercial Belfast – largely conform to expectations. Beyond merely describing places, Bermann attempts to read them for what they articulate about their inhabitants and the forces that forged their physical appearance. The essence of Ireland, her culture and her position within British imperial society, however, necessitates a look behind the drunkards on shabby streets and the polo players in generous urban parks; it can only be captured if an Irish collective mentality is delineated historically, as produced by circumstance and evolved along unique lines.

Conspicuously, Bermann does not dwell extensively on two of the most significant aspects of more recent Irish history, one momentous and one traumatic: Catholic Emancipation and the Famine respectively. He integrates these events into his allegorical overview. Those readers who possess some familiarity with Irish history will realise that the fairy tale rendition of the relationship between the British and Irish neighbours amounts to a rather crude condensation of the course of Irish history into a simplistic pattern. A keen sense of victimhood permeates this narrative and suggests a clear dichotomy between oppressor and oppressed. But the reductionist view is then subsequently nuanced and underpinned with characteristic examples that veer between the hapless and the tragic. These episodes and anecdotes paint a picture of Irish history not merely of victimhood, but also of delusion. Bermann recounts two instances when Ireland became the battleground for British political conflicts, both between rival pretenders to the royal English crown. They are both intended to illustrate how British rivalries give rise to the delirious hope on the part of Irish interests that aligning with either party would further an Irish cause. They also serve to illustrate how internally torn and split Irish society, most notably the elites, actually were over the centuries, and how easily they allowed themselves to be played off against one another, how gullibly they lent their support to causes only remotely related to their own interests. The immensely important aspect that, in the conflicts in question, and many others, Irish aspirations became pawns in pan-European power struggles, and that the Irish served as willing mercenaries for alien causes both at home and abroad, is only scratched tangentially – this phenomenon does not really suit Bermann's agenda, whose main focus is the Irish–British relationship.

The story of Lambert Simnel – one last stirring of the War of the Roses between the York and Lancaster branches of the Plantagenets before Tudor king Henry VII established a new dynasty on the throne of England – is not even very well known in British or Irish historiography, let alone common knowledge among the educated in German-speaking lands. The original of the ballad that chronicles this event – should it exist – could not be identified, but, since the poem foregrounds those figures present at the coronation of the pretender at Dublin's Christ Church Cathedral in 1487, it is imaginable that Bermann received his inspiration upon a visit there. It is significant, though, that Bermann should relate this tale in the form of a street ballad, thereby downplaying the importance of the incident, suggesting that it has become folklore, engrained in a collective consciousness as a curiosity and rendered with farcical hilarity – thereby offering a rather cynical commentary to the pitiful haplessness of the Irish insurgents. In the German version, the question of the unvarying refrain ringing out after every stanza seems addressed to all of Ireland: 'Bist du echt, Lambert Simnel?' Are you for real? Is this really the extent of your collective action in the national interest? The humiliation suffered at the infamous banquet where Simnel was forced to serve the assembled nobles not only illustrates the outcome of this particular affair, i.e. the pardon granted by the monarch which allowed Gerald Fitzgerald, earl of Kildare, to resume his role as deputy lord lieutenant and de facto ruler of Ireland only a few years later, but also casts the rebels in a rather ridiculous light, as bumbling and intimidated fools – for Bermann a striking metaphor of the Anglo–Irish relationship in general. His account omits the entanglement of occurrences such as this, and Ireland's fate as a whole, in European-wide political affairs, the power politics of European dynasties and confessional or political alliances. In this instance, the military power that the Yorkists around Fitzgerald could draw on consisted of a troupe of some 2,000 Swiss and German mercenaries under the command of the notorious condottiere Martin Schwartz, battle-hardened in the eternal conflicts between Spanish, French and Imperial German interests in Flanders. He was sent to assist the pretender by Margaret of York, duchess of Burgundy, widow of Duke Charles the Bold of Burgundy (1433–77), sister of the dukes of Clarence (allegedly Simnel's father) and Gloucester (Richard III), and aunt of the earl of Lincoln, another prominent figure in the Simnel insurgence. This contingent, as well as members of the Norman aristocracy of Ireland and Gaelic clansmen, formed the disparate army that was defeated at the Battle of Stoke Field on 16 June 1487.

Equally woeful was the fate of the Catholic cause, pinning their hopes on the deposed King Charles II at the Battle of the Boyne, which sealed the

dominance of the Protestant elite in political affairs, prepared the ground
for further confiscations of properties and plantations of Protestant settlers,
and thereby institutionalised an antagonism on the island of Ireland that
had heretofore not been as pronounced or irreconcilable. In deviations
such as these, Bermann suggests reasons for the situation he observed:
the landlordism, the cultural sway of the Protestant Ascendancy and the
political and mental rift that divided Irish culture and society. Bermann's
strategy of recounting the decisive battle as part of an afternoon stroll,
with irreverent reference to the hollowness of textbook accounts, serves to
whimsically downplay the magnitude of the event; it conveys a powerful
commentary not only on the ubiquity of history in the Irish physical
and mental topography, but also on the inadequateness of conventional
methods of identifying formative aspects of culturally alien phenomena –
in other words, the otherness of the culturally distant.

Here, as elsewhere, Bermann displays a strong appreciation of
the absurdities of Irish history, of the changing alliances and blurred
distinctions between factions, of the impossibility of defining Irish and
non-Irish, a distinction he strenuously upholds and concurrently constantly
undermines as too crude and too simplistic. Bermann's swagger cannot
conceal the fact that common, imported criteria fail to do justice to Irish
realities. And yet he tries time and time again, comparing Home Rule to
a semi-autonomy as, for example, enjoyed by culturally distinct regions in
Germany, such as Bavaria, and by framing the future association between
Britain and Ireland in categories derived from German federalism. When he
equates the campaigners for Irish independence, from a British perspective,
as the 'enemy within' ('der innere Feind'), he recalls the polemicism familiar
from recent German history in a variety of contexts, incessantly targeting
Catholics, Poles, socialists and later also Jews as enemies of the nation who
live in our midst. Given this acute awareness of contemporary political
issues, it strikes as curious that this Austro-German cosmopolitan fails
to mention ideas, espoused for example by Arthur Griffith, for a political
arrangement between Britain and Ireland that resembled that between
Austria and Hungary – a model that became known as the 'Dual Monarchy'
since the adoption of a new constitution in 1867.

Bermann only very occasionally slips into a terminology that,
characteristic for the time even among the more liberal-minded and worldly
contemporaries, borders on the racist. For the most part, he strenuously

avoids labelling the essence of Irishness as Celtic or Gaelic, unlike so many others who looked to Hibernia in search of unspoiled bardic originality, or with the aim of disparaging an allegedly inferior race. He does, on the other hand, issue very strong verdicts on the cultural and political affirmations of Irishness that he encounters, both through his descriptions and in explicit evaluations. His miniature of a celebration of cultural Irishness, including earnest judges, excited contestants and eager spectators, exposes a lack of substance in the popular pursuit of what certain organisations, the Gaelic League (for the promotion of the Irish language, founded 1893), the Gaelic Athletic Association (established 1884) and Feis Ceoil (literally: Music Festival, founded in 1897) among them, promoted as uniquely Irish. Noticing an over-reliance on ritual not matched by the enthusiasm of participants, he concludes that such revivalist attempts are destined for failure. He condemns sanctimonious, self-pitying, stale patriotism in the South as much as he despises the rousing, crowd-pleasing defiant rhetoric of the Northern unionist fanatics. His diagnosis – and herein also lies a communality between the seemingly so irreconcilable factions – identifies a mismatch between aspiration and reality as the pathological condition of Irish culture in all classes and persuasions. Bermann contrasts the alleged Irish stubbornness with what he perceives as imperceptible British assimilation machinery, with which he means economic and cultural forces that spread English lifestyle from continental Europe to the furthest corners of the Empire. He attributes here to British colonial expansionism a tendency that today we would call the levelling power of global capitalism and consumerism. At the height of colonial expansion, Bermann traces global lifestyles to British cultural dominance all over the world, including America. He also identifies the dynamics of modernisation that, he predicts, will eventually submerge the Irish conflict. In particular, he thinks of Ireland's potential to feed the Industrial Revolution – and that economic advantage will override political antagonism. He also believes that unionist Northern politicians will realise that they have nothing to fear from Home Rule as, through economic and cultural dynamics, their distinctness from Southern Catholics will diminish to the extent that the latter will become ever more entangled in global British cultural normalcy.

The brief excursion to the Isle of Man serves to exemplify Bermann's thesis about the power of cultural modernisation. Here, analogous phenomena may be observed, and they bring about similar effects. The

need to pay an entrance fee to gain access to spots of natural beauty is but
a symptom; the commercialisation of the mysterious, the transformation
of cultural uniqueness into an amusement park for pleasure seekers
from British industrial towns; the museality of time-honoured political
institutions – all these signify irreversible trends. The uniformity of
Manx capitalist and consumerist culture, the resortification of the island,
corresponds to the commodification of natural beauty and ancient relics
for the benefit of American tourists in Ireland. In Bermann's eyes, inevitable
modernisation leads to a cultural levelling not only within the British
Empire, but world-wide. In a report from the Sudanese capital almost
two decades later he detects the same British cultural mash of bacon and
eggs, sporting pursuits and carefree tourism as on the islands to the west of
Europe: globality has reached innermost Africa and turned Khartoum into
a hotel lobby and a tennis court, as it has done with the Lakes of Killarney,
the Giant's Causeway and the Manx Tynwald (parliamentary assembly).
Sweeping theses such as these about the levelling power of British cultural
coloniality invite modern readers to compare Bermann's predictions with
their own experience: a century later, has cultural uniformity indeed
subsumed political conflict that once was rooted in historical divergence
and cultural difference?

RESONANCES

A modern reader of Bermann's book might be slightly disappointed not
to receive an enthusiastic endorsement of a mysterious or exotic, but at
the least a touristically attractive, destination. Commonly held views
of Ireland are neither emphatically confirmed nor decisively dispelled.
Instead, the picture of Ireland in 1913 that emerges in Bermann's report is
decidedly contradictory, inconclusive, patchy even – delivered mostly in
a conversational register and often in a mock-epic, mock-legendary tone,
spiked with sarcasm and laconic put-downs. The book refrains from offering
a clear message and also from subsuming Ireland into a familiar master
narrative – of independence, nationhood, Catholicism and mysticism,
anachronism, exploitation and resilience, or of untamed natural beauty
to match the untamed spirit of its Celtic inhabitants. Many such grand
interpretative tropes were as available and ubiquitous in Bermann's time as
they are today, and he acknowledges several of them. Yet for all his historical

excursions, Bermann's core focus remains contemporary. He attempts to capture a different form of modernisation from the one he experienced in Germany. The contrary signals for example of a rather boring urban culture in Dublin and Belfast, the pandering to American tastes and selling out to the uniformity of mass tourism speak of an almost imperceptible inevitability of change, and of a degradation of the unique – should it have ever existed – to a political weapon: the identity politics of expediency.

Bermann's Irish impressions of 1913 are remarkable insofar as they manage to pinpoint many aspects that, to this day, are central to Irish sensitivities. Even on this short tour – of probably about three weeks' duration including the unplanned detour to the Isle of Man – he intuitively grasps some of the essence that defined the Irish situation not only on the verge of national independence, but also for many decades after winning it. He identifies revealing features that still resonate a century after his observations, such as the contradictions of the assertion of Irish selfhood amidst overwhelming and irreversible cultural influences from the neighbour across the Irish Sea, the immense diversity in outlooks and mentalities between Northern radicals and a more placid Southern flock, the attempts at creating a living Irish culture from the buried remnants of a constructed history while at the same time commodifying the past for sale to tourists. Among the contradictory and ridiculous features captured by Bermann is the strange dialectic that the colonial master's strongest allies are also their most defiant challengers – something that determines Irish political life to this very day.

Another paradox of the Irish transition from dependency to independence is related to the dynamics of colonialism. Colonialism is never clear-cut, binary or unanimously hierarchical. One aporia of colonialism is that it creates its own countermovement. However, since a return to an imaginary 'before' is categorically impossible – if a stable idea even exists of what originality might mean – the system that would replace dependency is modelled on the force which possessed the power to conquer and subdue the weaker party in the first place. The modern Irish Republic is a point in question: post-colonial societies are modelled on colonial societies, not pre-colonial societies. Even the retrieval of some elusive originality is mostly pursued with the methodology created by the colonial masters, and preserved in institutions established by them. This not only holds true for settler colonies such as Australia and Canada, but also for conquered territories such as India, South Africa, Kenya and many others.

The Dublin cityscape is full of colonial buildings that now form the heart of cultural and political Ireland. The style of government – the centralist and executive-heavy political system, the adversarialist parliamentary culture – is inherited from the British model. Complex grades of overlayering occur: school uniforms with Scottish plaid are used in the most Catholic of Irish schools, Shakespeare remains a staple on the English curriculum for senior years, the buildings of the National University of Ireland's colleges in Cork and Galway emulate Cambridge quadrangles, imperial measurements are still a common currency, and the dietary staples – or lack of uniqueness of the Irish cuisine that Bermann noticed – are features shared with the British neighbours.

For the German reader, the recognisability of certain traits of Irish life one hundred years after Bermann's visit seems almost uncanny – for example the restricted accessibility to large parts of the Irish countryside, the dogged helpfulness of passers-by asked for directions (*vide* Bermann's lament about his lost purse), or the pragmatic forgiveness dispensed by controllers and enforcers of many different persuasions. For Irish readers, too, one reaction to the text is how clichés and stereotypes emerge that still have some traction today, that are part of a persistent imagery of the Irish. Competitions and other rituals of self-assurance such as the Irish sing- and dance-off in the coastal park, the awkward role of the adjudicators – often priests then as now – and the unnatural relationship with the Irish language as an official assertion of cultural identity without an organic place in daily life – at least on the east coast, in the vicinity of the capital and in that quintessentially Victorian seaside resort – resonate strongly today: a slight stiffness in organised demonstrations of Irishness still pervades cultural and sporting organisations.

The modern reader will feel provoked to contemplate if any of Bermann's predictions have come true, if indeed Irish public life, as arguably the case throughout much of the Commonwealth, is still under the sway of the British model, if indeed Ireland has become a cultural rather than a political colony. For two decades or so the game of rugby has shed its reputation of being an exclusive, fee-paying-school sport and has become a universally popular game supported by the whole nation – a further reminder that ancient social and cultural divisions have disappeared as the Irish embrace a British elite pastime. However, as, at the time of writing, the United Kingdom attempts to assert its dissociation from the common European project, and the Republic of Ireland stands loyal to that project – and in turn receives European support for its legitimate concerns – old political divisions once again attain an uncanny actuality – one that, one cannot help thinking, has echoes of imperial pasts that many erroneously believed had been subsumed into more encompassing (European) identities.

Today, this book remains relevant in a number of respects, not least in that it represents the last comprehensive external and relatively unbiased report in the German-speaking world before the outbreak of the First World War and the associated events on the island of Ireland. Within only a few short years, Ireland saw the signing of a contract to achieve Home Rule, and therewith de facto independence, a civil war over the inclusion of northern counties in the emerging Free State, and partition of the island of Ireland as an accommodation of the conflicting aspirations, as portrayed by Bermann. The book represents a snapshot in time, yet in the light of subsequent developments, this historical moment turned out to be a pivotal one, a moment on the brink of momentous change. In a way, Bermann captures a pinnacle of conflict, the afterlife of which marks Irish history to this day.

The cultural identity of Irish society in the Republic still seems as ambivalent today as when it was mapped by Bermann. The renaissance of the Irish language and other unique cultural practices has not happened; Irish sports, music and dancing thrive, yet they have become normal and are no longer instrumentalised as demarcatory assertions of Irishness. The Irish language retains its status as a cultural treasure and a cherished symbol of uniqueness; yet, in spite of strenuous efforts on the part of its adherents and of political officialdom, it has not become a more widespread, more natural or integral part of everyday life: after fourteen years of instruction in Irish, the vast majority of school-leavers are anything but proficient in their native language. The sway of the Catholic Church has wavered because of scandals and rising religious indifference – and this problematic is one that cannot be pinned on former colonial suppression but testifies to a separate political culture and an emerging independent identity manifest in internal debates and legacies. In this respect, one must salute Bermann's clear-sightedness. At the time of writing, however, while over time the 'dreams' that Bermann invokes have lost much of their fanatical edge, the aspiration symbolised in his book by Sir Edward Carson is still incredibly pronounced and asserting itself in the context of Brexit negotiations with similar strategies and attitudes as over a century ago. Even the relatively recent subsumption of the conflict under multilateral structures and international principles of conflict resolution, as evidenced by the stipulations of the Good Friday Agreement signed in Belfast on 10 April 1998, has not fundamentally altered the fault lines, nor the entanglement of Irish politics in British domestic affairs and her relationship with Europe. The secularisation of Irish society in the Republic has removed the basis of accusations of 'Rome Rule', yet the echoes of nationalist association with 'external' agents (the European Union as guarantor of the Good Friday Agreement) might mobilise memories of Simnel's allies' forces being paid by the duke of Burgundy, the French royal assistance for Charles II and French revolutionary support for the United Irishmen, not to mention Spanish attempts to use Ireland as the weak flank of their imperial rival Britain in early modern times.

The Republic of Ireland has, as predicted by Bermann, matured into a relatively normal European country, yet the North remains fragile and the power of cultural assimilation is often held at bay by reminders of uniquely Irish conflictual legacies.

Note on the Translation

Bermann's style is marked by a distinctly journalistic rhetoric, by irony, sarcasm and self-deprecation (occasionally a little pretentious for modern tastes), as well as a light-handed switch between registers; it is also saturated with German and Austrian cultural references. 'Futsch', the term Bermann uses when he realises he has misplaced his train ticket to Drogheda, is an expressive and unique colloquial term for 'gone', 'lost' or 'disappeared' that has no direct equivalent in English. The same applies to translating German dialect, in this case the north-eastern Berlinish spoken by the chef in the Bray hotel where Bermann dines. Among the numerous cultural references in the text are also Bermann's quotation of the first line of the famous poem 'Das Wandern ist des Müllers Lust' [Hiking is the Miller's Delight], which alludes to the presumed German penchant for hiking, or his statement that German children have adopted 'Puppchen' as their national anthem, which refers to the popular song 'Puppchen, du bist mein Augenstern' [Dolly, you are the apple of my eye] from the operetta by Jean Gilbert (1912). Such cultural references are often only fully appreciated by way of explanation as they would otherwise get 'lost' in translation and become meaningless for an English-speaking audience. The notes that follow the text itself are designed to help unravel some of the allusions that might otherwise remain obscure. Asterisks in the text identify terms that are explained in the notes.

Other elements of Bermann's style include how he seldom expresses his opinion directly; mostly, rhetorical questions, slide observations, exaggerations, double-entendre, caricature and many variants of figurative speech convey his view of the things he observes. Some of his devices seem gratuitous; if a good pun offers itself, he is unable to resist, such as when the homonymity of the German words for lace and for an invective or punch-line ('Spitze/n') guides his association without actually making a substantive point. Some facets of his tone can be recreated in English easier than other aspects of his style, such as the fairy tale or epic mode that, on the one hand, has obvious parallels in English and, on the other hand, so overtly announces itself as pastiche that the translator may feel authorised to shed any restraint. The specific style of the journalistic opinion piece – infusing a telling observation with rhetorical inflections so as to expose contradictions and absurdities – in German often relies on modulations, parallelisms and other syntactical devices, and it operates prominently with the evocation of specifically German associations. The decoding of such references is necessary to understand Bermann's domestic agenda, for example the engagement with aspects of colonialism and globalisation that have a decidedly greater resonance in a culture for which agency on the world stage was then a relatively new, and far more controversial, issue than it was in British culture – only this way can we understand that Bermann, in castigating the English, targets a competitor on the world stage. The simulation of clandestine agreement with his German and Austrian readers, the winks to predispositions and presumed shared premises, are not only often lost in translation, but are just as often lost in time. Other demeanours, in contrast, integrate easily into today's horizons – a fact that is testimony to the longevity of cultural patterns in both the German and Irish contexts and to the astute perceptiveness of our author.

The present translation presents the entire text; it even retains passages – such as the ballad and postcard ditty from the Giant's Causeway – where the English version is completely unable to capture the sheer playfulness and hilarity emanating from the German. As both a native English and a native German speaker have collaborated on this translation, our hope is that the sensitivities of both source and target language and culture received due attention.

The translators candidly admit that they undertook the task of translating this book for their own amusement and gratification. But they also hope that an English and Irish readership unable to read the German original might appreciate being afforded access to such a seminal example of travel writing and a poignant spotlight on Ireland at, arguably, one of the most decisive junctures in her history.

LEESA WHEATLEY and FLORIAN KROBB
Maynooth, December 2020

CHAPTER ONE

Why Ireland?

'Don't go to Ireland', an English acquaintance told me. 'The landscape might be very beautiful, but it is a dirty and disagreeable country. If you want to see how beautiful it is here, why not visit the Cornish Riviera or the Scottish Highlands.'

'When I'm in a stranger's house', I said, 'I don't like to linger in the salon. The nursery is much more characteristic and even the privy! John Bull is a well-to-do man and I already know that the leather armchairs in his parlour are wonderful to sit in! I don't want to see how beautiful it is, rather what it is really like here.'

There comes a time in every person's life when he or she has to take a good look at the reality that is the British Empire – insofar as he or she is not one of the superior and extremely numerous aesthetes who do not concern and sully themselves with political and civic issues. You have to know what it's like in England or you cannot appreciate contemporary life to the full. This asocial intellectual aristocrat, this poor crippled creature, will at least want to have read *Shaw's works, even if Ireland and *Home Rule naturally do not concern him one bit. The English way of life does, after all, play into English literature to some degree; it is one of its defects and it should do better. But for the time being the Europeans will have to be more lenient towards the English. They really are still a bit peculiar, but nonetheless they have more or less conquered the world. This earth is British and is becoming more British by the day, if not in terms of political power relations then in terms of political structure and organisation. The fact that the Germans even elect a parliament is an English invention, as is the *Reichstag itself. Our political institutions are so permeated by the English spirit that we all have reason to concern ourselves with it in some form or other. No fully fledged central European citizen can remain indifferent as to what conditions are like right now in the Indian province of Bengal, in Canada and at the Cape. Everything English in this world is important to everyone in this world. All important issues of our times will probably be decided on once and for all on English soil. In the eighteenth century, Europeans anticipated that the major problem of political freedom was first and foremost a French problem. In the nineteenth century, reasonable people knew that the problem of the nation state would be solved for all of Europe in the German lands. We in the twentieth century should really think about the fact that the social question, the land question and the question of global white hegemony are determined in England and in the English colonies. In this sense, England is *the* representative country of our century.

This country rules the best part of the globe, either directly or indirectly, for better or for worse. Whoever seeks to study English world domination will have to traverse many a sea in a steamboat, many a continent in an express train and many a desert on a camel's back. We will surely not fully understand the English until we have drunk whiskey and soda with them in every colonial city between the North and the South Pole. But, I thought to myself, perhaps for the time being it will suffice for our daily concerns if I visit that English colony located less than a ten-hour journey from London, that colony England already ruled long before the first English soldier ever set foot in Asia, Africa or even America or Australia. Besides, it is really only of secondary importance how the English rule *Hottentots and Hindus. It is much more instructive to see what a European country looks like under English rule.

The first English conquerors came to Ireland shortly after the middle of the twelfth century. They were Anglo-Norman barons, and today their descendants still own the majority of the most beautiful parts of the island. Of course these forbears of English colonial policy did not just come to take over some land. Since England has existed, it has always feigned higher ethical purposes before nabbing a country, the only problem being that in poorer and less desirable countries, their higher ethical purposes do not flourish quite as well. Back then, the English had a wonderful religious motive. They were of course still Catholics like the Irish, and the Irish church was one of Christianity's oldest and holiest, held in the highest esteem far and wide. It came to light, however, that Irish bishops were not being ordained strictly according to Latin Rite; there was also something

amiss with *Peter's pence. Now it so happened that *Adrian IV, the pope
at the time, was an Englishman. England is often lucky like this with its
ethical purposes. The pope had to bring the Irish heretics into line, and
the king of England (*King Henry II) was happily willing to do so in the
interest of higher purposes. On this occasion, the pious religious spirit of an
otherwise notoriously secular monarch was aroused in the most edifying of
ways. Well, to make a long story short, the English came, and from the very
beginning they came as enemies of the Irish brand of Catholicism and Irish
nationality. They have remained in Ireland ever since and the country will
never be rid of them.

That is Ireland's history in a nutshell. It was exactly the same in India,
the only difference being that English rule did not begin with the same
violence, rather with commercial benignity. In both countries the higher
ethical purposes evaporated over time – yet the English stayed. Every
time one of these higher ethical purposes was gloriously implemented in
Ireland, hundreds of additional acres fell into the hands of English lords.
Apparently, that is how on this earth a resolute people of conquerors and
their leaders are rewarded for their idealism. This is England's speciality in
world history: the strong lacquer of humanitarian and religious hypocrisy
that so cleanly coats the weapons of these magnificent and admirable
thieves. All conquerors in world history have at one time or another
ripped foreign countries apart, maintaining that it was only for their own
good. But for the Romans this was nothing more than empty pompous
rhetoric. In London, however, their belief in their own higher purpose was
unshakeable; their race is unbelievably talented in feeling morally superior.
And perhaps it is exactly in this time-honoured moral snobbery that
England's significance for world culture can be found.

In the long run, though, it is not possible to relentlessly pay lip service to
higher cultural purposes while digging into other people's pockets. It might
be feasible as long as the superior nation has not yet completely subdued
the foreign country with their morality. But there comes a moment when
there is no longer any reason to postpone the work of redemption; you
can scorch, singe and murder as long as you lay siege to Jerusalem, but
you will have to respect the freedom of the cross when the cross has won
out and Jerusalem has been conquered. The English still have each one
of their colonies to themselves, which is as much as to say that they have
monopolised them to the financial benefit of their aristocracy and their

merchant class. All great conquerors acted this way. But the English, and this is a great advantage given all their damned hypocrisy, have repeatedly smashed in the skulls of the recalcitrant natives with the battle cry: it's for your own good! As a result of this, the moment always arrived when this solemn promise had to be honoured. Indeed, it was usually a moment when John Bull was not feeling the best. But nothing compares to the power and attention garnered by rhetorical phrases repeated over and over again. If you tell a Berlin shop assistant often enough that *Kant was the funniest and most fashionable author, they will eventually all be reading Kant. That would not befit Kant, the commercial clerks, or the nation. But preaching to the English middle class for centuries that they are the selfless saviours of this world – that is beneficial. For they might, indeed, actually redeem the world.

In India the time has come when the ancient humanitarian pretence suddenly becomes a moral power and – the drama possesses considerable irony – forces the old hypocrites to make good on their claims. India is increasingly governed on its own terms; the native population are being given rights and taking part in government. *The victory of the Japanese, the *commotion in the Muslim world and to some extent the *conspiratorial Hindus with their bombs have of course contributed something to this change of affairs. But such a tenacious and strong race of conquerors as the English should have been able to keep a much firmer grip on the prey between their teeth – had the benedictory rhetoric not ripped open the predator's mouth. In the end, it would be safe to say that the English really are the most humane and kindest people of them all because they play the hypocrite where others would never even dream of doing so.

That's exactly how things are now in Ireland. England is about to give Ireland back to the Irish. Of course they are not doing so completely voluntarily and without compulsion, but under duress of the political ideals which, very much against their proclaimer's original intentions, have taken on a life of their own and have turned rhetoric into necessity.

Since America's independence, this tremendous and unpredictable movement is spreading through the British Empire. Everything that political manoeuvring has clawed together and kept together with an iron grip, the British programme of cultured rule – the consequence of that blessed national hypocrisy – is now undoing. Whether this empire can stay intact when its individual lands are doing well is more or less the only question of real significance for world politics today. That is why it is so incredibly important (and it is important for us, too!) to observe what is currently happening in Ireland. The English are about to release one of their victims. As a consequence, this country will remain very English for evermore. All the qualities of the English race will surely be revealed. The question as to whether it will be possible to convert an independent Ireland to patriotism for the British Empire is nothing other than the question as to whether the British Empire can remain British in the face of advancing civilisation.

Perhaps this concerns us Germans, too. But Germans are more familiar with Central Asia than Ireland, and upon returning from my trip even well-educated people asked me how impressive the *Hekla was. After all, Germans are much more inclined to visit Iceland than Ireland. Ireland is indeed not the British Empire's finest reception room. This room in their mansion is only just being cleaned up and it still looks a bit messy and wild. It is impolite to be peeking through the cracks in the door at a time like this. I realise that my behaviour might be regarded as frivolous. I went to Ireland when on the Cornish Riviera I could have stayed in so much nicer a guesthouse.

Chapter Two

The Inniscara

At the beginning there was London. Coming to Rome for the first time, you wonder in amazement how you could have ever lived in another city. You are seized by the same sense of awe in London, even if it is not as painful. But the reasons are different ones.

If someone has previously lived in *Bautzen and goes to *Chemnitz for the first time, then Chemnitz seems to have all the intense garish attractions of sophisticated urban culture. Suddenly Bautzen is looked upon with affectionate pity as provincial. Now, however, this good man arrives in Berlin for the first time and, after five minutes, he realises that the abundance of lifestyles in the big city, the sense of order and comfort, are incomparably greater than in Chemnitz, i.e. that Chemnitz is also in essence a provincial town. Well, the city that makes Berlin look like a nice quiet provincial town lies on the Thames and is called London. As sure as Orvieto is more beautiful than Berlin, it is also certain that Berlin has many advantages over London – but Bautzen, too, must have its special merits, since otherwise all its inhabitants would emigrate. But there is no denying that a centre's significance always corresponds to the size of its orbit. London is the metropolis of the mightiest culture in the world. Most people come here to make a racket in all kinds of ways, which is what we call a city. The people are of all colours. London blanches them. London is the greatest assimilation machine in the world. Indian princes and Russian Jews are poured into a funnel and, while it is not exactly Anglo-Saxon world rulers that emerge, they emerge as indifferent creatures with the 'Made in England' stamp. The Indian prince is made into a gentleman, that is a person who feels compelled to find everything English simply divine. And so he can now go back to India, continue to play cricket and during the intervals rule over millions of people in a way that pleases his London club.

Russian Jews tend to be a tougher breed than Indian princes, but London also knows how to make the typical national dish of roast beef out of them. It is hard to believe just how easily the immigrants undergo this process of superficial Anglicisation. Fixed ideas are contagious, and Englishness is nothing but a compound of fixed ideas. Fixed ideas that you have to eat certain dishes for breakfast. Fixed ideas that you are destined to save the world. Fixed ideas that mentioning the word 'trousers' is immoral, and that a respectable human being does not utter the word 'damn'. Above all the fixed idea that England is always right no matter where and when, and that the big fat English codex of fixed ideas is more sacred than any Bible. The English gentry have, not to the detriment of their class, unleashed this codex upon the world – behold how it now mushes the world to a pulp. Within the space of an hour every *Negro prince can play the perfect Englishman by simply acting as if he believes in a handful of fixed ideas. Of course the few dozen truly English men, the real rulers of the world, secretly laugh at this superstition. But they know very well that it is exactly through the power of this superstition that they rule the world. It is like Islam, which is making such tremendous progress at present: it replaces the most complicated paganisms with three or four simple rituals and doctrines. The most intransigent African who submits to these suddenly becomes a member of a powerful global organisation and is as distinguished as the most refined Arab or the noblest *Haussa. It is just as easy to become part of the equally noble global movement that is the Anglo-Saxons; three or four simple rituals suffice (eat bacon and fried eggs for breakfast, read the sports news every day, keep the Sabbath holy). This successful club is not an exclusive one, which explains the constant influx of new members. In today's world the cogs of an enormous machine are turning. This machine absorbs people of all races and produces Anglo-Saxons. London is the heart, the engine of this gigantic assimilation machine. It is in London that all the metal in the world is re-minted and given the Anglo-Saxon imprint.

Alas, what I wanted to say is that this place, London, is half a day's journey from Ireland. All over Ireland, London newspapers are read on the very same day they are published. For centuries, hundreds of thousands of Irish have been coming to London.

Yet I have been told that Ireland is not an Anglo-Saxon country. It does not bear the imprint. It is not assimilated.

Well, if this is the case, then Ireland must be a truly extraordinary country. For us continentals, the big question making all of us anxious at present is how do you even begin to not be an Anglo-Saxon? (We can also call this the struggle against the Americanisation of the world. America – that means all nations already washed away in the Anglo-Saxon flood.) Apparently, you can learn this from the Irish. The journey across St George's Channel may not be of good repute but I will have to risk it.

I take the Great Western Railway's Irish express to Fishguard. My companion and I are once again amazed at how we are placed in a third-class English carriage. In Germany, our railway employees only treat travelling nobility and imposters in this way. I remember Cook, the great *Thomas Cook, only allowed his tourists to travel third class in England as a matter of principle. He claimed that the English third class did not correspond to the continental first class, but rather exceeded it. Now, on this train there are also carriages for first class; these are probably reserved for lords and imposters. That's the difference: our lords and imposters sit on comfortable seats, while the middle-class sit on wooden benches that cause bruising on delicate body parts. In truly democratic countries, lords, imposters and the middle class would all sit on the same benches, either all comfortable or all uncomfortable. In aristocratic England, the middle-class citizen sits on really soft comfortable seats and worships the lord from afar, who sits on even more comfortable seats in his separate temple. This English aristocracy still prevails because they have understood the importance of giving the middle classes *bread and games: a tremendous national awareness of power and a taste of the average comforts of life, of which the continental middle class can only dream – in spite of their equal social standing. However, there is also the rabble. They scream so loudly that they, too, will have to be given their comforts. That is the great skill of this clever aristocracy. If the people want to travel first class and are strong enough to impose their will, then do not open up the first class to everyone, rather spruce up the third class by cushioning the seats and hanging pretty pictures on the walls. Across the British Empire the same problem can be heard in the same way: the subjugated peoples are being shown that even in third class the seats are soft and comfortable on board the all-British world express. These people consequently leave their masters in peace as they travel first class. This thought underlies all the major reforms in the English colonies and all civilisatory impact following the great conquests. It's actually not a bad idea, given how things stand today.

Outside the carriage window an enormous garden is in blossom. It is a first-class landscape, or else the third class is better arranged and designed than the continental first class. At home the forests are more beautiful, in England the parks – and where our countryside is plain, the English one is parkland. It is difficult to pass judgement while whizzing past like this; but nonetheless, these farmhouses look like villas and the numerous castles all seem fit for a king. It made me think of my beloved Jersey, where the farmers go to church on Sundays in top hats and gloves. I know all this has its drawbacks. I know the English tenant farmer is emigrating to Australia, not because he is hungry but because in Australia he will be a free man for his money and no longer a tenant of the squire. Indeed, there are people who are not satisfied with third class even when the seats are cushioned. Aristocracy is infectious.

The train races through a medium-sized town. Every house looks the same, but each belongs to a single family and each has its own little garden. Living in a detached house just outside the city, smoking a pipe in the little garden in the evenings and respectably going to the neo-Gothic church on Sundays – this is what they call 'suburban life'. A life just outside the city gates. The indispensable *red monthly magazine with its entertainingly dull short stories is also part and parcel of it – life in third class is indeed well cushioned. A powerful force is making its way through the world, whereby everyone wants to come to the dubious compromise between slavery and pleasure that is the English middle class. Herein lies the Anglo-Saxon conquest of the world.

Darkness gradually descends. Red flames glow through the summer evening on either side of the railway: we are in the Welsh coal-mining district. Definitely a fourth-class area where sooty men work by day, or knock back whiskey in revolting taverns or engage in excessive industrial action – well that's what you read in the newspapers from time to time. There must be special trains for the workers because I cannot imagine that soot-covered men should all of a sudden climb aboard and sit down beside me on the plush red upholstery of my compartment. It seems that England's industrial workforce still travel in a special workers' train, but it is also probably somewhat better equipped than the travelling prisons we call fourth class back home. Then there are those disreputable people whom English society does not care to provide transport for at all, namely the dreadful wretched masses I saw in east London. As long as the great social question of our time has not been solved, the best trains will not convey fourth class and even the most basic ones will not carry fifth class, in England as elsewhere. For the time being, however, I think the most important question relates to the upholstery of third-class carriage seats. I tend to travel third class, you see.

The train stops. Bright railway lights illuminate steep rocks. It must be seaside cliffs because in front of them is a darkness that is different from the darkness of the mainland. The compartment doors are flung open; a porter silently steps aboard and takes my luggage. At home he would not voluntarily come aboard like this and I, sitting as I am in third class, would probably have to lug my own little suitcase. Here, the railway company pays the porter. It really is very pleasant to travel third class in England.

My companion and I follow the porter and we see that the small train station is directly on the landing stage. A plump mass towers up right beside the platform: it is the steamboat *Inniscara*, which is to take us across the nocturnal sea from Fishguard to Cork. I rack my brains as to what 'Inniscara' means and how it is pronounced. It must be an Irish place name. So this is where Ireland begins, when I step on deck...

The porter turns around, scrutinises our attire and at first glance does not know where to bring us, finally asking, 'saloon or third class?' I was asked the same question this morning in the travel agent's in London, whether I wanted to travel first or third class on the boat. The splendid third class on English express trains sprung to mind and I decided on the more economical option. Fine, I tell the porter. He gives me a censorious look and as soon as we are on board we do not go left where it looks pleasant, but rather turn right where a filthy steep flight of stairs leads down to a very dark and very unwelcoming deck. Something dawns on me and I tell him I would like to remain outside for the time being. In a familiarly official tone, the porter announces that this is forbidden. He pushes open a kind of cellar door. Noise and stench hit us. A steep and narrow ladder leads down into the overcrowded ship's hold. We see a bar where untrustworthy-looking fellow passengers knock back the drink, and benches that I certainly will not be lying down on. Underfoot, meanwhile, the floor is sticky with twenty generations' worth of sea sickness.

I exchange glances with my companion and then tell the porter that we will pay the supplement to travel in the 'saloon'. The porter immediately becomes nice and polite as he escorts us to a much more comfortable part of the ship.

'Who would have thought!' exclaims my companion. 'After the marvellous third class on the train.'

'It seems we are in Ireland', I reply. 'And in Ireland, it seems, the English are not inclined to travel third class.'

We pay a small fee and are allocated a splendidly spotless cabin with fresh sheets that are a pure joy, and handy buckets clean as a whistle for all eventualities. I am quite tired but there is something rather appealing about staying on deck when a ship departs. And so we go through the appetising dining saloon and the small pleasant smoking room and step out onto that friendly first-class deck where we picturesquely lean against the railing and look at the dimly lit quay. The ship's crane rises and falls as it grabs crates and packages, gently placing them on the lower deck. The high cliffs are in front of us. The sea must be on the other side. But today it is not there; just a black void. You can be unromantic about the whole thing and say that the crossing will be pleasant, or you can be a bit more imaginative and predict that we will never make it across this dark infinity.

'How do you do?' someone beside me asks, someone who actually has no business making such enquiries. I see a tall red-head with a round face, and like every upright Brit he is wearing a mac and a flat cap.

'Where are you travelling to?' this man asks me with ardent interest in his voice. Now, it is not exactly difficult to guess where I am going since this steamboat is neither puffing its way to the summit of the Jungfrau in Switzerland nor to Honolulu, but rather to Cork in Ireland, as it states on the ticket. And indeed this is what I reply in what English I can still muster at one in the morning. 'Oh you are travelling to Ireland!' the man says, tremendously surprised and enthusiastic. 'As you will see, it's the most beautiful country in the world! Come, have a drink!'

And now we are sitting in the pleasant little smoking room and I have to sample real Irish whiskey and tell them where I am from and what people in Berlin think of Home Rule and whether *the invasion is about to begin and do I not think that Ireland is the most beautiful country in the world and that the whiskey is 'very lovely' and do I take more whiskey or more soda. It is a typical English conversation – apart from one thing. This first Irishman I meet is advertising Ireland, something an Englishman would never think of doing. The Englishman who advised me not to travel to Ireland comes to mind. For more than eight hundred years, Ireland has been politically united with England; therefore English patriotism should also encompass Ireland, and Irish patriotism England. However, if I tell an Englishman that the Isle of Wight is beautiful he is flattered; if I say that the south of Ireland is beautiful he couldn't care less. Meanwhile, the Irishman is angry if I even mention the Isle of Wight. This is what the union between England and Ireland looks like in the minds of its participants.

The *Inniscara* is still docked in the English port and this is palpable. It seems that this ship really will carry me across a dark abyss. Like myself, the red-haired Irishman at my table has come from London. He is wearing the English mac and cap, the English short pipe sits between his teeth, he struck up the conversation with the set phrase 'how do you do' and is currently in the process of saying the evening prayer of the faithful, which here goes by the name of whiskey and soda. The man is a product of the assimilation machine. There is nothing Celtic about him apart from the red hair on his head. He bears the Anglo-Saxon imprint. In keeping with his Anglo-Saxon manners, he harbours fixed ideas: the idea of the Irish fatherland and hatred of the 'Saxon' strangers (which, however, are not one and the same thing).

The *Inniscara* raises the anchor. This English ship with a Celtic name, with the comfortable English first class and the filthy Irish third class, truly transplants you from England to Ireland – over the black abyss.

Inniscara, Inniscara. It sounds sweet, musical, strange, Celtic. I want to know how to pronounce it and ask the red-head.

He pronounces the Celtic word as if it were an English one.

CHAPTER THREE

Cork

The morning turned out to be dull and foggy. We are standing on deck at a spot that is pleasantly warm from the steam engine. There are twenty Irish boy scouts in front of us on the unappealing third-class deck (it seems that this is permitted now), wearing loud Irish-green neckerchiefs and yellow embroidered harps on their sleeves, not to mention the green shamrock leaves. Standing there decorated in their national symbols, these tall boys obviously feel extremely important – not least on account of their paraphernalia. They open their Irish nostrils wide and breathe in their country. The Irish coast begins over there. A green stretch of coast, it kindly opens up and lets the steamboat in.

Now we are faced with a labyrinth of canals, bays, islands and foothills. It is like a Norwegian fjord, just not as forceful, rather softer, cosier. The sea pays the land a friendly visit, flowing deep inshore. Small towns with *big cathedrals are located on the banks and each town has its nice suburbs with spacious houses and well-maintained gardens. The bay becomes narrower until it forms a mere canal, and finally the mouth of a river. A city lies between green hills – you immediately understand why Ireland is called the 'Emerald Isle'. Charming. The boat stops. The city is still there, and has been for a long time, or so it seems. Okay, we will disembark. You can recognise a main street, but the hotel that adorns it is somewhat mediocre. No matter, we clean ourselves up and get off the boat. So this is Cork city in the south of Ireland! There is indeed a main street and, well, another main street. The latter is called the Grand Parade. My guidebook tells me that it's a very beautiful street and its main attraction is in fact a statue of King George II, but the statue is no longer there because loyal Irish subjects tossed it into the river one day. That was not very nice of them – even if they were rebelliously inclined, they could at least have left in place the few attractions that the poor traveller wanted to admire.

However, what is the point of a guidebook other than to line up the indispensable tourist attractions for the traveller? Well, then, what does my richly illustrated *green-covered guidebook have to say?

It opines that St Finbar founded an abbey in the seventh century. How exciting! Furthermore, Desmond McCarthy, king of Munster, surrendered to the English King Henry II in 1172. As if on cue, as soon as you set foot in Ireland, things kick off with the old Irish kings – here we have encountered a key concept. But unfortunately I cannot take a look at King Desmond McCarthy; he is of course long since deceased.

The guidebook suggests I might take a look at the Bank of Ireland building. Or the country club. The choice is difficult; in the end I go to the Catholic cathedral and am pleasantly surprised. The *church was only built in 1879 (by W. Burgess) and is nevertheless an important work of art. Apart from picturesque ruins, there aren't very many old Catholic churches in Ireland. Most cathedrals have been newly built since *Catholic Emancipation, but, it seems, this hasn't always been a success. This church here, although Romanesque in style, is a beautiful brand-new one – what a miracle! It has something to say and is saying it loud and clear: 'I am the old church of the *Irish apostles – I am the new church that has not died, I reign over Cork and over the entire island!'

The sacristan tells me that the church is one of the most beautiful examples of the old French Gothic style. He is mistaken, but I still give him thruppence. He brings me a book and says I must write my name in it. A gentleman like myself does not come to his church every day, he tells me.

(A depressing suspicion overcomes me: has this man noticed that I am a foreigner on account of my accent? I was really counting on Ireland! The people here speak bad English – I also speak bad English, so they could have kindly taken me for a real Irishman.)

After visiting the church, there is once again an awkward interlude in the sequence of Corkonian attractions and diversions. This extremely lively and enlivening provincial city stretches out along the banks of the River Lee, unstirring. Since nothing much is going on, perhaps a spot of lunch is in order. The bars and restaurants are terribly enticing. After rambling down the main street, or rather down both main streets, we sit at a nicely laid table and can start sampling Irish national dishes. But no, the menu is exactly the same as that of Lyons in London, where I suffered such an upset stomach. I can have roast beef, a steak too rare or too well-done, a huge selection of spuds, and a cup of tea. It doesn't cost any more than a nice luxurious breakfast in a fine German wine restaurant. Still, if you pour spicy Worcester sauce on one English lunch after another, coat it in mustard, sprinkle pepper on it and top it off with fruit jelly, the bland and boring stuff actually eventually acquires some sort of flavour.

Now and again I look at my watch, but it's still not tomorrow morning. I stroll the streets and discover that there are two categories: dirty ones and boring ones. The shops are closing right in front of me as it is one of the countless Irish holidays.

All of a sudden I see a poster: a horse show is on somewhere outside the city. Ha, I storm straight onto the open top of the electric tramway. And once again the journey takes me through charming suburbs with gardens that display Italian vegetation under cloudy skies. A fenced field. Beggars. Pushing and shoving. Tickets, please.

I go through the turnstile and all of a sudden know that I made a mistake. I come straight from London to Cork and, because there is no early train out of here, I expect that Cork, indeed the south of Ireland in general, should be as busy and interesting as tumultuous deafening London. But I am in a country where fine pigs are fattened and noble steeds are bred. This kind of a country needs market towns and they should look just like Cork.

Countless agricultural machines spin around the big field, steam engines heave. Rakes, flails and scythes move in rhythm. It is a colourful picture. Well-fed farmers with flat caps stand in front of the machines all business-like, forming small groups as they look on.

Horses standing in the big wooden sheds are about to be presented in the ring. Loud crowing sounds from a hut – and to tell the truth, Irish prize hens are certainly not small.

My travel companion is not happy. He expected sensational things, at least something of the hustle and bustle of a fair. But no, none of that here. Artificial flowers are on sale at one of the stands. Some country women are buying these flowers and their great-grandchildren will still have them gathering dust in the vases they inherit. Otherwise – seeds, manure, a bar where men sit legs astride drinking Irish whiskey with joyless dedication. A modest tea tent is provided for the women. That's it. And yet all of Cork is out here.

I can tell by the look on my companion's face: he is wondering whether he came all the way to Ireland for this. I tell him this is why I came. Earlier this morning the bays and islands – tomorrow the mountains and lakes. This here is indeed a pleasant bonus. The nondescript things are of course boring, and yet they are the heart and soul of all of life. Ill-fated is the country that boasts only tourist attractions; almost all picturesque regions on this earth are infertile and all interesting peoples dressed in rags. There is no lack of either in Ireland; but there are also fattened pigs and potatoes on this poor island. They are of less interest but are the future and the hope of this country. Ireland is only a few hours from London and London gets its meat from Australia while Ireland starves. Both could be fed on Irish bacon if Ireland were to become a little more boring. The English are terribly afraid that the food supply for their industrial cities could be cut off should war break out in Europe. Yet they tolerate the fact that in their own country more and more fertile agricultural land is being turned into pleasure gardens and hunting grounds for the aristocracy. On the neighbouring island of Ireland the singularly nonsensical agrarian practices of the gentry have forced the actual tenant farmers to emigrate in their hundreds of thousands out of sheer necessity, and today the best part of arable countryside in Ireland lies fallow while the rest is farmed inefficiently. Now that an anti-Ascendancy *majority is in power, England understands that every new tillage field in Ireland and every new cow on luxurious Irish meadows strengthens the position of the Empire. Sound agriculture in Ireland protects London and Birmingham from the threat of war better than one hundred *dreadnoughts, which cannot feed hungry citizens. Each and every potato an Irish farmer sells to an English importer ties rebellious Ireland more firmly to the Empire. When Irish farmers thrive, to whom are they to sell their produce other than the English consumer? This kind of thing binds two countries together more strongly than ten volumes full of political propaganda. There is nothing more important and more interesting in Ireland right now than the potato fields.

From this vantage point, all good Irishmen and, what's more, all good Englishmen should be in favour of filling in the famous Lakes of Killarney and growing potatoes on the reclaimed land. I hope that this commendable action will be carried out, but please, not this week. For I will soon be travelling to Killarney and I want to experience evergreen, wildly fragrant forests and bodies of dark waters. This is what I want to dream of. After visiting the horse show, I am indeed very much in favour of agricultural centres such as Cork – but I think after a day here one should sleep exhilarated and dream of something else. No passionate Irish patriot should expect me to dream of potatoes.

Chapter Four

Glengarriff

The train out of Cork offered me a polite apology: it was indeed a train, but unfortunately only a short one. It offered views of romantic ruins and, what's more, at one particular spot sight of the confluence of two Irish rivers – on the whole quite a beautiful journey. This is what the colourful posters and illustrated brochures said, and it all looked very nice indeed. But for now I will reserve my judgement and crane my neck to see romantic ruins. That is the first task for someone travelling through Britain – to keep their consumption of tourist attractions to a minimum, as otherwise they will go mad with all the posters, brochures and travel guides floating around and will die in frenzied pursuit of said attractions. Regarding ruins, they are more abundant in Ireland than fully preserved buildings. As per usual, the abbey in question was destroyed by *Oliver Cromwell, but sometimes it is simply an abandoned farmhouse of someone who has starved in the course of Ireland's grim history.

On we go. While travelling I do actually notice why the train had to apologise. In the face of English influences, this train knew how to maintain its Irish national character: third class is a pig sty and as uncomfortable as could be. A similar image haunts me when, gripped by fever, I have visions of Austrian passenger trains. It's quite clear that in good old Ireland the seats for ordinary passengers are nowhere near as comfortable as in England. I for one am very happy that the island is not too big and that no train journey takes too long. We are already approaching *Macroom. Just outside this dump of a town there is another important set of ruins, and then thank God the train ends and bids us farewell. Since I am in possession of an open ticket with all the bells and whistles, I am allowed to climb aboard an impressive motor vehicle. The *Tourist Development Co. Ltd has promised me further ruins and, what's more, ancient druidic altars in all shapes and sizes. When I bought the ticket in London, a poster guaranteed a delightful trip. In Cork, a brochure screamed: the most beautiful trip in the whole kingdom. In Macroom the motto has become: the most beautiful part of Europe!

For the time being the countryside is reasonably cultivated, hilly and very green. The motor omnibus races along as if it had now become very self-important and thought itself a lord's private automobile. We climb uphill slightly and then something strange happens: these few hundred feet of elevation give the land an excuse, as it were, to let its mask slip and to reveal the original state of the countryside. The few bad fields we saw up until now disappear from sight, but rich meadows do not always take their place. Swampy bogland and bare stones unveil themselves. You would think yourself at the summit of a range of high mountains or on the swampy plateau of an Alpine ridge. But you are actually not that high up at all, yet along the edge of the road wonderfully opulent flowers are in bloom, and yes, surely this bogland could be drained, and surely that slope is too good for grazing sheep – we are after all in Ireland, a poor downtrodden country. The villages we travel through consist for the most part of cabins which the cattle in England would hardly care to sleep in. But the biggest and most impressive building in every village is the school and that is laudable.

Undoubtedly, there are druidic stones among the many stones we pass by. The chauffeur swears to it; it says so in the brochure, too. In any case, there are plenty of stones. Steep rock faces appear to the left and right of the road, treeless but covered with deep-green moss. The heather is already in bloom. These rock faces jut out from an abundantly fertile soil and incredible floral splendour. Now and again you can see oak forests. The oak trees here are not as straight as ours. The branches twist into strange gothic forms, and there is also fern in these forests!

The area becomes more and more sequestered. One spot quite high up in the mountains – well what you call 'high up' on this island – is called *Lone Gouganebarra. Solitary Gouganebarra is a dark lake in a beautiful, deep basin of wilderness. In the seventh century *St Finbarr founded a hermitage on a little island here precisely because it is so isolated. And now they have plonked a hotel here, and Thomas Cook brings tourists who faff around the lake exclaiming 'Oh so very isolated indeed!' This is the brochures' fault.

If I hadn't read any of them or had had the good fortune to mislay my damned guidebook, over the course of the next hour I would have casually remarked on what a pleasant pass we traversed. It is indeed very nice and would also stand out in the Alps, given how steeply the exposed rock drops off at either side and how green the ferns are and how radiantly the heather blooms. But of course I already know that the O'Sullivan clan used to make their way through this pass from Keimaneigh to the plains, where they used to steal cattle ('The tourist can literally see the wild figures with their swords gleaming cheerfully'). Of course the guidebook says nothing about the red heather, and as a conscientious tourist I am not allowed to even look at it. The bus driver stops and pulls a ceremonial face. Since it is only myself and my German companion in the large vehicle, nobody says 'very fine indeed!' – but the words spoken with an American twang well-nigh hang in the air. But they do not improve the air. The air is abundantly fragrant. It is delicious and warm, mixed with just a pinch of sea salt. But without the O'Sullivans and the brochures it would be even better. Ireland is much too close to America.

Just after the gap you can see silver water shimmering; a bright bay comes into sight. Then there are daring cliffs, yellow gorse bushes, vistas of green and blue, and then another forest, but not a Nordic one, rather an almost tropical forest with evergreen trees and boisterous undergrowth. The driver points to a hedge and clearly says 'Few-scha'! My English is not that good, or perhaps I cannot yet judge the unusual Irish accent correctly, so I look at the hedge to find out what 'Few-scha' is. Indeed, this human-sized bush with countless red blossoms is the very fuchsia we plant in little flower pots. And here the entire narrow pass is bound by forests, glowing red forests of fuchsia. The leaves of the *arbutus gleam brightly in the undergrowth. I saw this tree on the *Riviera di Levante and was proud of how far south I had made it, to the country where fat red strawberries grow in the forest in untold abundance. Now on an island in the north of Europe I find this friendly miracle once again. Glengarriff is the name of this subtropical place on the rugged Irish coastline, and those who come here find it very hard to leave.

Just behind our nice, clean, tiny little hotel is a maze of trees, stones and fern. Climbing down on all fours, you arrive at a small dark river between massive boulders. An old ivy-clad bridge leads across the river. It was destroyed a long time ago, and who could have destroyed it if not Oliver Cromwell? The Irish have fond memories of this great man. He wanted to exterminate them one by one, but he did not quite succeed. Still, within just a few years he managed to reduce the native population by a good third; *between 1641 and 1649 around six hundred thousand people were killed or sold as slaves to the West Indies. Then one day Cromwell unceremoniously confiscated all of the survivors' land and settled his soldiers there. With unbelievable tenacity, the Irish race has since managed to reclaim everything it lost. It is only in Ulster in the north of the country that the descendants of Cromwell's soldiers can still be found in enclaves. They have remained fervently anti-Catholic Puritans and are now protesting against Home Rule, i.e. against the peaceful conclusion of the old bloody feud.

So the *Lord Protector also has this bridge in Glengarriff on his conscience. But may he be forgiven for this particular sin! Because if the bridge were intact, if it were just a normal bridge to cross over the river, then it would not be half as picturesque.

Of course, such ruminations are becoming of a tourist who seeks nothing but diversion. On one of the glorious beach walks near Glengarriff we came across a tiny little hut. A small potato patch at the front, and beside every third potato plant a proud plaque stating the name of the variety: 'Queen of Ireland', 'Magnum Bonum', 'The best of all!' We go into the yard and ask for a glass of milk. The old farmer's wife busily goes into the house, which consists of just one single, smoky room. A red-haired young lad is sitting at the open fire with a pipe, while a dog is lying in front of him. The farmer's wife fetches two clean glasses and fills them with excellent raw goat's milk. We drink one glass after another, enraptured by the view of Glengarriff bay with its islands, its old romantic castle, its sharp contours and its soft luminous surf. 'You have a really beautiful view here!' I say. 'The view is of no use to us', the woman replies, 'we are too poor!' But she absolutely refused to accept payment for the tasty milk, and in the end when I popped a few pennies into her children's piggy bank she insisted that that was just a gift and not payment for the milk.

The moral of the story is that a tourist like myself is a good-for-nothing so-and-so for whom a cabin can never be dilapidated enough, who thinks children dressed in rags are ever so picturesque and is outraged when he finds a boring crop of potatoes at a scenic viewing point. Glengarriff isn't exactly a poor place since the big hotels set up shop and Americans pass through the town, but look at the state of the main street! Nevertheless, in the evenings there is friendly banter on the street. The men with torn caps and short pipes stand around in groups. One group is reading the Cork newspaper and talking about Home Rule, the redemption that is supposed to come. Meanwhile, two ancient women converse in deep guttural sounds. It is the first conversation I have heard in Irish. You often see the strange *gothic lettering of the old Irish language on a shop sign or a noticeboard on the street, but you really don't get the impression that they are serious about the whole thing. In this part of the country at least, the old language seems to take a back seat.

As it so happens, the inhabitants of Glengarriff manufacture the famous Irish homespun cloth, and many a coachman wears a jacket that the ordinary folk of Berlin could never afford. Irish lace is also produced here. Who knows if the poor people really earn any money from this. Usually the most expensive and finest things are those that poor cottage workers profit from the least. What use is the beautiful view to them then?

It makes no difference. In this country, you cannot escape depressing thoughts. When the great English novelist *Thackeray travelled the island some seventy years ago, he wrote one page on each picturesque area, but three on each and every well-cultivated one. Perhaps he also liked cliffs better than potato fields. But as I already mentioned, you have a guilty conscience in this country, and if you are an Englishman like Thackeray, this guilty conscience must really bear down on you quite heavily. For more than a thousand years, this beautifully fertile country has endured the most awful history imaginable. When the bloodbath had come to an end, the political, religious and economic oppression remained in place; when Irish Catholics were emancipated, their most fertile fields still remained the property of English lords. And now fair-weather tourists travel this island, delighting in desolate bogs, lush and lonely mountain valleys and the picturesqueness of grotty villages. Tourists do exactly the same thing in southern Italy – where incidentally conditions are even worse than in Ireland. They are irritated by every well-built house because it does not fit in with the landscape the tourist office promised. Or they totally resent the country for its poverty. Other people are hit with a guilty conscience, as if they were somehow responsible.

At this juncture, allow me to establish the fact that I did not blow up the old bridge and I am also not a big fat landowner who bleeds his Irish tenants dry. But still – the Few-scha would glow even brighter, the forests even greener, the lakes even clearer, if Ireland's history was not as it is and if there were a few less romantic huts as reminders. At this moment in time, tourism is really taking off in Ireland. It will not exactly do away with the country's history because it feeds on it – Ireland's history populates the countryside with splendid sights, with druidic stones, with ancient kings and ruins in every shape and size, all meticulously decorated with ivy. But the tourist industry should help clear away the huts, these dreadful holes, even if then the ladies from Connecticut or thereabouts find Ireland a lot less delightful.

CHAPTER FIVE

The Park of the Lords

very single guidebook wanted me to go to Killarney. At home in
Berlin you rebel against these guidebooks and plan to live life as it
comes while travelling. But here in Ireland the guidebooks win over
and a peace-loving person assents to their dictate.

Once more I am not travelling by train, but rather in a large open-top
motor vehicle along with thirty Americans. Instead of improving the trains,
such bus routes are now being introduced all over Ireland. It is very pleasant
for the tourists; it costs a lot more, but it is very pleasurable. Hopefully the
natives will get together the necessary dollars so that they, too, can travel
their country in some sort of half-reasonable comfort. Indeed, there is no
law that states the Irish may not use the motor cars. But in reality they are
packed full of Americans.

So off we go, sitting aloft, through isolated passes, past rocky deserts and
green bogs. A miserable-looking hut here and there, everywhere else grazing
sheep and black cattle. Then we make the descent to the jagged coast of
the Atlantic Ocean. The omnibus company wants me to have lunch in a
certain hotel, so I have to. There are wonderfully big and expensive hotels
in this part of Ireland with violet rhododendrons in endless gardens, with
their own coastlines, golf courses that stretch for kilometres, everything
beautifully enclosed by walls – in short, in these ultra-modern times, it is by
no means just the parks of the English lords that cover the most beautiful
parts of Ireland, rather often it is also the pleasure grounds of American
tourists. And so I am forced to have breakfast in one of these unbearably
beautiful hotels and it's not exactly cheap. Then back to my lofty seat. It's
great that it is so elevated because otherwise I would not be able to see the
sea. In Ireland, when an area starts to become beautiful, it is immediately
shut off from the world of mere mortals by a towering hedge. Behind this

hedge, some lord or other has his park and this park extends exactly to where the beautiful scenery ends. Those who have paid for the privilege to sit aloft in a touring car can just about see over the high hedge into these parks. You can see the sea shimmer through the trees, a splendid country house on wide expanses of lawn. All of the views, the shoreline, the oaks, the arbutus and the blossoming rhododendron belong to the lord. If you peek over the hedge, you might just catch a glimpse of them.

And then we head inland again. There are no hedges here. The land still belongs to the lord, yet the views aren't as good, and hence His Lordship isn't really that bothered. Tenants who do not possess a penny to their name grow a few potatoes, while the rest of the ground remains untended. Hardly a tillage field in sight, and where there is one, the stalks are scattered around among the abundant colourful weeds. Now we travel over another pass. Anywhere else you would say that the road goes uphill. Here you go from fertile seashore to complete Alpine solitude within the space of half an hour. Not a tree in sight. And now a descent of a few dozen metres past small, still, silvery waters. A broad, bright valley opens up, a wonderful view of a chain of lakes, of mountains and dark green forests. And what happens? A hedge. Another lord's park.

We speed along towards Killarney. The hedge cheerfully keeps us company. But no matter, like all the Americans I have paid my fare and sit aloof – I am allowed to observe that the world is beautiful. I am looking forward to Killarney: lakes, mountains, forest. There must be plenty of walks!

The next morning, after I have suffered my way through an English breakfast, I stand at the front door of my hotel and look at Killarney's main street. Well, German villages have cleaner main streets. Alas, it is not because of the dirt and the dilapidation that Irish dumps seem so depressing, but because of their provincial insignificance, because of a shocking lack of character and appeal. How fondly I remember Tivoli, that Italian dump, when I'm in Ireland. There is decorative dirt and there is squalid dirt. Irish dirt is hardly ever decorative, although sometimes it can be. In Ireland, dirt does not just mean poverty, it signifies slavery. These Anglo-Saxons, these lords of the land, know how to look after themselves. Every tourist centre in England looks neat and pretty in comparison to Killarney, which is supposed to be the main attraction of the Irish tourist trade! But there's no use in wailing! I am going to the shore instead. I take the road to the left. Three minutes later I am standing in front of a park fence. Between me and the lake stretches the *earl of Kenmare's park, and whoever wants to reach the shore must go through His Lordship's park. Now His Lordship could do one of two things. He could either allow me, the wanderer, entry. That would be hospitable, generous, aristocratic. Or he could completely close up the gate and keep all of Killarney's beauty to himself. That would be snobby, haughty, exclusive. However, His Lordship, the earl of Kenmare, does something completely different: the noble lord demands an entrance fee of sixpence. If I pay him sixpence, he is not snobby, rather hospitable. All this makes perfect sense. And yet, something in my middle-class soul resents this practice, and I think to myself that I will just get to the sea by a different route instead. So I don't pay the sixpence and imagine how disappointed the earl must be right now.

As I turn around, a coachman speeds past and suggests that I might like to rent his jaunting car. Now, an Irish jaunting car is a truly enjoyable experience. A trap on two high wheels, drawn by a single horse, it rides like a fairground contraption rather than a coach. It looks as if the horse's saddle has slipped onto the horse's rear end. There is a high ridge in the middle, to the left and right under this ridge there is a narrow seat. The horse is not in front of you but beside you. The coachman sits at the front atop this ridge while the passengers must hold on tightly or else they slide off. It's great fun and rather quick, but, as the song goes: *'hiking is the miller's delight', and when it comes to hiking, every German is a miller. So I cockily reject his offer. I won't be driven to the lake's shore, rather I will walk there. I will sit in the grass. I will – –

In the first instance, there is a wall between me and the lake. Followed by a hedge. Now there's no denying that Irish walls are indeed beautiful; green trees tower above them. Irish hedges are even more beautiful: they blossom and smell fragrant. But in the long run, people don't like to be going to and fro between walls and hedges on a dusty country lane. Eventually, there are no more walls and hedges – instead, there is now a fence. This is where the lord's park ends and another one begins, this time one of the two hotels located on the lake. That's of absolutely no help to me. I do not have the privilege of staying in either of these hotels; all of my rich uncles from whom I might expect an inheritance are in the best of health and have plenty of children of their own. Well, I will keep going! But straight ahead I face another high wall, and behind it lies yet another park of some lord, or perhaps it's only the lord's second cousin, how would I know? But I start to realise that, given the present social order, I will certainly not reach the lake unless I pay the earl of Kenmare half a shilling. I turn around full of regret, pay the fee and swiftly learn what an Irish wall looks like from the other side. I have an enormous park at my disposal, indeed nature itself – thanks to the earl's permission. And I see all the things that the earl of Kenmare owns. A broad lake that roars as it throws up waves. Mountains as high as some of our German mountain ranges, but steeper and bolder. They jut out into the lake creating wild cliffs. Meanwhile, violet blossoms peek out of the deep green undergrowth. A dark stream flows through a narrow valley towards the lake, which is swimming with islands dotted with old ruins. There is an abundance and richness, as around the lakes of northern Italy, and a sternness and solemnity reminiscent of the northernmost parts of Scandinavia. But if the Irish people refuse to pay their sixpence, they do not get to see their own country.

In the hotel, I ask the innkeeper if I really have to pay the earl of Kenmare this tithe if I want to visit the area. She says not at all, I could alternatively book tour package 3c, the 'big tour' which includes lunch on a boat. The destination is a mountain pass, the *Gap of Dunloe, and it seems that in Killarney people would rather eat small children than forego this ritual excursion. If I were to follow my initial instincts I would probably prefer to eat small children – I am actually very much against such outings that you absolutely *have* to have done. But we humans are cowardly and weak when it comes to the superior stance and united front of guidebooks and hotel porters. I put my name down and the next morning a jaunting car awaits me at the hotel entrance. It takes me down that road with the hedges again. But today I can see over the hedges because I have paid to sit up on high. The car gradually brings me uphill as we travel between the hedgerows. Soon the area turns desolate and bleak once again. All of a sudden a rider gallops towards me on the street. Then another one, and another, ten in total. They all want me to rent their horse because I will soon have to alight from the vehicle when I get to the mountain pass. I wonder whether lords with hedges usually reside in Irish mountain passes. But no, they prefer their lake views. I don't need a lofty seat and I will finally be able to walk some of the way. And so ten very disappointed riders trot along behind my car. Incidentally, there are more vehicles of all shapes and sizes on the road – all the hotels in Killarney send their day-trippers off at the same time. It was like a fairground at the entrance to the pass with all the hustle and bustle. It is customary to drink a glass of goat's milk in a particular farmhouse here. All the tourists do it. In the meantime the front of the farmhouse is teeming with a hundred horsemen and their animals. They are all of the opinion that I should mount their horse. An old woman tries to sell me thick woollen socks, while a man with a trumpet says he can make a fine echo and that I can take him with me for one shilling. I don't like echoes. He is indignant, swings around on his bicycle and pedals off in a huff. I stick around for a while because it is just too comical seeing really old American women climb onto gentlemen's saddles and gallop off.

A delightful procession then makes its way through the mountains. Hundreds of horses trot along in front of and behind me; young girls laugh, old women shriek and squawk, drivers curse, and among all this solitude prevails – that is how gloomy the cliffs and the small mountain lakes are. Every sign of human life in the vicinity is completely miserable and does not warrant attention. Only now and again do you see a cottage, with a corrugated sheet roof along the road. A young girl is usually lurking outside the front door asking if the traveller is thirsty and wants to have a ginger beer – chemical lemonade with vitriol and paprika, or, to be precise, a drink that would only ever please the singed palates of irredeemable old whiskey drinkers. Apart from this inconvenience (and it is easy to ignore it), the area is unassuming, like a lunar landscape. I sit down at the side of the road and let the riders pass by. When they are further away, going over the humpback bridge up ahead, they look good, romantic. A young blonde American miss with white feathers on her hat scorns her Irish driver, who is leading her horse by the reins. Laughing, the horse gallops away on her all of a sudden, past the frightened Sunday riders. The spectacle presents a joyful silhouette on the bridge, a Valkyrie with a healthy dowry.

The dust settles. I can slowly continue on my walk. The man with the trumpet is waiting at the next bend and says for three pence he will now blow his trumpet. I thank him but refuse. He sounds his trumpet nonetheless, and then comes after me saying that he has now blown his trumpet, there was an echo and I may give him a penny. Another man behind the next boulder shoots off a small cannon, while at the darkest lake a photographer takes my picture, not because he thinks I am ever so photogenic, but because he wants to catch me somewhere later on and sell me the developed photo. That's what the poets call the tranquillity of the mountains.

You can see the lake glistening in the distance when you reach the end of the gap where the valley leads on to the other side. Everyone is delighted and the horses trot off. I rejoice; now I will get to the lake, whether the earl of Kenmare likes it or not. My boat with the breakfast basket is already waiting for me at the shore. I see the traffic building as all the riders dismount. Now we arrive at park gates, and at the gates there is a charming little ticket booth. If you want to pass through to get to the lake you have to pay *Lord Bandon a shilling. The ransoms of medieval highwaymen seem harmless in comparison to this. All this happens in our civilised times. In Ireland, it is perfectly accepted and legal that the entire country is in the possession of a handful of English lords.

The breakfast is nevertheless very tasty. We are sitting on the grass eating yet another sandwich. Three paces on, members of a Thomas Cook party lounge on the grass, ceremoniously being served by their liveried guides as if they were in the dining room of the Astoria hotel rather than under the very blue sky on a very green island on the shore of a very blue mountain lake. Nothing beats proper international classiness.

I take my last few sandwiches aboard the boat. It's time to explore this lakescape more closely. What follows is exquisite – a long, magical boat trip taking in the three lakes. The lords' arbutus trees are so very green, the lords' sky glows pleasantly, their eagles encircle the stark mountain peaks, which also belong to the lords. They own history, too, these lords: old abbeys and castles on the shoreline were wrested from the Irish and destroyed by lords of former times. *Ross Castle, Innisfallen Abbey. Ivy creeps up the old ruins. When the Irish pay their entrance fee, they too are allowed to witness how cultivated their country was in ancient Christian times, and how bravely Irish soldiers once defended these castles against the English intruders. But the Irish soil they fought for nowadays belongs to the lords. Ireland has become these lords' back garden.

CHAPTER SIX

Pat and the Lord
An Annotated Fairytale

'Once upon a time in the County of Kerry, or maybe it was a different county in Ireland, there was a red-headed man named Pat who loved to sing a tune. And he had reason to sing, because his land was green and fertile, his pigs thrived, and his cattle never had to go into the shed since the fields stayed green even in winter.'

Hang on a minute. This requires commentary: If it didn't always rain in Ireland, it would have a truly Mediterranean climate. The country is not poor, rather it is rich and fertile, it's just Pat who is impoverished.

'Pat might not have always made for an agreeable sight, looking a bit wild with his rough, homespun coat, but he was a decent fellow with a placid, upright and pious demeanour. He honoured his chieftain like a god and his priest like no god had ever been honoured. Of an evening he would listen to the songs of the village bard, who sang of olden times and the deeds of the ancient kings.'

COMMENTARY: If we were to believe patriotically enthused historians, the Irish bards were, up until recently, passionate lovers of the arts and gems of historical scholarship. The eighteenth-century poet *Eoghan Rudhan O'Sullivan was a farmhand. One day, when his landlord's son could not get to grips with a Greek text, he helped him out. In Kilkenny in 1817, a farmer called his eldest son to his deathbed and recited his family tree several times over, which went back to 210 BC, and naturally enough to the ancient Irish kings. Yet nowadays in Ireland *illiteracy rates are staggeringly high.

'However, at that time there lived a strong man across the water called Lord John. He was not only called a lord, he was indeed a lord by profession. It so happened that Pat's beloved chieftain got into a quarrel with another chieftain – sure what else would they be doing? So, Lord John sent some of his many, many sons across the water to help the enemy of Pat's chieftain, whose cause was doubtlessly most righteous and just. John's sons killed Pat's beloved chieftain and later on the other chieftain as well, because in the meantime it turned out that he was in fact a traitor of the worst variety. Pat didn't have much to do with all these goings-on, but John's sons told him that they were now his overlords as they made themselves comfortable in front of his hearth stretching out their long legs and beating Pat's sons if they did not hurry along to slaughter the calf and serve the porridge. However, they paid nothing but compliments to Pat's daughters. Although they boisterously pulled at the village bard's beard when he came along in the evening, the young lords also began to unconsciously hum along to the sounds of the harp. They were also very taken with how Pat's wife prepared the porridge. As time went by, they married Pat's daughters and got along just fine with Pat. In the end, Pat just had a few more mouths to feed.'

> COMMENTARY: The first English settlers in Ireland turned into true Irishmen in the blink of an eye. Old Norman noble families relinquished their names and started calling themselves 'Mac' and 'O'. Centuries later, when new Englishmen reconquered the country, these 'degenerate' dynasties were the invaders' most treacherous foes.

'Lord John got quite angry when he no longer heard anything from his sons and so he sent new sons across, but they did the exact same thing. Pat's house was starting to get a bit overcrowded, but he remained the same as always. It was Lord John who became indignant and cut off all communication with his sons who had degraded themselves by marrying Pat's daughters. One day, Lord John made a very important discovery. Pat, in his naivety, worshipped St Patrick's crozier, the holy staff which Christ's hand had touched, or so believed Pat. John, on the other hand, all of a sudden thought that this was idolatry; around that time, he had received a beautiful new prayer book and was convinced that God could only be worshipped with these prayers. And so, he once again sent new sons across the water, and these ones were more irate than the previous ones. For starters, they burnt St Patrick's staff, then they attacked Pat's revered priest and chased him away. They then sent over a new priest and the new prayer book, which Pat didn't understand. Pat had to pay burdensome tithes to this new priest, while his own priest was left to starve. Neither Pat nor his sons-in-law, John's degenerate sons, were too pleased. They preferred the old priest and had more faith in St Patrick's staff.'

COMMENTARY: The Reformation was a spiritual movement across Europe and iconoclasm was merely an attendant symptom. In Ireland, the Reformation consisted solely of burning the most sacred and holy relics and of banishing the monks so as to give English reverends hefty sinecures without any parishioners. No one ever tried to convert the people to the new teachings, nor were the Bible or the Book of Common Prayer ever even translated into the local language of the time.

'And so it came to pass that Lord John once again sent more sons over to Pat. It was not as easy for these sons to marry Pat's daughters because Pat no longer shared the same religious beliefs. That's why these young lords started to pester Pat and his sons. Some of Pat's sons, however, had no manners and bravely put up a fight. Unfortunately, John's sons were much stronger, and they threw Pat's sons out of their house.'

COMMENTARY: Irish history of the sixteenth and seventeenth centuries is full of desperate rebellions and insurrections, followed by mass confiscations of land. Any time an Irish chieftain rose up in rebellion, the land was confiscated from the peasants of the area, and English settlers were quick to occupy it. But these settlers, too, at least in part, were swiftly absorbed into the native population. The methods used to confiscate Irish lands were often very irritating and provocative. During the reign of *James I, the authorities informed landowners in *Connaught that their titles had to be re-registered, and registering incurred additional fees. The decent people paid these fees, but they did not receive the new documents. A short time later, the government declared all these lands as confiscated – because they had not been registered.

'One day, yet another one of Lord John's sons came trotting up to Pat's house. His name was Lord Oliver, and he was especially fierce and strong.

Back home he had even beheaded his own king. He displayed excessive force when he met Pat. And because Pat would not accept his rule straight away, he chased and kicked Pat into the remotest corners of the country. He slew Pat's sons wherever he could find them, while he *packed others onto slave ships and sent them off to wild negro countries to work on Lord John's sugar plantations under the whip like wretched animals. And Pat's fields were then taken by our Oliver without further ado. Oh, poor old Pat, how badly off you were back then! The bard was struck on the head with his own harp, and the old priest had to go into hiding.'

> COMMENTARY: Oliver Cromwell's particular Irish policy has already been mentioned. The Lord Protector ordered the massacres of all hostile garrisons of the towns he conquered. Following the *Siege of Drogheda, he wrote to his parliament that not even thirty of the defenders were left standing. These were guarded closely while they waited to be shipped to the plantations in the West Indies. *Cromwell concluded: 'I hope that all honourable hearts will give the fame and the glory for this event to God alone.' Edifying words indeed.

'Having done such great deeds, Lord Oliver went on his way, but his brothers remained with Pat. At the same time, Lord John had yet another quarrel with his king: this time over a difference of opinion regarding the prayer books. The king ran off, fleeing to Pat. Pat thought to himself that he could obey Lord John's hereditary king because John's sons had said over and over again that one must always be loyal to his king, and if one of Pat's sons had not been loyal, they would have had him hanged and quartered. And so it was that Pat and his sons remained loyal to Lord John's king. However, other sons of Lord John, who were already in the country, rose up, while yet more of Lord John's sons came across the water, and boy they were strong fellows. Pat's family suffered a terrible beating and then Lord John made it known to them that as punishment they were no longer deemed human and each of John's sons was allowed to spit in their faces whenever they felt like it. They no longer had any rights other than to cultivate the land for the foreign settlers, land that no longer belonged to them and no longer provided sustenance for them.'

> COMMENTARY: The decisive battle was fought in 1691 between the Stuart King James II, who had been chased out of England, and his

great rival William of Orange. Following their defeat in the civil war, Irish Catholics were formally and unjustly made into pariahs without any rights. In the meantime, any time a viceroy has spoken about the majority of the Irish population in a royal speech, he has used the terms 'the Irish enemy', 'the common enemy', 'the enemy within'. *(Don't we know this practice all too well??!)

'Pat's sons then said: What's the point of staying at home? We are starving on our fathers' lands. We don't want to serve Lord John's sons any longer. We would prefer to go abroad and see if we can play a trick on them from there. And this is exactly what they did, leaving the bleak paternal home behind. Their father Pat, however, stayed at home. He had grown old here and hoped that better times were on their way. The sons emigrated to far-flung lands and, anywhere they could, they played a trick on Lord John. Lord John thought this was terribly unpleasant of them, not to mention unpatriotic, and he simply could not understand their behaviour because everything he had done to Pat, he had only done for Pat's own good.'

COMMENTARY: Mass emigration from Ireland began in the eighteenth century. Between 1691 and 1745, the number of Irish who lost their lives in French military service alone was 450,000. Countless emigrants sailed to America, where they became the most ardent pioneers of independence. Eight Irish people signed the American Declaration of Independence, while Irish officers led Washington's army and fleet. The American-Irish never stopped staging conspiracies against England and to this day the Irish voters in America are the mortal enemies of every policy that shows goodwill towards the English.

'As time went by, things became a little unpleasant for John's sons who had remained on Pat's farm. They grew bored because there were no longer so many little Pats running about the house. So they decided to move back across the water to the big city their father had come from – there to have a good time. But before they left, they lectured poor old Pat and those sons of Pat who had stayed put, saying: "Just remember that every single inch of your land and every single blade of grass in your fields belong to us. We are heading off to our father's city and we need money there, lots of money. Beautiful women, noble steeds and playing cards await us. And you, of course, have to foot the bill. So sell your last drops of blood and send us money, otherwise we will tear the roof down from over your head. That is the law and it is, naturally enough, for your own good." With that, they headed off, leaving Pat's family in despair. Pat was terribly hungry and became thinner and thinner every day. He even stopped singing, despite the fact that he had always hummed away to himself even in the worst times. Meanwhile, the lord in John's big city needed lots of money because champagne is, after all, rather expensive. When Pat's sons could not afford to send any money, strange men came and tore down a piece of Pat's house. A few more of Pat's sons and their wives and children once again had to emigrate to foreign shores, while other sons starved to death. Pat himself was becoming ever weaker and he feared he would never see better times. His house became emptier and emptier, while the rain leaked in through the broken roof. In fact, it rained during the entire duration of this true story and it is still raining on Pat today.'

> COMMENTARY: The nineteenth century is the century of the scandalous evictions for Ireland. Even the most unspeakable slaughter of earlier times was not as bad: it is better for a farmer to be slaughtered than driven from his land. Up until two or three decades ago, a 'landlord' squandering his income in London could evict an Irish tenant farmer without any prior notice if he was unable to pay the outrageously high rent on time, or if the landlord simply took a dislike to him. According to official figures, which are much too conservative in their estimation, almost 110,000 tenant families were evicted from their farms. Machines were even invented to remove the roofs from the houses. This naturally enough resulted in a huge increase in the number of emigrants. In the last sixty years, four and a half million Irish people have left Ireland. On 4 May 1860, *The Times* reported: 'If this trend continues, Ireland will become completely English and the United States completely Irish. Then there will once again be an Ireland, but a huge Ireland, and an Ireland in the New World. We must prepare ourselves to face this consequence of seven centuries of misgovernance. Until the end of time, hundreds of millions of people spread across the largest inhabitable area on the globe will remember that their ancestors had to pay the tithe to the Protestant clergy, to pay rent to the absentee landlord and were forced to obey the laws that the two of them made.'

'Pat's dearest sons were thus evicted from their father's house, and were now clenching their fists somewhere out there in the world. Meanwhile, Pat kept himself composed in resigned patience, waiting. But his situation worsened. All the while, Pat's lords were living in the city, misbehaving, and tongues started to wag even in Lord John's home country. Those who started mumbling and grumbling were probably not able to deal with the insolent tyrants by themselves, and so Pat and his sons came to mind as possible allies. In turn, they promised Pat support. Perhaps John's sons had become more good-natured and could no longer look on at how miserable Pat was. In the meantime, Pat still had a few sons left to spare, who over time had become much stronger for their part and ever more like John's sons. They bravely helped against the lazy paunches and gluttons. And one day, Lord John came along and said to Pat in a bitter-sweet tone, for he actually loved his ill-mannered sons the most: "Dear Pat, I think you should have your land back. You just have to pay for it in instalments over many years."'

COMMENTARY: Over the last years, a veritable agricultural revolution has taken place in Ireland. Ten years ago, a Conservative government for the first time approved a considerable sum of money to enable Irish farmers to buy the land they had previously cultivated as tenants so that they could build a house fit for human habitation in place of the terrible huts. A second parliamentary decision from 1909 increased this sum to 125 million pounds, and in 1913 the chief secretary for Ireland introduced a bill in the House of Commons according to which another 160 million pounds should be used to help liberate Pat from his debt. It is reckoned that within twenty years, every Irish farmer can own his own turf, if he does not lose it once again on account of mismanagement.

'And so Pat lived to see better days after all. He was very grateful to Lord John, even though John is of course also human and knows exactly why he is doing good. Pat was once again in charge of his own land. However, in one particular corner where there is a beautiful view, where trees provide shade around a pool of water, in this beautiful corner where Pat used to sit and his children loved to play the most, that is where Lord John has built a walled garden and a charming country house. Pat's house did not have a roof anymore, but good old John lent Pat money so he could have a new roof made. And Pat stepped out of his front door and looked around his fields. How his heart sank! The beautiful chapel where he used to pray to St Patrick was destroyed; he could still see the blood at the back entrance where one of his favourite sons had been killed. The big wheat field was trampled flat, the forest cut down and the meadow had become bog. Pat fell to the ground in pain, digging his poor, red fists into his fertile soil as he wept bitterly. And if no one came along to help him up, then he is probably still lying there today.'

> COMMENTARY: It remains to be seen whether the land reform will help the Irish farmer if he does not receive capital and guidance. Fortunately, agricultural co-operatives have done a lot of groundwork, but if they are not expanded vigorously, Ireland will not be able to withstand the competition posed by Canadian and American agriculture, despite its close proximity to London. The Irish have also almost forgotten the art of agriculture. For centuries, Pat had no particular reason to exert himself for his absentee landlord who was anything but like the English squire who acted as the good-natured patriarch of his tenants.

That is the story of Pat the Irishman. And if you don't believe it, you will be charged a shilling.

CHAPTER SEVEN

The River Shannon

From Killarney to Limerick. This is another one of those cities very picturesquely situated on a river, but otherwise of little interest. The river is the Shannon, Ireland's answer to the river Rhine. The city, on the other hand – –

Well, when speaking of the city, it is only proper that the old Irish king *Brian Boroimhe should be mentioned, who is also called Brian Boru by those who like a bit of historical variety. Incidentally, all Brians, Bryans and O'Briens across the land and as far afield as America claim to be descendants of this ancient king, because he was a very powerful king and you really couldn't pick a finer ancestor. Brian Boru freed the city of Limerick from the Danish Vikings in 968. In other respects, too, the most important historical events in Limerick unfolded at very suitable historical dates. Indeed, the city has such an interesting history that it can completely get away with having nothing of interest in the present day. There is a new town with poker-straight streets, and there is an old town with an indescribable amount of filth and dirt. In between the two districts, historical buildings hang around, bored to death. The wonderful *Norman cathedral shimmers through the foliage of an overgrown garden. Of course, over time the cathedral was taken away from the Catholics and now belongs to the *Anglican Church of Ireland, which has almost as many cathedrals as it does parishioners.

I stroll on. As a diligent tourist I seek out the *Norman castle. Eventually I stumble across a hideous garrison with fine romantic towers jutting out of it. The English call their garrisons 'barracks', and they really are ugly – this one has boldly been inserted into *William de Burgh's castle. A khaki-clad corporal is standing at the gate and asks me if I want to visit the castle. Yes, I do. The corporal says that this is forbidden. I play along with his game and reply meekly, 'Oh well, what can you do'. The corporal says I could ask for permission, to which I reply, 'The next time I'm in Limerick, I'll do just that'. Then he tells me that he is the commanding corporal on duty and thus hereby grants me permission. Very well, I go through the gate with him. At that very moment, an elegantly dressed civilian cycles through the barracks' gate. The corporal stands to attention – the cyclist is his lieutenant. He just got changed out of his uniform because as a gentleman he cannot be seen wearing his uniform in the city.

We ascend a wobbly set of stairs to the top of the tower. The corporal points out evidence of bullet holes stemming from all periods of history. Standing at the top, I look out over the battlements at the beautiful broad river and a city that is still rather unremarkable. The corporal tells me that the Tower of London is of course much more impressive; he is from London, after all. His regiment was ordered into the Irish military police. The corporal appears to see this as a form of demotion. Leaning against the battlements, he rants on about the nasty Irish, who are so terrible for not policing themselves. He indignantly shows me the ribbon on the sleeve of his infantry uniform, a symbol of his obedience and decency. The letters RMP are embroidered on it: Royal Military Police. I think to myself that the entire British army is nothing more than a royal military police charged with ensuring that subjugated countries don't make off with themselves. If possible, the force is to take over new countries as well. That's how it has been up until now. The latest craze in London is to see if these countries cannot be trained to look after themselves.

I look at the map of Limerick. I look at the city before me and find what I am looking for. The bridge over the Shannon. It is a visible sign of oppression stretched across Ireland's longest river. It is the reason why this poor corporal has to play the policeman watching over Ireland, instead of seducing lots of dark-skinned women and winning the *Victoria Cross somewhere interesting – and closer to the heart of Africa. My guidebook tells me there is a stone monument on the bridge, known as the Treaty Stone. I for one will certainly not be going over to see this monument and to feel moved in its presence. I believe the guidebook when it tells me there is a stone monument on the bridge over the Shannon. But there is a story behind this particular monument. In 1691, a treaty was signed on this stone between besiegers and besieged, between the English and the Irish. Meanwhile, the Shannon quietly flowed beneath listening to everything.

A short time later, Limerick was appealingly renamed, a name you still hear today: 'The City of the Broken Treaty'. The English masters had ceremoniously arrived from Dublin, promising the Irish nation the most pleasant-sounding terms in the name of William of Orange if Limerick would just capitulate and forget about the Stuart's cause. Roman Catholics were to enjoy the same privileges they had under the Catholic-friendly Charles II. Those who took to arms in support of Charles' successor James were not to be punished and were not even going to lose their property or possessions. The Irish were to remain Catholics and citizens, and they were to retain the right to vote in parliamentary elections. This touching display of peace and goodwill brought an end to the Siege of Limerick and the *Irish war between the Jacobites and the Williamites.

A few years later new *Penal Laws were introduced in Ireland. They permitted Catholics to breathe, but that was about it. Catholics were not allowed to hold any public office, to vote for or be elected to the Irish parliament, to purchase property or buy a horse worth more than five pounds. If a younger son in a Catholic household converted to Protestantism, then he was entitled to take the entire family estate from his father and older brothers. All Catholic bishops, cardinals and monks were exiled. Catholics were not allowed to practise any professions or even attend a school of higher education. That's just a small compendium of the measures; more expansive historical works on Ireland have a lot more to say on the matter.

I remark to the corporal: 'Since the Treaty of Limerick was broken, that means that the Siege of Limerick is still ongoing, the only difference being that nowadays Limerick is under siege from within this barracks and by you, corporal. There has to be another capitulation, it's called Home Rule. Then you can dispose of your police armband and, as an obedient British soldier, go conquer dozens of dark-skinned women somewhere out there in the Empire.'

The corporal doesn't really care for world history, and instead he asks me if I have already sampled some Irish whiskey. The big building on the Shannon is a very good distillery, he tells me.

I am not hard of hearing and so I support the British army.

* * *

That's Limerick, the port city at the mouth of the Irish Rhine. Apart from broken treaties, the city exports bacon and ham as well as marvellous lace. Limerick is also famous for its beautiful women, but they seem to go into hiding when a foreigner wanders the streets looking for something to see other than butchers, cinema façades and small-town architecture, something easy on the eyes. Another noteworthy thing about Limerick is that you don't even have to stay here forever – there is a train out of here. And so that evening I was in Killaloe by the Shannon. My tip – pronounce Killaloe 'Killeluuh' and really draw out the 'u' at the end, it's as long as an *Irish mile.

A pleasant porter carried our luggage into a hotel on the riverbank. On the other side of the bridge you could see the old towers of a town. My companion says: 'After dinner we'll go across the river. We have to see Killaloe!'

'Yeah, we have to see Killaloe,' I reply. 'How else can we possibly get along in life if we haven't seen Killaloe!'

The July sun sank into the Shannon. We had eaten dinner in an exquisite dining hall – fresh salmon from the Shannon and other delicacies served on fine porcelain and silver. Now we were sitting in soft, roomy armchairs in the spacious conservatory. The little table was set up in such a way that the whiskey nightcap could make it straight into your mouth, that is if you weren't already puffing away on a soothing pipe. The Shannon shimmered silvery in front of us. We could hear the swooshing of a weir. Across the river, the first lights went on between the old towers. Night fell on the garden in front of the conservatory. The river paled, disappearing into the soft fog.

'No', I said, 'we don't have to see Killaloe. It's better to have just witnessed it from this incredibly sophisticated reclining chair – a silhouette of walls and towers on the other side of the nocturnal river. I'm sure Killaloe has a main street, over there, where all the lights are on. They are probably the bright lights of lots of regular little cinemas. Do I really have to know this for sure? What's more, the exact tourist attraction we are meant to visit is probably the spot where king Brian Boroimhe's palace used to be. That's all very interesting, but when the fog rises over the river and I puff away on my pipe, soon enough I can probably conjure up an image of what king Brian Boroimhe's palace looked like. That's better. On this beautiful evening I do not want to believe that Killaloe is a miserable Irish provincial backwater, made up of dust and historical pretention. It must be the old royal city on the Shannon where the people are sad because the kings of old are dead – cold and lifeless and forever regal. This is probably how the Irish see Ireland when they have emigrated to America and, on dark summer evenings, sit there dreaming themselves across the ocean towards home. They are clever, for they hardly ever return. Fog rises up from the Shannon, enveloping Killaloe – the fog probably knows exactly what it's doing.'

'You're right,' my travel companion replies. 'It's really very agreeable in this conservatory. Let's have another whiskey and soda.'

'It's not only agreeable,' I say, 'it's positively comfortable. The English travel to Killaloe to fish for salmon. They built this marvellous hotel so they could stay close to the famous weir where the salmon leap. They set up these unbelievably expedient armchairs so they could sit down and rest after a day's sport, which by rights a tired person should be allowed to do. They created whiskey to make the evenings evaporate away and carry the body off to sleep. That's not just agreeable, that's genius. The Irish are sitting on the other side of the river, and maybe they are talking about Brian Boroimhe, maybe not. In any case, they cannot afford this level of comfort. Maybe it is even more "agreeable" in their pubs over there; there's probably music and a different kind of whiskey – a more potent one – that makes the evening lively and cheerful! Perhaps. But when you have been travelling around Ireland for some time, you are allowed to give yourself an evening off and view the world from an English point of view, i.e. as a fiefdom where gentlemen indulge in salmon fishing surrounded by the greatest comfort. That's how things are in Ireland – the Irish have their ancient kings while the English have comfortable reclining chairs and couldn't give a hoot about king Brian Boroimhe. On the one hand, the Shannon is the Irish national river, on the other hand it presents an opportunity for well-off English and Americans to indulge in a spot of salmon fishing.'

'Let's have another whiskey,' my companion replies.

He is a man of few yet incisive words.

* * *

The next morning we travel upstream on a steamboat. Near Killaloe, the Shannon forms a large lake called Lough Derg, a gentle body of water surrounded by green hills and even greener pastures. Sometimes there are ruins or a castle tower on an inlet – after all, you wouldn't want to assume that there are no lords with their parks here. Or you see a church tower waving across the water – Irish national saints were founding churches everywhere, you see. *St Anmchadh from the 'sacred island' Iniscaltra even made it to Germany (where they probably couldn't pronounce his name correctly) and became a hermit in Fulda. Legends, legends – it really is like on the Rhine, the only difference being that the countryside along the Rhine has very much awoken from its reverie, while the Shannon dreams on. *The hill with a strange hole in the side is a prime example of this. According to the Irish, one day the devil took a bite out of the mountain. But for the greedy guts his eyes were bigger than his belly and, just like the English years later, he bit off more than he could chew. And so he spat out the piece of rock in *Cashel, County Tipperary, where it can still be found to this day.

The lake now turns back into a river and the hills have disappeared, as if the devil dined much more successfully here. It is simply a slow, winding, viridescent river between meadows full of reeds – and it goes on for hours on end. Sometimes a broad sail appears, sometimes you see cattle grazing along the banks. That's it.

A few Irish fellow passengers hang around on deck merrily playing a game of patience. The aim of the game is to slot a cunningly twisted iron ring into another one. It's terribly exciting. One of the men holds out the rings to me – I should try it too. I politely take the rings and twist them about over and over again. The Irish have a right laugh at me, for of course I cannot solve the puzzle, even if I wanted to. When I, this strange foreigner, have spent enough time amusing the children of this land with my ineptitude, I hand back the toy. I can think of a much more suitable game of patience to play at this exact moment in time: to watch how the river winds and twists its way along the flat, reed-lined banks. So this is the heart of Ireland: water, vast cow pastures, everything as green as can be, and topped off with a cloudy sky. I must say that for the whole time I have been in Ireland, I have been very lucky with the weather, something that is unheard of in the country's annals: it doesn't rain that often, but it always seems as if it's about to rain. The people live in an eternal damp mist, and it is particularly bad here on the river.

So, that's what Ireland looks like when you have passed by the picturesque spots, the repositories of legend, the ruins. Green solitude for the cattle. I again look in vain for fields full of crops – where are they? A sullen, dreary air of melancholy hangs in the air. The heart of Ireland beats rather listlessly.

The journey comes to an end. A few woeful cabins appear. *Banagher station. From here we take the train to Dublin, and then further afield. I can't stand being on an island for too long without going to the sea. I first have to take a look at the Irish Sea before I continue to tour the countryside, towns and cities.

Banagher on the Shannon. This place has just one delectable building: the train station for getting out of this backwater. This complete shit-hole. Pigs run about the village's main street looking exceedingly depressed, because that's their purpose in life. What's more, it starts raining, again, and the train leaves in three hours. What does a man do in Banagher on the Shannon when his train isn't leaving for another three hours?

We look for a pub. Not that we harbour high expectations! True to form, the entrance looks dodgy.

Yet, to my surprise, in Banagher on the Shannon I step into the nicest, cleanest and most endearing pub I have encountered on my journey so far. The rotund innkeeper is dressed completely in black and has big gold bracelets on her arms. She gives us a radiant smile that literally dries the wet clothes on our bodies. She doesn't want to know if we want to eat, and if so, what we want to eat – we are welcome, long-awaited and cherished guests. I take a look around. This is not the kind of comfort we paid for in Killaloe, this is quite simply 'Gemütlichkeit'. Someone will try and tell me that this word is untranslatable. But, contrary to all expectations, it seems that this word does indeed exist in an Irish dictionary. This polished, rounded old English furniture is the comfiest you can imagine. You might sink into a plush American lounger, but this upright middle-class armchair soothes the soul. A waitress neatly sets the table with the whitest of bleached linen and robust old crockery. She then serves us a proper, steaming pot of soup. The innkeeper sits at the head of the table. We assume that we have to pay afterwards, but for the time being she is a kind housewife sitting at her own kitchen table, and if a customer makes a fuss and won't eat, as an honourable housewife she gently obliges him to do so. It doesn't occur to the customer to order this or that from the waitress – it would be rude and ultimately futile. The rotund innkeeper, however, immediately and intuitively knows that the customer would like just another little drop of oil on his salad. And she chats away about all sorts of things, with the discretion of a lady, the politeness of an attentive innkeeper and the kindness of a stout country mammy. We stretch out our feet under the table and feel at home. So it turns out that the jovial, hospitable Irish aren't a literary invention after all. What's more, there are completely unexpected rewards in the middle of Banagher on the Shannon. A crazy idea comes to mind: what about staying in Banagher for eight days? Of course that's not really an option– from time to time, I would have to step outside, and this prospect is no less disconcerting than before. So I have to make do with these three hours, but they fly by. Yet, the whole time we are here, there is one thing playing on my mind: will this fine Irish lady be insulted when it comes to paying up? Well, while we are drinking our coffee the innkeeper disappears and the waitress, a lot less timid than before, brings us the bill. But we still want to thank the innkeeper for making us feel like invited guests. And she deserves every bit of it, as she brightened up quite a dull day.

We board the train, leaving the Shannon behind us. On our journey thus far, we witnessed all the things the Irish Rhine flows past – past the ancient Irish cheerful disposition, past very modest country folk who nevertheless enjoy their own brand of Gemütlichkeit. Then it flows past green, melancholic islands full of reeds, ancient Celtic castles and legends, an English establishment for very comfortable salmon fishing, and finally past the city of the broken treaty, under the bridge that has symbolised Ireland's oppression for centuries. All of Ireland lies on the banks of this, the national river. And it is to Ireland's credit that the small pub in Banagher is also to be found along the Shannon. In some ways, this pub must be the dear old Ireland that the Irish around the world rave about.

CHAPTER EIGHT

At the Irish Sea

A few days later I wrote a letter to Berlin:

Where am I? Gosh, I'm just around the corner in Bray, County Wicklow, Kingdom of Ireland. It's a seaside town right beside Dublin, but *Heringsdorf on the Baltic is actually easier to get to from Berlin. And if I can let you in on another secret, Heringsdorf is nicer too, not to mention the North Sea resorts. Bray is lacking the beautiful sandy beaches, and then there's the minor peculiarity that, for someone from Central Europe, it's quite difficult to actually go swimming here. There's seawater alright, but look at the state of the men's changing rooms! The cabin doors can't be closed because they don't even have doors in the first place. The diving boards and the steps leading into the water are perilous and you would have to be an acrobat not to fall off them. Once you actually make it into the water safely, you find yourself standing on hard pebbles. If you crawl out you are given a dirty towel. Now, in Heringsdorf all this is quite different. Why, you might ask, am I not bathing there? I could be all hypocritical and instantly regurgitate the spiel from the tour guides in Bray and the surrounding area. It really is quite pleasant – there are steep cliff walks ablaze with crimson heather, there are extensive parks, a waterfall, imposing hills and deep river valleys, and everything is so wonderfully green. Nothing but wonderfully green. Bray is in the heart of green Ireland and Ireland is so green because it's always raining, which can of course spoil your seaside strolls.

I'll admit it – it would have been much nicer and cheaper in a German seaside resort. And now for the even bigger confession: I didn't go to a German seaside resort because for the whole summer I didn't want to see anybody from Berlin. It's akin to fasting, so that afterwards your usual food tastes even better. If you don't cast off all your usual habits while travelling, then travelling just doesn't feel right. And so, once a year, I have to denounce my habit of hearing Berlinish being spoken, finding Berlin dishes on the menu and running into actors from the Berlin stages.

When I arrived in Bray, I made my way to the promenade and noticed that it consisted exclusively of guesthouses – all of them the same size with the same garden at the front. I went into the seventh-last one – I am very much in favour of the number seven. I went inside and was delighted at how very English everything was. A woman with English blonde hair stood in the entrance to the hall, as well as a very tall, very angular gentleman. They spoke English, saying it was a very lovely day, despite the rain. I negotiated with the ever-so English landlady. She brought me the guest book, and I wrote: from Berlin, Germany. And then the very English lady turned on her heel and said as German as could be: 'Ach!' And since she was still as British as could be, she sent the angular gentleman over to inform me that she was, in fact, from *Wilmersdorf. Five minutes later I was sitting in the exceptionally cosy drawing room beside the blonde English lady, who has lived in Berlin for years and now spends her holidays at the Irish Sea. A group of English ladies sat around us, occasionally uttering 'indeed?' because of course we were talking about Berlin and what a great city it is.

Then dinner was served. The soup had a bit of a kick to it. It had a strong German taste, not so much of herbs or a stock cube, but rather of hearty meat broth. Then the fish dish arrived – 'Aal grün', boiled eel in herb sauce – a Berlin speciality. At this point a chef dressed in white appeared at the dining room door. He looked at me to see if I liked it, too. I said everything is 'very good indeed'. The chef replied *'det freue ihm'. He was from Rixdorf, you see, this chef. He emphasised the name *Rixdorf, because he came to England before Rixdorf assumed a historically coloured name (Neukölln). This chef spoke north-eastern Berlinish with a thick London accent. And when he heard there was a gentleman from Berlin in his dining room, he really made an extra effort and cooked proper Berlin fare, but the food still had a certain London flavour to it.

After dinner it all became very Anglo-Irish again. I was sitting beside five tall gentlemen in the smoking room who wanted to know what we thought of the *Balkans in Germany and was the invasion not about to begin and were we not shaking in our boots at *the thought of France. I talked until my mouth was dry and then rang the bell. The maid came over and I asked for a whiskey and soda. The girl pulled a face in response, telling me I was in a non-alcoholic hotel. On hearing this, one of the gentlemen stood up, and returned a short while later with a huge bottle of whiskey. He had it in his bedroom – for rinsing out his mouth. It was really good old whiskey. Nothing beats a non-alcoholic hotel.

Afterwards we frequented a music hall. A very good, extremely entertaining cabaret show was on, but the actors did not stop talking about Germany, and mocking the Germans, and thereby I learn exactly how the clowns will behave when the *German invasion begins.

By the following evening, I had managed to calm down somewhat – a big military concert was to take place and it simply had to be oh-so British. Incidentally, it was very pleasant as well. It started off with a regiment of bagpipe players from the Scottish Highlands – bare legs, colourful, handsome plaids draped over their shoulders, even a leopard skin on one occasion. Little Scottish bonnets placed atop unkempt mops of hair. The music sounded like belly-dancing music, but was still quite martial. Next up were the drummers and pipers from a regiment of grenadiers. They marched with beating drums, or rather with dancing drums. The stocky conductor threw his cane in the air just like the famous *Mister Meschugge. The drummers dressed in red held their drumsticks above their heads, swinging them like Indians do their weapons of war, and only then did the wood strike the hide. Next up were marching bands from two battalions – staunch, red as lobsters, soldierly. All of the musicians march to the far end of the promenade, where a very important musical general assumes command. Now the melodious army lines up – English, Irish, Scottish. A marvellous battle scene by a quintessentially British man called *Eckersberg really bears a striking resemblance to the battle music you hear on festive days in *Wannsee, the only difference being that in Bray 'Heil dir im Siegerkranz' ('Hail to Thee in the Victor's Wreath') features as 'God Save the King'. But it's the same melody, and with the impending invasion the English will realise that things won't change all that much. I already told the gentlemen in the smoking room that the entire clandestine plan for a German invasion is in fact based on this similarity in national anthems.

From all this you can see just how different battle songs are in Wannsee and in Bray, County Wicklow, Ireland. But in Wannsee you drink a wheat beer while enjoying the music, and if there was wheat beer or even any kind of tasty, enjoyable beer in Bray, you couldn't properly enjoy it anyway, for on the entire length of the promenade there are at best bars and hotel restaurants, but not one single beer garden, or beer hall with inviting tables. That's not how things are here – the bottle of whiskey lives beside the washbasin. I have landed in the strangest surroundings. This experience alone makes my extensive travels worthwhile.

I say this to the British lady from Wilmersdorf in the hotel, and she laughs at me. Why am I constantly reminded of Berlin when I am actually pining for local charm? Because the urban masses of Berlin possess local charm and because urban masses all over the civilised world share this charm. Ireland doesn't start until you get to the next village further inland. But here in Bray is where Dubliners come on commuter trains to spend a day, just as Berliners go to Wannsee. And all resorts outside urban centres are like Wannsee. A seaside town close to San Francisco, Cape Town or Sydney can't be much different.

So should you even bother travelling at all? Yes, you should, because those who have only been to Wannsee and maybe *Swinemünde will not enjoy such profound insights. That's not to mention the mileage I'll get out of this back in Berlin. 'So you were in *Ahlbeck, Mr Mayer? I was in Bray, County Wicklow, myself. That was quite an experience indeed! The Emerald Isle. Erin. There was a radiant blue sky and crystal-clear waters. When I was taking the air on the banks of the River Dargle...'

Mr Mayer is now ashamed and deeply distressed that he only made it as far as Ahlbeck.

CHAPTER NINE

The Meistersinger of Ireland

O n any given Sunday, people in England are not allowed to do anything other than go to church and be bored, but in a respectful kind of way. Things are a little bit different in Ireland. People are very religious here, too. The well-dressed people attend their Sunday service, but the huge Church of Ireland church is never quite full. The not so well-dressed people, the real Irish, kneel at the doors of the Catholic cathedral in their droves, because there isn't enough room for all of them inside. Meanwhile, the Catholic clergy do not demand that their congregation quietly go back home after mass and bore themselves to death for the afternoon like the Anglicans and the Presbyterians – quite the opposite, in fact. Sunday afternoons in Catholic Ireland are spent singing and dancing, and the clergy are right in the thick of things.

The clergy is part of everything going on in 'Irish Ireland', not just on Sundays, but during the week as well. 'Irish Ireland' means the Catholic counties that, in contrast to Protestant Ulster, still consciously want to be Irish and love Ireland. The priests and chaplains rule over the *Gaelic League, which is trying to resurrect the ancient Celtic language, they rule over the *Ancient Order of Hibernians and *Sinn Féin, as well as any number of other nationalist organisations and associations. That's also why they have to preside over the many competitions in Irish singing and dancing held on Sundays. In Ireland, they don't just sing and dance for pleasure, they do so in opposition to the English, the Saxons, the Protestants, the lords. It seems well-nigh impossible that people might sing and dance in Ireland without there being some sort of religious and national agenda behind it.

A green Irish meadow situated just above the seashore. The very European and very ordinary promenade can be seen in the background.

The fashionable visitors from Dublin and from England are sitting on the benches dotted along the promenade, all looking very respectable indeed, barely raising their eyes when loud brass bands or Irish boy scouts in their green shirts march past. Up on the meadow, respectable-looking hats are in the minority – second-hand flat caps dominate, but the odd clerical biretta can also be seen. Those who pay just three pence entry can have a slightly elevated position on the grass; and there they sit in avid anticipation. Those who sacrifice another three pence in the name of their fatherland are allowed into the inner circle and can take an actual seat. A stand has been set up for the music, with a platform in front for the singers and dancers. Committee members with green badges run around looking all busy. The committee member with the quietest voice takes to the podium and makes a speech. It must have been a very pleasant speech and will surely be printed in the weekly paper. Then the music starts. Up until this point, I was in a provincial backwater somewhere in Europe, looking on at some sort of local festival. As soon as the music starts, however, I am in Ireland, in Irish Ireland. The young boys in their sloppy uniforms play music that is cheerful, melancholic and dramatic all at the same time. It is Celtic, it is Irish. The skipping rhythm of the Irish dances also underlies the country's anthems, while conversely the lonely Irish bogs and the blood and the agony of Irish history are somehow encapsulated in the dances. And time and again the melodies are infused with a solemn plea and with muted national pathos. The talent of the young boys in communicating this through their music is remarkable. It's just like Bohemia, where every village musician is truly gifted.

The competition begins after the music. The first row of seats is teeming with excited children – the *Meistersinger of Ireland are rarely older than sixteen years of age, and they are usually female. What's more, dancers are more abundant than singers. The pretty girls dance and the not so pretty ones sing. For the time being, they still have their long coats on over their white or blue cotton dresses and their green sashes; they sit beside their mother or sister shaking with stage fright. To start off, a young schoolboy shows off in his green shorts and pointedly green tie. At the same time a fiddler takes to the stage. The fiddle plays along to an authentic Irish dance. It's not really music, rather a breathless, monotonous tootling reminiscent of quiet villages, humble shepherds and rural amusement. The fifteen-year-old boy steps forward – all of a sudden he is no longer firm and sturdy.

His feet pound the podium. He moves forcefully on the spot. The dance seems similar to the *Bavarian Schuhplattler, minus the crudeness, or rather the way the divine *Nijinski would dance the Schuhplattler on a bad day. The dancer's upper body doesn't move, only the legs are alive, twisting and turning as they make the body airborne and then the legs fall on their tippy toes with a short, quiet thud on the boards. This is an Irish *hornpipe. But it might also be a *jig or a *reel – the difference is only apparent to professional Irishmen.

Following this dancer, a young little miss with the affectation of a prima donna takes to the stage. Irish girls can be very pretty, but there is also a more humdrum type with broad shoulders and angular noses. What's more, these plain girls dress rather oddly and adorn themselves with cheap jewellery. The singer steps forward, placing her hand on her forehead. This is supposed to mean 'I am terribly reluctant to perform'. Then the performance begins – a sentimental, melancholic Irish song with English words. There is a round of applause – her aunts are sitting in the audience. The judges with the green badges take notes, looking important. This performance will surely earn her a silver shamrock.

Next up is a really small child not yet ten years of age. It is delightful to watch her hop and skip across the stage. *Peter Altenberg would enjoy this. I take out my programme to look at the child's name. It's probably a really sweet girl's name, but I can't read it because, although the programme is written in English, the participants' names are printed in crinkled Gaelic lettering. Indeed, the entire festival is propaganda for the revival of the national language. A respected priest even says so during the first interval, but he says so in English so that everyone understands. He's a fine specimen of a priest. He makes jovial jokes as he speaks warmly of Ireland's old songs and dances, as well as its ancient language. In reality, he maintains, Irish is only spoken on the isolated, western-most fringes of the island and is not the language of present-day Ireland by any means. It is, therefore, dear to those who are displeased with present-day Ireland. Everything on this meadow is devoted to Gaelicness, but the fine old priest continuously speaks the language of the Anglo-Saxons. It seems that the audience supports the Irish language in theory rather than in practice.

This was evident just a short while later when a sweet little schoolgirl timidly took to the stage and recited a long poem in Irish. The audience was delighted, but nobody could tell me what the poem was actually about.

The jolly priest now has an important task to perform: he is giving out the prizes that were won in earlier performances. A cheerful crowd forms around the podium as committee members, clad in green, lug piles of heavy books onto the stage as well as small packages filled with silver medals, small crosses and shamrocks. The somewhat less charming young miss from earlier receives a hefty music book, and for a split second an air of apprehension reigns among the audience in case she might sing all the songs in the book. A tiny little chap no more than four years old struggles as he climbs up on stage. He is dressed like the embryo of an ancient Irish druid wearing a green tunic and a dark yellow throw made of home-spun cloth. He's as cute as a button. The priest gives him a little silver cross – and he deserved it for his hornpipe dance. We all applaud. The boy is delighted, as if he had just won loads of chocolate, and the priest shows him how to take a bow. Meanwhile in the corner, ten teenage girls compare their prizes, delighted if they got a better prize than their best friend. The boys have already come to fisticuffs because such-and-such a pal won't let them read the book they just won. For the most part, they are English books.

After the interval there is more singing and dancing, and after a while it all becomes a bit monotonous. But two boys and a girl dance a very nice reel. They reach out their hands to one another and jump into the air at the same time. They then advance in a line, clattering the soles of their shoes on the stage, performing a drill more so than a proper dance. They have a tense look on their faces as they concentrate on the next steps rather than enjoying themselves. But they are young and it is a charming performance. They know very well that they are doing something worthy of praise: they are dancing for their people and it is a show of support for Home Rule and of opposition to the Ulster Protestants; all very important indeed. The audience also looks quite serious, and there isn't a drop to be had at the entire event, not even Irish whiskey.

But at the end, the musicians powerfully swing their instruments as they play the song *"A Nation Once Again". An Irish melody with English lyrics. That's how it is in Ireland these days. It's doubtful as to whether the *Gaelic League will succeed in translating the lyrics, either. It's easy for people to learn this straightforward English language, and they never forget it. If a Mongolian person emigrates to America, he will speak better English than his native language in just one year. There can be no doubt that the entire Irish nation has by now linguistically crossed over to the

English-speaking world, and, despite all the Irish poems, it has also joined the English literary world. And it is an exodus from the linguistic realm of anonymous bards into the linguistic realm of Shakespeare – this should by no means be forgotten. Maybe the language of Shakespeare is stronger than the associations promoting Irish culture, despite the important role priests play in them.

Nonetheless, the ancient melodies still reverberate across the land, and Irish children learn them. In Germany, children dance the tango and have adopted *'Puppchen' as their national anthem.

CHAPTER TEN

The Capital

Every textbook says that Dublin is the capital of Ireland. Like most things stated so apodictically in textbooks, this is not the whole truth, rather an approximation. Dublin was at one time Ireland's capital, and in the future it will be Ireland's capital once again. Today, London is the capital of Ireland, and Dublin is merely a kind of minor centre. Just as the lord deputy of Ireland used to stay in England and would only send a subordinate to Ireland.

Walking around Dublin, you can see, feel, even smell that it was once a capital city. There are impressive public buildings in the classicist style, while just up the road young people dressed in rags fight in the dirt and the drunks stagger about the place. There hasn't been an Irish parliament here for more than a century – and since then Ireland has continuously gone backwards. In former times, this city was second only to London in the British Empire. The Irish peers had to live in their palaces in Dublin for better or for worse because the *upper house of the Irish parliament sat there. The wealthy gentry came to Dublin, as someone in every family was either a member of parliament or wanted to be one. At the end of the eighteenth century, Dublin was one of the biggest cities in Europe. Today, it is a provincial town with some metropolitan, indeed cosmopolitan affectations – a strange mix of Paris and Ballygobackwards. A town with hardly any industry, but with an industrial proletariat. The Guinness brewery is the most significant industrial enterprise in the city, but in Dublin the consumption of alcohol is certainly of superior economic importance than its production. A good deal of traffic goes through Dublin port on account of emigration. In dusty little shops you see exquisite old porcelain, pictures and furniture – the city is slowly retreating into its own second-hand emporia. Aside from one or two busy main roads, the streets are empty and quiet, unless a drunk is making a scene. Then you once again happen upon incredible English elegance, beautiful women and noble steeds: the viceroy has an official residence here and thereby upholds some of the city's former elegance.

To understand what Dublin is, you have to know what it was: a colonial capital. This thoroughly Irish city was the stronghold of all oppressors of Ireland, first the Danish Vikings, then the Anglo-Normans and then generations upon generations of the English. At one time when Ulster was still the stronghold of the wild *O'Neill clan and as Celtic as the back of beyond in Brittany, the English already had a tight hold on Dublin. Speaking Irish in Dublin was forbidden. By law it was permissible to beat any Irish person to death. This was solemnly declared in the *Statutes of Kilkenny in 1361. Pales were struck down into the ground all around Dublin to make sure that nothing Irish could make its way in. Down through the centuries, Dublin Castle was Ireland's answer to the *Zwing-Uri. To Irish ears, 'Dublin Castle' means bureaucratic oppression, police rule and colonial tyranny. When you visit the most important church in the history of Irish Christianity – St Patrick's Cathedral – you will find it full of memorials to men who fought against the Irish of Ireland. Of course since the Reformation it belongs to the Church of Ireland, which, from an Irishman's perspective indicates all things English and anti-Irish. An even more beautiful old cathedral, Christ Church, is located just down the road. At least this church was built by the Anglo-Norman conquerors and was never a national relic of the Irish people, like the church of the holy St Patrick was. Naturally enough, Christ Church also did not remain in the hands of the Catholic majority, who had to build brand new churches in the shadow of their misappropriated national shrines. When talking about the two denominations in Ireland in an erudite tone, you say 'church and chapel', whereby church of course refers to the Anglican Church of Ireland. In this peculiar country, the big cathedrals are for the minority, while the smaller ones are for the majority.

Dublin Castle, St Patrick's Cathedral and Christ Church Cathedral are all located quite close together on the right bank of the Liffey in the old part of Dublin city – a labyrinth of gloomy towers and battlements. Trinity College, the national university, is located somewhat further down the road. Up until 1792, Catholics were not permitted to attain an academic degree here, and Catholic academics have only been allowed to participate in all the perks and privileges of the filthy rich university since 1873. Nevertheless,

Trinity College is still a stronghold of English Protestantism. The college sends an MP to London, and at the present time this MP is *Sir Edward Carson, the leader of the *Irish Unionist Party and the most determined enemy of the Irish people. The Bank of Ireland with its ionic columns is just across the road at College Green. This is where the *autonomous Irish parliament sat until 1801 – a parliament that was elected by the English colonialists. Just when the Irish were allowed into parliament, it was closed right in their face, and the Union was enforced with all the corrupt methods known to man. Since that day, Dublin has no longer been the capital city of Ireland.

You can tell that this city has had a major historical role to play: it was the launchpad of the old British assimilation machine. It is from here that Ireland has been governed against the Irish. And yet time and again this city has regained its Irishness – and that is a very peculiar thing.

If there is anything that is as strong as the crushing might of Anglo-Saxonism, it is the adaptive power of the tenacious Irish nation. The Norman barons were speaking Irish, wearing Irish cloaks and using Irish names only a few decades after they had chased the old Celtic chieftains from their land. Cromwell's soldiers slew the Irish farmers and then became Irish farmers themselves (where they weren't all grouped together in clusters). *William of Orange saw off the last proper Irish rebellion at the end of the seventeenth century – a rebellion led by the last Catholic king of England. In the eighteenth century, Ireland became more Irish than ever; it witnessed a veritable Irish renaissance. While England was fighting against America and the French Revolution was raging on, the Irish could no longer be kept in check. Britain had to tolerate the fact that 40,000 *Irish Volunteers armed themselves so as to protect their country against a French invasion. These armed forces were too strong to be ignored, resulting in the high point of contemporary Irish history: the Dublin Parliament. This parliament, made up of English Protestant colonialists, had become so Irish that it fulfilled all national aspirations, it issued a declaration on national human rights and did away with the barbaric Penal Laws. From 1782 to 1801, Dublin was the capital city of a truly autonomous Irish state. The city experienced a tremendous boom.

And then the disastrous *1798 Rebellion took place, a side-show to the French Revolution, a bloody race war without any obvious political purpose. The English saw and took their chance to violently suppress recently liberated Ireland and to destroy its autonomy. Since then, Irish history has taken place not in Dublin, but in London. The great Irish leaders were members of parliament in London. The Irish had gained political rights and now had to exercise those rights in London. Since then the country has been ruled from London, even though the viceroy and the traditional bureaucracy have remained in Dublin Castle. The British assimilation machine no longer works its magic from Dublin, rather from London.

And London is more powerful. When the Irish were subjugated pariahs in Dublin, they remained Irish and turned their oppressors into Irishmen. The Irish as free citizens have all but lost their national specificity since they started sending MPs to London.

Dublin's main street is called O'Connell Street and this is even written in Gaelic lettering on the road signs. The beautifully straight street is marred with monuments, each one imbued with more nationalist symbolism than the last. But does this actually matter? What matters is what you can buy in the shops on this thoroughfare. And what you can buy is nothing but English products. The pedlars run around screaming as they sell the morning papers from London. For sure, they also sell nationalist newspapers with the most valiant patriotic editorials and columns in Irish with their conspiratorial messages. But the reports on the latest horse race in London are read with much more enthusiasm, while the back page flaunts advertisements for Lyons tea and Pears soap. Irish nationalists wear top hats in the London style, they take lunch in a typical London city restaurant, where there is not one Irish speciality to be found on the menu. The whiskey is the only thing that has remained Irish, as the Scottish one is not as potent.

Dublin has been a big provincial English city with traces of Irish nostalgia ever since it lost its status as a fortress of subjugation. Essays on Home Rule and Irish grammars are on display in bookshop windows, but the newest sixpenny novellas by popular London authors are what people are buying. During the season, the newest London hit shows receive mediocre stagings in the local theatres. The excellent actors who speak Irish dialect are popular only in London and have no audience here in Ireland. George Bernard Shaw wrote his political comedy *John Bull's Other Island* for Dublin, but it was performed in London.

Dublin is an English city with more noise, dirt and whiskey than all other Irish towns and cities combined. And maybe with a little more music and local flair. It's not easy to pinpoint what is still Irish about this city, but when you roam the streets and see reminders of the past, you soon understand.

What is Irish about Dublin, indeed about the entire island, is the longing for an Irish national identity that has long disappeared. The painful longing for the painful experiences of a miserable past. The Irish are not like the Poles, whose nation state was destroyed; the Irish never had one in the first place, if you ignore good old Brian Boroimhe's nebulous kingdom. For a century, the only thing that was Irish was resistance against the enemy. The result of this is not a truly modern, homogenous nation, rather only sorrow and lamentation over lost nationality. There's no denying that this unites a people. But what the Gaelic League is putting out there as unique Irish cultural capital – the Gaelic script, bardic rhetoric, druids and ancient kings – is merely sanctimonious historical hocus pocus. If Dublin were destroyed tomorrow by an earthquake, if all the monuments of historical oppression and all the symbols of the persistent struggle for assimilation were to be reduced to rubble, and if the new, united Irish nation had to rebuild the city amidst the ruins, they would build a quintessentially Anglo-Saxon city. The only thing that gives Dublin a sense of Irishness today is the memory of English oppression. The English know very well why they now want to make Dublin into a proper capital city again, this time of an autonomous state within the British Empire. From Dublin, the complete Anglicisation of the island will be conducted once Ireland gains self-governance.

When an Irish parliament once again resides on College Green, it will undoubtedly erect ten more patriotic statues with harps and inscriptions in Irish. But each and every member of parliament will wash themselves with Pears soap, will drink Lyons tea while dining on bacon and eggs, and will prefer to read Shakespeare and even more so the latest penny novels. Basically, he will be a man of colonial England with a sentimental penchant in his heart for something quite un-English.

An opponent of the Irish once said that the Irish don't really know what they want, but they won't rest until they get it. This is the key to the Irish question. This utter restlessness is the only thing that characterises the Irish today, in addition, of course, to a peculiar disposition determined by climate and race. Culturally speaking, Ireland is an Anglicised nation, but its Anglo-Saxon culture does not make it a nation of rulers. When Dublin becomes the capital of Ireland again, a unique variety of Englishmen and women will form a new, Anglo-Irish state. These people will be distinguished from Londoners the same way that Bavarians are from Eastern Prussians. Dublin will become a kind of British Munich. As soon as Home Rule is introduced, the assimilation of the Irish will reach completion. If, for the thousandth time, Irish autonomy is thwarted, Dublin might perhaps become a Gaelic-Celtic city once again, even if it isn't exactly clear how this would be achieved. Perhaps it might be achieved in the same way that Catholic clericalism could triumph permanently in Ireland – by renewed persecution of Catholics.

If Home Rule fulfils the Irish people's longing for Ireland, there will no longer be an Irish people.

CHAPTER ELEVEN

The Hero of Tullow

Queen's* Theatre, Dublin. It's the second performance of the evening. The first is at 7 p.m., and then at 9 p.m. for a second run. However, the playbill states: 'Two genuine plays, not edited in any way, rather especially written for two performances in one evening.' That really puts me at ease.

The German reader will get a faint whiff of provincial cabaret at this point. But the Queen's Theatre is by no means a shanty out-of-town set-up, rather it is an impressive building. Nevertheless, I wouldn't like to be here when a fire breaks out. If you have time to kill in Dublin during the summer and don't want to go to the cinema or to one of the monotonous music halls, then your only choice is to go to see a performance in this theatre, the only one open at this time of year. What else is there to do on a summer's evening in Dublin? The shops all close at 7 p.m., and at 8 p.m. it's already obvious that the Irish whiskey is making itself felt. Drunks stagger along the broad main streets, which during the day look somewhat metropolitan and even a little elegant in places. In the ineffable side streets there is nothing but vile, loud chaos. Not even Naples has such an impoverished, miserable district. It's as if a pack of drunken ruffians have been let loose on the city. Indeed, an evening jaunt in Dublin isn't really any fun at all. You could dally in front of the ionic columns of the Bank of Ireland, the former seat of the autonomous Irish parliament, and listen to the two speakers holding an impromptu open-air people's assembly. One speaker, a black man, wants to promote a new diet and very affordable therapy; the other speaker, a bald-headed man, is spouting off about a religious sect. Both of them are standing on the small, open vehicles that form the national mode of transport here. Both of them are roaring and shouting, and they are joined in their activity by the tipsy crowd surrounding them. Two extremely tall policemen are standing beside them looking rather sedate. Fine specimens they might be; still, policing Dublin cannot be considered an easy task.

After a while, the black man's new diet will become just as boring as the bald man's new religion, so it's just as well that the show is about to begin in the Queen's Theatre. A seat in the dress circle costs one shilling, but, since the theatre is full, I don't get a regular seat for my money, rather a spot on a makeshift bench placed across the centre aisle. So I sit myself down here, and should the audience break out in a panic, I couldn't be more in the way.

There's also an upper circle and a gallery, and in the gallery the people of Dublin only pay thruppence for their seat. Looking up there is comical. You can see a few rows of heads with grimy flat caps sticking their necks out, and they all seem to be hanging right over the stalls. Prominently displayed in huge writing above their heads is the following notice: 'Rowdy behaviour and especially smoking are strictly forbidden!'

Below, the music starts. It's blaring circus music, but at the same time it is still soft and replete. We are in Ireland – the land of music. Then the curtain rises. The stage is a somewhat rudimentary interior of an Irish farmhouse. The music keeps playing. All of a sudden a made-up woman in a simple blue dress takes centre stage. A spotlight falls on the meek heroine, surrounding her in a mysterious circle of light. The entire gallery starts whistling, but here that simply means that the audience is very pleased. The woman immediately starts gesticulating, and in her monologue reveals that she is very virtuous, that her father is very virtuous, and that all the Irish are very virtuous, but the evil English villainously oppress them. And now two scoundrels take to the stage; the gallery is up in arms! One of the scoundrels is the woman's cousin, but he is pro-English. The playbill labels the other rascal a 'minion of Dublin Castle', but they could have been even more scathing in their choice of words. By using brutal force, the despicable cousin tries to make his virtuous cousin into his wife, while the older rogue spies on them. But then a tremendously noble Irish gentleman comes to the rescue, drawing his sword and disarming the cousin. At the same time, an exceedingly pleasant country lad appears – a 'salt of the earth' kind of fellow, as the playbill calls him – and gives the old rogue a good kick in the you-know-where. The gallery couldn't be more pleased. The blue-clad heroine's father appears on stage as well, behaving both nobly and patriotically, but nobody pays any attention to him because the spotlight has turned to illuminate a very remarkable, noble priest. It is the eponymous hero of the poignant drama, *Father Murphy – the Hero of Tullow. Straight away he starts talking about Ireland's suffering, accompanied by the music. For the time being, he's not encouraging an uprising, rather he points up towards the rigging in reference to God. But as soon as the priest has left the stage, the two scoundrels are back again. They have brought English soldiers dressed in scarlet uniforms with them. They shoot down the heroine's father, kidnap the heroine and set Father Murphy's chapel on fire. What is a priest to do in such a situation? Have himself elected as the general of the Irish insurgents, of course, because otherwise the gallery would not applaud.

And in the next act he has indeed become a general armed with a sword as he continues his patriotic pontificating. Although the English rascals spy on him, the salt of the earth keeps watch, behaving not only cleverly but also heroically. Then the *Battle of Oulart Hill commences and it's no fun at all. English soldiers fire their guns, but Irish farmers are much more admirable in how they shoot theirs. The salt of the earth gives a redcoat a kick, while Father Murphy takes centre stage as he unfurls Ireland's green flag emblazoned with a yellow harp in the middle. The orchestra plays the Irish national anthem – a deeply moving, solemn, rousing tune that can only be compared to the Marseillaise. The audience is beside themselves! The entire theatre yells, whistles and stamps their feet as one.

The rest of the play was also very good but rather sad. The likeable hero and the salt of the earth are terribly brave. They free the kidnapped heroine. The hero comes to blows with the mean cousin six or seven times, looking much more heroic in his green national uniform than the villains in their red coats. The salt of the earth always appears just at the right moment and masterfully administers the older rascal a few kicks in the you-know-where. The English are alternately called bloodhounds and murderers, much to the delight of the audience in the Queen's Theatre. But to what avail? Given that Father Murphy is so noble, he allows himself to be lured into a trap and the evil cousin wastes no time in torturing the poor priest. This doesn't take place on stage, but you can very clearly hear the clattering and rattling of the torturous instruments.

In the end, the tortured Hero of Tullow is bound to a stake while the minion from Dublin Castle fetches a cat o' nine tails. But behold, who brazenly delivers a murderous shot through the window? The salt of the earth. And who storms in with a shiny sword? The nobly green Irishman. Who is deservedly bumped off? The two scoundrels. Meanwhile, Father Murphy has laid himself down to breathe out his life and only has just about enough time to give a long speech in the spotlight, prophesying that Ireland will be free someday. National anthem. The gallery is beside itself. It's a good thing that nobody suggests marching to the viceroy's castle right now. And if the scoundrels weren't dead already, members of the audience would be waiting for them at the stage door and would give them a right going over. In the end, they could barely open their mouths as the audience roared and yelled at them indignantly.

For sure, the behaviour of these grim plotters was truly terrible, whereas the Irish were nothing but virtuous green angels during the 1798 Rebellion, as indeed they always are. (For example, they burned 180 Protestants in a barn that year.) The dramatist allowed himself a certain degree of poetic licence with the figure of Father Murphy, who was in fact conveniently hanged in Tullow and is called the Hero of Tullow only on account of this geographical detail.

I returned to my accommodation through the noisy streets. A visitor who doesn't exactly look like everyone else has to be careful in choosing his route, because otherwise he will be mocked and pushed about by the inebriated lads.

This is what you have to see in Ireland. If you only travel through the green countryside and the grubby, quiet provincial towns, you will not fully understand this country. The rabble in the capital city and likewise the anti-Irish, ultra-conservative and ultra-Protestant rabble in the second capital Belfast are more fanatic and wild than any other rabble in all of Europe. The country folk want peace, better living conditions, political independence and a solid connection to the British Empire, while the rabble in Dublin still rejoices when the English are called bloodhounds and when war and rebellion are the topic of conversation. The English are clever because they allow the Irish to scream their heads off in the theatre. They believe that the Home Rule bill will link Ireland with Great Britain for all of eternity and will relegate the bloody past to the annals of history. When peace reigns and the people of Dublin become more enlightened, when Irish whiskey is consumed somewhat more sparingly, then perhaps the lonely summer theatre in Dublin will become a little bit more European and, who knows, maybe 'God Save the King' will be played at the end of the performance, as it is in all respectable summer theatres across the British Empire. Dubliners will probably initially acquiesce without applause, but I, for one, would be very happy if they would just be quiet.

CHAPTER TWELVE

The Death of King Brian Boroimhe
An Epic Interlude

A cloud hung heavy over the world when Brian Boroimhe, the hero of the O'Brien clan, was still just a young man. The living were awaiting the thousandth year since the coming of our Lord with much trepidation, as theologians across the western world had announced that the Lord would appear for the Last Judgement in that very year. For some, this news crippled them into idle devotion, while for others it whipped them into a frenzy of pleasure and excess. But the young Brian Boroimhe took a look around the Emerald Isle. Would the saviour still find the land of his apostles? Would St Patrick and *St Columba, standing at the Lord's right-hand side, hide their heads in shame for Ireland? The wild Danes, plunderers from the Nordic pagan world, descended upon the sacred fields with fire and sword, and the people cowardly submitted to their bloodstained cane. Malachy, the *Hy-Niall, high king of Ireland at Tara's famous hall, was too weak at the time. He might have been able to tame a wild horse, but he wasn't able to chase the Vikings from his lands. And so Brian rose to the task of cleansing his land before the Day of Judgement. Strong men from the mountains of Munster rallied around the hero. Brian Boroimhe attacked the heathens in the name of the cross and of the impending Judgement Day, and victory was on his side. He then decisively reached for the ancient crown, which wasn't sitting tightly on Malachy's head. And so the tamer of wild horses willingly bowed to the tamer of heathens, as a good man bows down to the better man. The land greeted its liberator as *ard reagh, high king of the Irish. He majestically took his seat in Tara's hall, famous far and wide, enveloping all the chieftains and the kings of Meath and Ulster, of Leinster and Connaught, with his shield. He wore purple robes, resplendent gold shoes and a golden belt, and held the ornate gold spear in his hand. Bearded wise men and sages sat next to the king of kings, and every single bard with his harp sang royal songs in his praise.

And so it was that a fresh wave of Danes came across the sea. Ship upon ship, they had been propelled from the uncanny abundance of the misty lands to the north. And once again King Brian raised the army's flag with the cross and the harp, once again his sword struck the enemies of God and the holy Irish church. Brian Boroimhe won countless treasures and blond-maned hostages; the bards' songs extolled him as *'King Brian of the Tribute'. But Brian held worldly treasure in little esteem, for there was greater treasure to be won. Grinding their teeth in anger, the Nordic kings of the sea submitted to the Christian fate, planting the cross on the battlements of their defeated castles. The Day of Judgement was looming ever closer. More Danes arrived in more Viking longboats across the dark sea. His sight firmly set on the impending day that was nigh, Brian was victorious once again.

And then the day heralded by the theologians arrived. Brian Boroimhe quietly sat in his hall, somewhat worn out. His work was done, and he was ready to be judged. But something incomprehensible happened. Sun after sun sank into the sea and the anticipated day never arose from its depths. The only thing that arrived were more Danes, but not the saviour's Day of Judgement.

King Brian arose once again and defeated the Danes. The years passed by and yet more Danes arrived in their longboats. Time and again, Brian took up arms against them. But his beard was becoming grey, his brow weary. He no longer listened to the bards' songs in Tara's famous hall, instead he sat in his chair dreaming. His thoughts often became confused because he no longer knew the purpose of his deeds. He stood before a wild abyss of infinity.

Yet more Danes traversed the undulating sea in their longboats. *Brodar the Viking and *Sigurd the jarl of Orkney descended upon the land like Nordic wolves. Kjarli Canutson prepared speedy ships so he could plunder the Irish, too. The Norsemen residing on the Isle of Man joined in on this expedition against Green Erin. Blond warriors, proper hooligans, came from the coast of Scotland and from distant Norway, greedily looking for spoils. *Sitric, the sea king of Dublin, threw off the yoke he had borne for so long. He tore down the cross that Brian Boroimhe had planted on his walls. The banner with Odin's sacred raven fluttered in the wind over St Patrick's city, warriors everywhere were summoned to war. Messages in runic characters called people to arms in the name of the Nordic gods.

But Brian Boroimhe sat in his chair dreaming. *Morogh, his belligerent son, reluctantly reproached him. *Torlogh, son of Morogh, stood grumbling among his group of battle-greedy young men.

'The judge didn't arrive', the ard reagh Brian said. 'More and more Danes are coming to our waters all the time. I am tired. I have carried the banner of war so many times against the heathens. You may carry it now, my son. But I don't know the purpose of it all.'

And so Morogh, son of Brian, called Ireland's sons to the field of battle. The valiant clans arrived with leather helmets on their heads and cloaks streaming in the wind, maces and swords in hand. The O'Neills and the O'Sullivans, the MacCarthys and the O'Briens, from Ulster, Munster, Connaught and Meath. The battle songs of the bards reverberated across the land. Holy bishops blessed the departing warriors.

Morogh lined up his Christian army on Clontarf beach. The battlements of Dublin waved from afar; St Patrick's defiled cathedral begged for help. Torlogh, son of Morogh, led enthusiastic young men into battle, heady from the melodies of the harp. 'Brian Boroimhe is with us', they said among themselves. 'The *Hero of Sulcost, Defeater of Danes, is old, the victor of so many battles. But we are all fighting for him, the sacred high king. St Patrick and St Columba are by our side today!'

This was the talk among the young men. But ard reagh Brian Boroimhe turned his head away from the troops. He wandered the shoreline between woods and waves, far away from the cries of battle, and had an exquisite rug laid out in front of his regal tent. There he sat, praying quietly. It was Good Friday, a day of prayer. 'The sacred king is old, but he is praying for us', the Irish legion said. But Brian Boroimhe wasn't thinking about the present skirmish. He had witnessed many battles. The Danes kept coming across the dark sea and he knelt on the shore. 'Come', he implored the saviour, 'come, as you promised, and put time to rest. Will evil from across the sea keep tormenting us for evermore? Lord, please grant us a blessed end to all of time.'

The resounding *battle bugles of the Vikings reverberated all around, drowning out the rich, full tones of the Irish harps. Odin's sacred flag menacingly rose from the battlefield, encircled by ominous ravens. Brodar the Norweg and Sigurd the jarl of Orkney descended upon the enemy with battle chants. The Danish women watched from the castle walls and roofs, their blonde hair streaming in the wind. They mumbled runic spells so that their men may be successful in battle, while Odin's *Valkyries, invisible to the mortal world on their fiery steeds, swooped down over the battlefield to carry many a dying warrior to *Asgard. The Irish cried out to their Lord and St Patrick as they rained down blows on the shields of their opponents, metal on metal. The flag of the cross fluttered green in the wind.

Brian's armed guard, his loyal servants, stood in front of his tent with austere countenances. The king nodded in approval of their silent wish: 'Go!' They were no longer obliged to stay, and so, eager for battle, they stormed off towards the sounds of the war harps. The old king kneeled in prayer on the beach, the sea breeze toying with his long, snow-white beard. The only person left was an old servant standing silently behind the king.

And Turlogh, son of Morogh, pounced on Sigurd the jarl of Orkney. The shimmering shields gleamed in the light. Armud, the Isle of Man's king, chidingly challenged Morogh, son of Brian, to a duel. The huge armies fought man for man. Warriors from Ireland against O'Neill's clansmen, Northumbrian Vikings against wild-looking, bearded O'Mahonys, Canut's Jutes against the MacCarthys and the O'Sullivans.

Morogh, son of Brian, defeated Armud, the Isle of Man's king, but Brian Boroimhe's son was severely wounded. Torlogh, Morogh's son, struck down Sigurd of Orkney dead in the dust. But Brian Boroimhe's son was bleeding from hundreds of wounds. A messenger galloped to the shore on a breathless steed: 'Come, ard reagh! Your son is dying on the battlefield.' But King Brian Boroimhe shook his weary, grey head – what was the point? More Danes would come.

Another messenger galloped up to them on a panting steed: 'Come, ard reagh! Your grandson is on his deathbed, covered in his own blood. Who is to lead us now?' But Brian prayed quietly and from the bottom of his soul. Had he heard the news? Did he understand that Ireland's young men, the people's hope, were being slain? That the kingdom was dissipating before their eyes, the glorious prize of so many battles? Brian Boroimhe was weary. He knew that more evil would make its way across the sea, infinite evil for Ireland. Because the Lord had not appeared for the Day of Judgement, and there was no end in sight for the deluge of time.

And Ireland's sons looked on as their leaders died in the dust. Fierce hands clasped the searing hilt of their swords even tighter, while black cudgels whooshed down in unspeakable rage. The blond Valkyries tirelessly swooped down onto the battlefield as the dying eyes of these Nordic warriors saw the invisible sirens and the gates of Asgard opened wide to receive them. However, the triumphal sound of the Irish harps became louder and louder. The daughters of the north standing on Dublin's towering battlements covered their heads in lamentation. Suddenly taking fright, Odin's ravens fled from the wilting flag. The Irish warriors cried out 'Christ and Saint Patrick'. King Brian Boroimhe heard the distant sounds of victory. A flush of royal blood once again rushed through his weary head. But sighing, he turned his heavy head to the sea and loosened the gold strap on his sword and threw it into the water. More Danes would come after his day, new enemies in blood from across the sea.

Groaning in pain, Brodar the Viking led the last strike. Like a flash of lightning, his strong limbs were filled with the terror of righteous desperation, with the fear that sweeps defeated heroes from the glorious battlefield like sheep that sense the wolves' revenge. He stormed off screaming, surrounded by his army, pallid and aching. Heavy trails of blood marked their path of flight. Brodar made his way to the beach to board a longboat and escape across the sea.

The old servant stood behind Brian Boroimhe keeping a lookout. 'Save yourself, King Brian, the enemies are closing in on us!' 'Deliver us from evil', King Brian prayed. Weapons clattered in the woods. The Danes raced between the trees towards the sea to save themselves, eyes alight as their yellow manes of hair blew in the wind. Brian Boroimhe stood on his exquisite rug in front of the crimson tent, an unarmed old man praying as his beard fluttered in the breeze.

Brodar's shield-bearer raised his maimed hand. 'Look, Brodar Jarl, this is how we avenge the death of fearless warriors. This is King Brian, the enemy of the gods. Kill him, Brodar Jarl, before we flee.'

But Brodar replied: 'That old man? He is but a humble monk, a tonsured priest. King Brian Boroimhe never kept himself away from the battlefield.'

The old man turned to face him, and regal splendour shone from his eyes. 'You are lying, you pagan. I am Brian Boroimhe of the O'Brien clan, ard reagh of Ireland in Tara's famous hall. I fought a much tougher battle than you today.'

In utter astonishment, Brodar the Viking looked the old man in the face. Then he loudly cursed the gods of Asgard. The tremendous figure powerfully swung the axe high into the air. Brian Boroimhe gently tilted his silver head towards the weapon. 'Deliver us from evil!' he prayed. Then the axe came down upon the king's head. Brodar was ashamed as he ran off, for he did not feel like a hero who had bravely slain the enemy. The clatter of Irish weapons sounded from the woods.

Bitter, heartfelt tears were shed for King Brian. The bards lamented at his splendid tomb in Armagh.

And new mortal enemies kept arriving on Ireland's shores.

CHAPTER THIRTEEN

A General Note on Ancient Irish Kings

B ack when I still wasn't entirely sure where Ireland actually was, one thing I did know was this: all Irish people are called Pat and claim to be descendants of old Irish kings. This was confirmed when I subsequently read *William Makepeace Thackeray's novels. In each and every one of the satirist's works there is at least one Irish figure who tells of his regal ancestors and, apart from that, speaks his own peculiar brogue, drinks a bit too much and is generally something of a scruffy gentleman. The study of English satirical magazines is important for the cultural aspect of the Irish question. In such magazines there are more jokes about the Irish than about *Baron Mikosch, and almost as many as about the Jews.

In reality, the Irishman portrayed in the satirical magazines resembles a real Irishman, much the same way as the Jewish man of satirical magazines resembles a real Jewish man, that is to say only slightly. Even Thackeray, for whom Ireland was otherwise not disagreeable, only saw his Irish characters with the eyes of a satirist, i.e. superficially. On one occasion he made an Irishman the key figure of an entire book, namely the curious adventurer *Redmond Barry-Lyndon, a kind of male counterpart to the delightful schemer *Becky Sharp in *Vanity Fair*. Thackeray has this likeable Barry-Lyndon Esq. portray his wicked adventurous life in fabricated memoirs, which begin with a terrific genealogy of the noble house of Barry. *'I presume that there is no gentleman in Europe that has not heard of the house of Barry of Barryogue, of the kingdom of Ireland, than which a more famous name is not to be found in Gwillim or D'Hozier; and though, as a man of the world, I have learned to despise heartily the claims of some pretenders to high birth who have no more genealogy than the lackey who cleans my boots, and though I laugh to utter scorn the boasting of many of my countrymen, who are all for descending from kings of Ireland, and talk of a domain no bigger than would feed a pig as if it were a principality; yet truth compels me to assert that my family was the noblest of the island, and, perhaps, of the universal world; while their possessions, now insignificant and torn from us by war, by treachery, by the loss of time, by ancestral extravagance, by adhesion to the old faith and monarch, were formerly prodigious, and embraced many counties, at a time when Ireland was vastly more prosperous than now. I would assume the Irish crown over my coat-of-arms, but that there are so many silly pretenders to that distinction who bear it and render it common.'

At this point, the honourable man states that the family papers of the illustrious Barrys of Barryogue unfortunately no longer exist. He goes on to explain how he himself grew up in impoverished circumstances, how he began his career as a con artist, then moved on to become a common soldier, an officer's footman and finally a police spy in Berlin.

I have a faint hunch that this case is not typical of the Irish nation. But if all Irish people really claim to be descendants of ancient Irish kings, then they must all be right, and this needs to be demonstrated.

I fetch a map of Ireland dated to the time of *King Henry VII – i.e. just before the Reformation and the violent oppression of all things Irish. The area around Dublin is white on the map; back then the English resided in this protected area known as *the Pale, and they did not permit any Irish into their tightly controlled reservation. The remainder of the island was divided into clan territories. As in the Scottish Highlands, each territory was ruled by a patriarchal Celtic chieftain. The chieftain was simply known by the name of his clan, and did not bear any other titles. Thus, he was 'the' O'Neill, or 'the' *MacCarthy More. The other members of the MacCarthy or O'Neill clans, be they bards, farmers or swineherds, might have been baptised Patrick or Hugh – but to the outside world, they were of course a MacCarthy or an O'Neill. Looking at the clan names – O'Brien, O'Flaherty, O'Kane, MacMahon, O'Connor, O'Moore, O'Rorke – they are the exact same as the names of the Irish policeman in New York, the Irish cobbler in Dublin and the Irish MP in London. And they are all the names of kings because, in the endless rough and tumble of early Irish history, each one of the clans in turn played an important role at some stage or another when the chieftain of the respective clan was allowed to call himself king for a while.

Now, hand on your heart Mr Miller, unfortunate as you are to be
called Miller, if you perchance happened to be called Staufen, Bourbon
or Windsor, wouldn't you, too, hope that you were begotten by the
*Hohenstaufens, Hohenzollerns or the Capetians? God knows, perhaps
you are a rich and busy man who has no need for such conjecture – but
in Ireland people have a lot of time on their hands and little money, so
they play party games such as 'Irish Kings'. Germany is above all else a
thoroughgoing and exact country. If Mr Staufen claimed to be *Barbarossa's
heir, a very knowledgeable scholar would waste no time in proving in
the minutest of detail that this is of course nonsense. But here in Ireland,
when some O'Brien, Bryan or Brian claims to be a descendant of King
Brian Boroimhe, of which there are already plenty around, he might not
be able to provide proof positive, but there is also not a mortal, no matter
how bespectacled, who can produce any evidence to the contrary. Among
the hundreds of thousands of O'Briens there are perhaps only two or three
who are actually descended from King Brian, while the rest are descendants
of the king's swineherds. Who's to say whether the young O'Brien lad
looking after his pigs in Clare isn't actually the one true prince? So long
as this matter isn't cleared up, all Brians, Bryans and O'Briens are to some
degree entitled to bestow regal titles upon themselves while soliloquising in
private. All of the Irish are clandestine princes – and a land like this should
be ruled with prudence! But the English have only themselves to blame.

For when they started to systematically and violently Anglicise the Irish,
the ancient Irish kings were of course thorns in their sides. Then the English
gentlemen came up with the novel idea to thoroughly exterminate the small
clans: they searched for Irish family trees and carefully burnt each and
every one of them. They diligently hunted down the chieftains' minstrels,
heraldists and genealogists, openly admitting their aim to ensure that from
that point on no Irishman should know his grandfather.

The consequences of this delightful system have been outlined above –
since no one knows for sure which Irishman is a descendant of the ancient
kings, all Irish are now their descendants. It is incomprehensible that the
English were absolutely dumbfounded each and every time the Irish rose up
in rebellion! A country where all swineherds are potential princes cannot be
a peaceful country and, given the nature of princes, it cannot be a humble
one either. The mystery remains, however, as to who herded the Irish pigs
during all of those princely uprisings.

The English made Ireland into a land of nostalgic fantasising and must now bear the consequences. Every lazy pretender to the English throne found enthusiastic followers in Ireland because all Irish people are pretenders to the Irish throne. A moving story is that of the young boy *Lambert Simnel, who came to Ireland in 1487. He told everyone he was the son of the *duke of Clarence, the last heir to the House of York.

The *duchess of Burgundy instigated the conspiracy, sending two thousand German mercenaries to support the pretender to the throne. The entire island of Ireland was immediately convinced that the pretty young lad was a *York and the rightful heir to the English throne. Archbishops and earls were present at the ceremonious coronation of the pseudo-Clarence in Dublin, where he was crowned with a diadem taken from a statue of the Virgin Mary.

The whole affair soon came to an unexpected end. King Henry VII, the first monarch of the House of Tudor, dealt with the young Lambert Simnel as he had with others. The rebellion was suppressed, and Lambert was captured. King Henry wasn't a bloodthirsty king, but he possessed a rather sardonic Anglo-Saxon sense of humour. He didn't just allow the young pretender to the throne to live, he also gave him an honourable position in the royal household – as a scullion. A while later the Irish earls and archbishops who had supported Simnel also made their peace with the king, and were invited to dinner at the royal court in London. When the men sat at the king's table, a sheepish young servant came into the banquet hall to serve wine. It was the same young lad whom the barons had crowned their king just a short while ago with much loyal enthusiasm. You can imagine the awkward moment of embarrassed silence at the king's table, as not one of the guests dared to drink even a drop of wine. That is, until the former pretender made his humiliated way to the decorous, old and jolly *earl of Howth, the only Irish peer who had never recognised Lambert as king. The earl gave him a jovial pat on the back: 'Well, you can fill my glass up, but only if the wine is good! I'll drink the entire glass for its own sake and for my own sake, and for you, too, because I think you're just a poor innocent fool.' The king gifted the earl money for this topical speech. Lambert Simnel made a good career for himself, too, dying as a well-established royal falconer.

The story is so very Irish. Every Irish waiter who serves you a pint of beer could actually be the son of a king, and you can tell by looking at their faces, too. The entire country lives under the notion of historical pretence. Those who are a bit more sensible, and don't consider themselves a closet prince, still believe their people to be a chosen people of covert kings. Ireland is imbued with a completely fanciful romantic sentimentality that is prone to stifle all political and social realities. As long as Ireland is governed by foreigners, this untenable state will hardly change. Ireland will only have what it currently dreams of when it is governed by the Irish – the heirs of the ancient Irish kings will be restored in their rights. Every Irish policeman appointed to his position by Irish national authorities will have found a small piece of his lost crown. There is only one remedy for dreams: to realise them. Then people will wake up once and for all – and I bet you that in a free and independent Ireland not one soul will claim to be the descendant of ridiculous ancient kings.

CHAPTER FOURTEEN

The Ballad of Lambert Simnel, Pretender to the Throne

Lambert Simnel sat on his golden chair
All Ireland at his feet,
The House of York's most truest heir
The beautiful boy to greet.
All lords and ladies before him bowed,
As eager servants around him crowd.
            Are you real, Lambert Simnel?

*Fitzgerald Tom, the noble Lord,
From Norman times of renown,
And *Lincoln the Earl, they carried his sword
And his sceptre – although not the crown.
That Henry held onto so mightily fast,
The ruler and king – as yet unsurpassed.
            Are you real, Lambert Simnel?

From a statue of the Virgin Mary so pure
A crown from the brightest of gold
Tore *Lord Lovell, the angry and bold,
For the boy there his claim to secure.
Thus Lambert in his youthful fame
As Ireland's king they proclaim.
            Are you real, Lambert Simnel?

Fitzgerald bowed before the lad,
Count Lincoln he laughed and he cried,
Lord Lovell bent his knee – yet
Lord Howth, the fat one, denied,
His oath of allegiance and loyalty
And joined not in cheers of jubilee.
        Are you real, Lambert Simnel?

The harps were sounding throughout the land
In praise of the glorious boy,
Lords, ladies and squires were all to hand
To join in the swaggering joy.
When Henry the king they remember
They swore there to never surrender.
        Are you real, Lambert Simnel?

In London in his palace wide
The Tudor couldn't ignore the tide
That Ireland he'd have to forswear.
But he swiftly accepted the dare.
I who Richard the Third did defeat
Fear no pretender so youthful and sweet.
        Are you real, Lambert Simnel?

Henry Tudor assembles his might
And leads it towards the foe.
His ships on the sea, with the coast in sight,
On shore soon the soldiers go.
All over Ireland they played the lewd game
And many a farmstead went up in flame.
        Are you real, Lambert Simnel?

The battle is fought at Stoke on the field,
Poor innocent Simnel he quickly must yield
In one bloody fray,
His hopes swept away.
Regardless of lineage from Clarence or York
Quickly desert him the nobles and lords.
        Are you real, Lambert Simnel?

On his splendid horse in armour and chain
The victorious king sat up high.
He laughed out loud: 'Put him into our train,
The hapless chap needn't to die.
If Ireland's king your role cannot be,
Deep into my kitchen condemn I thee.'
        Are you real, Lambert Simnel?

When Henry sat down to his victory fest,
The Irish were there one and all.
Count Lincoln he harboured regret in his breast,
Fitzgerald, too, heeded the call.
Lord Lovell suppressed his indignancy,
But wished that not present he had to be.
        Are you real, Lambert Simnel?

The Tudor then in a gesture of grace
Offered clemence to all who were there:
'The adventure is over, I rule in this place.
Let's eat now, partake of the fare!
Enjoy you the drink that's on offer galore,
My splendid new steward the wine he will pour.'
        Are you real, Lambert Simnel?

So pale the lad who emerged through the gate,
Clad in the most ragged of clothes.
And yet 'twas him, the king of late,
Lambert, in misery's throes.
Blood-red a sign on his forehead was shown,
The stigma from the Virgin's crown.
        Are you real, Lambert Simnel?

'Indeed, cupbearer, now it's your turn
To pour their cups full of wine.
Thereby the lordships' thanks you will earn,
They'll cherish your service benign.
To those who but recent allegiance you swore,
Lowly service today is your chore.'
        Are you real, Lambert Simnel?

Who'll be the first to drink eerie cup,
To whom will the turnspit serve it up?
The hall falls silent in grave-like chill,
As everyone fears the victor's will.
'If you, traitors, swear me your loyalty not,
This king assures you: you'll all go to rot.'
            Are you real, Lambert Simnel?

Fitzgerald trembles, remembers his oath
To a prince he himself helped to groom.
Count Lincoln turns suddenly white as a cloth,
Expecting impending doom.
Lord Lovell fears mighty the Tudor's ire.
For treason the punishment surely is dire.
            Are you real, Lambert Simnel?

Yet merry Lord Howth at the table sat,
This lover of feasting and singing so sweet.
Cheerfully he instructed the lad
In words with wisdom replete:
'You might not be in spirits quite high,
The Burgundy, see, is still splendidly dry.'
            Is he real, Lambert Simnel?

To servants is the task assign'd,
He passes his patron the chalice,
Lord Howth took the lead in downing his wine,
And soon was forgiven their malice.
They drank to the Tudor's lasting fame,
While the boy from the hall disappeared in shame.
            Were you real, Lambert Simnel?

CHAPTER FIFTEEN

Analogies

The best way to characterise the people of Irish Ireland is as follows:
they are the Jews of the Occident.

Note the striking similarities: an ancient civilised people,
persecuted for centuries because of their religion, eventually assumes
the language and culture of their persecutors and do not retain much of
their own historical character other than their ancestors' religion, certain
historical-genealogical fantasies, a terrible accent and a strong sense
of solidarity. Other traits include an instinctive aversion towards the
oppressors, some physical peculiarities and their role as stock characters
in satirical magazines. Those who know the Irish will be able to discover
many more minor traits that make them one hundred per cent Jewish,
for example that particular tendency to emulate the dominant foreigners'
physical appearance, as well as the typical Jewish anti-Semitism of those
who have become assimilated – these traits can be found in the Irish, too,
not to mention the somatic idiosyncrasies caused by inbreeding.

However, one major difference is immediately apparent: the majority
of the Irish nation have not left their Palestine, rather they still live there,
farming the land, working with their hands, climbing to all ranks of the
social ladder and practising all professions – with a particular predilection
for the military. The majority still form a national unit, despite the degree
to which the national spirit has been transformed and expropriated by the
foreign government. As is well known, there is, nevertheless, a large Irish
diaspora. Thousands of Irish people live in English-speaking countries
around the globe. Even in non-English-speaking countries, Irish immigrants
have often played an important role. Take the American Irish, for example,
and compare them to the American Jews, and you will soon see just how
similar they are in their very nature, perhaps the only difference being

that the American Jews don't speak English as their native tongue. What the *Jewish jargon is to the German language, the Irish brogue is to the English – a variety with a strange syntax mixed with individual words of a dead language, altogether somewhat comical and yet full of expression. And just as Yiddish jargon has nowadays become a kind of ancillary literary language, the same can be said of Hiberno-English. There are three kinds of Irish poets: those who write in Gaelic (these are neither numerous nor particularly good), those who have penned masterpieces of literature permeated by the Irish spirit but written in excellent English, and finally those who believe that the best way to capture the day-to-day life of the people is through everyday, i.e. vernacular, language. Similarly, the Jews of today write their books in Hebrew, German and Yiddish. But the names *Heine and Schnitzler, Swift and Shaw clearly demonstrate which of the three modalities is the most seminal.

The revival of Hebrew language and literature, just like the very similar Gaelic Revival, strives for the renaissance of a dead cultural ideal. There is an Irish version of Zionism. Just like Jewish Zionism, up until now it has been a purely partisan issue, with many of the best Irishmen deliberately keeping their distance from it. There are a few turncoats who believe themselves to be fully assimilated with the English way of life and so vehemently abhor all things Irish that it is obvious to any psychologist just how Irish they ultimately still are. Apart from these few individuals, the majority of the Irish want a new, free Ireland, but not all of them want a Gaelic-speaking Ireland, nor do they want the ancient *Brehon law to be reintroduced or to ban Shakespeare's work in favour of bardic songs – in short, they are not in favour of replacing an extremely lively, strong culture, even if it is originally a foreign one, with a historical masquerade. These Irish people, who are in the majority, are just like the *Jewish Territorialists for whom a future Jewish state cannot be modern and un-oriental enough. The Gaelic League, on the other hand, are striving for what the fanciful Zionists term the *'Re-Orientalisation' of the Jewish people – in itself not a completely unattractive historical-political romantic notion. One thing the revival of the Hebrew language has going for itself is that the Jews around the world speak diverse languages, and thus any Jewish colony in Palestine would be a Babelian confusion of tongues if a standard *lingua franca* were not introduced. Lots of East-European Jews still speak Hebrew, and they do so with ease. But only very few people, namely those in the west of Ireland, speak any Irish, and no Irish person has French, German or Spanish as their native language. The vast majority of the Irish think in English, and it would be a monstrosity to rob them of this, their native language. It's quite different of course if Irish is taught in schools as a classical language so that the youth can better understand their people's cultural history.

But today, the Gaelic party in Ireland holds a different view. They say: we aren't the only race that has almost completely lost their native language, and other races have successfully managed to fully reinstitute their native language, for example the Hungarians and the Czech people. Prior to 1848, the educated people of these nations spoke German – nowadays they might well scold anyone who speaks German in their presence. And why do the Hungarians speak Magyar today? Because in the end, they were granted Home Rule, national self-government. When the Magyars took the reins of government, they set up Magyar schools and spoke Magyar in public offices and in parliament, no matter how difficult it was at the beginning, and today even the Germans in Hungary are being Magyarised in their scores. The Czechs did a very similar thing in Bohemia. According to these examples – –

And now, as an upright Austrian, I would like to have a serious word with the Irish: Austria is suited to all sorts of things, but not to political argument by way of analogy. There are certain Austrian matters that a foreigner will never understand, especially if that foreigner is living in Ireland, where I am constantly asked if the Austrian language is easy to learn. The lower classes of Hungary and Bohemia never stopped speaking their native languages, rather it was the middle class and the aristocracy who thought it more refined to speak German. The *democratic movement of 1848 put the national languages back into the spotlight in the most natural manner. Apart from the insignificant and poor rural regions in the west of Ireland, more or less the only people who can and want to speak Irish in Ireland are the educated classes. This means you would have to force the people's 'native language' on them, rather than have it flow freely from their tongues. This would be futile, and there is also no political reason to do so. The Czechs and the Magyars are wedged between foreign ethnicities; if the Magyars didn't start speaking Magyar again, then an independent Hungarian state would make no real sense. Ireland is an island, a land destined for independence by its very nature and geography. And if Ireland were to stop speaking English, then England would surely find itself obliged to violently conquer Ireland all over again, just for entertainment purposes.

The Gaelic League has nevertheless achieved some success. A law has been passed stating that every Irish child has a right to Irish lessons in primary school if the parents so wish. And Irish is indeed actually taught in every third or fourth primary school. Only those who pass a test in the ancient national language are permitted to hold a number of public offices. There are some Irish newspapers, while others contain Irish sections. As already described in a previous chapter, Irish songs are sung, Irish words are proclaimed and Irish dances are performed across the land. But it's much easier to do Irish dancing than to speak Irish because the language is extremely complicated for minds that are used to easy-peasy English grammar.

In the end, things will come down to a sing-off between William Shakespeare and the bard *Daibhi O'Bruodair from Limerick, between Swift, *Goldsmith and Shaw, and the Irish author and lexicographer *Aodh Buidh MacCurtain. With all due respect to the Irish bards, they don't exactly have the strongest hand. Nevertheless, the Gaelic League can refer to the Czechs once again, whose respectable epigonic literature resisted being thwarted by the German masters *Goethe, Schiller and Grillparzer, although at times it did allow its national distinctiveness to be somewhat diluted by them. That's all well and good, but there were never any great German authors of Czech origin, and there are plenty of great English authors of Irish origin. And should all of the Irish start to speak Irish again, just as they had before the English invaded their country, if they could completely forget the language they have acquired over centuries, then each and every person would have to re-learn it in order to be able to read the Irish authors Swift, Goldsmith and Shaw, the parliamentary speeches of their great heroes *Parnell, O'Connell and Redmond – in short every noteworthy pronouncement made by Ireland in the last few centuries just so the world would listen.

There's no use in the Gaelic League's campaign to cleanse Ireland of English culture, because everywhere they will have to inflict damage on the nation. And it is for this reason that I do not believe in the Irish Renaissance, even if the Gaelic League had two hundred thousand followers instead of just a hundred thousand. There are two minor impediments – firstly Swift, and secondly there is the small matter that, when an Irish child goes into an Irish shop to buy cheese for a penny, he does so in English. And that's what matters – not whether the cheese is wrapped up in a newspaper editorial written in Irish.

Chapter Sixteen

George Bernard Shaw, Irishman

Many great English men are of Irish origin. Almost all great Irish men are of English origin. Oliver Goldsmith, the author of *The Vicar of Wakefield*, lived in Killaloe, but he was Protestant, and therefore not a true Irishman. The great satirist Swift was dean of the Anglican St Patrick's Cathedral in Dublin, where he was also buried. If, during his lifetime, someone had said to him that he was Irish, someone from the despised Catholic rabble, he would have taken it as quite an insult. He stemmed from the Protestants planted in Ireland to rule over the Irish, and to his mind he was as Irish as his Gulliver was Lilliputian in Lilliput. And yet the Irish honour him as their great poet. Nor could he help it – he imbibed an Irish temperament from the disdainful climate, he absorbed the derisive spirit of the oppressed and the utopian dreams of the enslaved. And in the end, he also lived long enough to make a famous political plea for disenfranchised Ireland, while still quietly continuing to despise the Irish. But on the other hand, he was an Irishman, just as *Beethoven was German and not Dutch, just as Nietzsche was German and not Polish, and just as Dumas was French and not a negro.

The *Duke of Wellington was Irish and Protestant, Parnell – the great leader of the Irish Parliamentary Party – was Irish and Protestant. All of these men had English blood flowing through their veins because only very few true Irishmen converted to Protestantism. The same applies to today's great Irishman, our favourite poet George Bernard Shaw. He is a descendant of the English colonists – and a man of Ireland.

He says so himself in the book he wrote on the Irish cultural question. He writes the following about his ancestors: *'My extraction is the extraction of most Englishmen: that is, I have no trace in me of the *commercially imported North Spanish strain which passes for aboriginal Irish: I am a genuine typical Irishman of the Danish, Norman, Cromwellian, and (of course) Scotch invasions. I am violently and arrogantly Protestant by family tradition; but let no English Government therefore counter my allegiance: I am English enough to be an inveterate Republican and Home Ruler. It is true that one of my grandfathers was an Orangeman; but then his sister was an abbess; and his uncle, I am proud to say, was hanged as a rebel.' And so it is that Bernard Shaw was also born a rebel. This disposition stems from the Irish climate, while his English blood provides him with the strength to see his rebellious nature through. Perhaps he is today one of the loudest advocates of old Irishness exactly because his forefathers were English colonialists – the ancient Celtic dreams do not attenuate his voice. Indeed, he says this himself: miscegenation is more or less the same in Ireland as it is in England. There were Celts in England, too, in ancient times, while Scandinavians, Anglo-Saxons and Normans also settled in Ireland. It's not the blood that's Irish, it's the people's dreams. An Ireland with the cold sense of reason of the English would be England, not Ireland.

'But your wits can't thicken in that soft moist air, on those white springy roads, in those misty rushes and brown bogs, on those hillsides of granite rocks and magenta heather. You've no such colours in the sky, no such lure in the distances, no such sadness in the evenings. Oh, the dreaming! the dreaming! the torturing, heartscalding, never satisfying dreaming, dreaming, dreaming, dreaming! No debauchery that ever coarsened and brutalised an Englishman can take the worth and usefulness out of him like that dreaming. An Irishman's imagination never lets him alone, never convinces him, never satisfies him; but it makes him that he can't face reality nor deal with it nor handle it nor conquer it.'

These words are taken from Shaw's comedy *John Bull's Other Island*. It is perhaps the only one of the more important works by the author that has not been performed on the German stage. It has been published in *German translation by S. Fischer. The printed work has a lengthy and intense 'Preface for Politicians'. I prefer the play itself, it is more potent and lucid. Here, an Irishman has captured his Ireland. The preface is incisive and shrewd. It demonstrates how disgraceful the Catholic clergy is and the extent to which the efforts of the Gaelic League are a romantic diversion. Ancient Celtic mysticism is thematised in the play, or rather personified, while the Catholic clergy also has a human face, and therefore can't be completely wrong. The same applies to all the problems that are so clinically analysed in the Preface for Politicians – in the play (for us mere mortals) these problems are given a human face, so that the audience empathises with the characters and their plight. An Irishman, a poet, has given his opinion on Irish problems. No one should doubt his authority.

John Bull's Other Island might not be a powerful play, but it is a wonderfully distinguished piece of poetry in the intricately rich style of the young Bernard Shaw. I must summarise the play, in fact the entire piece should be reprinted in every book about Ireland because Ireland is so deeply ingrained in this play.

First off is Broadbent – a tall, single-minded, successful, liberally inclined man fed on steak, i.e. an Englishman. He travels to Ireland as he has business to do there. Since he doesn't want to undertake such a risky expedition to a strange and unknown land on his own, he decides to take an Irishman with him. He finds a terribly authentic Irishman who speaks the same splendid accent as a stage Irishman, who can down half a bottle of whiskey in the blink of an eye, who possesses that genuine natural wit of the Irish, as well as the sentimental disposition, the shabby clothing, the red hair and big red nose of all Irish cartoon characters – and who incidentally turns out to be Scottish. Larry Doyle is the one who exposes the Scottish man's true identity. Doyle, himself an Irishman and a civil engineer like Broadbent as well as his business partner, has been living in London for decades. He is as capable and competent as only the Anglo-Saxons can be, and never lets himself be seen dreaming of Ireland and a certain woman he left behind there. He left her behind because he wanted to escape all the Irish dreaming and fantasising: 'I had only two ideas at that time: first, to learn to do something; and then to get out of Ireland and have a chance of doing it. She didn't count. I was romantic about her, just as I was romantic about Byron's heroines or the old Round Tower of Rosscullen'. Well, it turns out that across the water, surrounded by English competence and efficiency, he continued to dream of Nora Reilly when lost in thought about Ireland. And now that his friend Broadbent is going to Ireland and will see her, Larry Doyle is going to come along after all.

And so Ireland is over there in ancient Rosscullen. Ireland is Patsy, who has his own cross to bear, as well as a wild fear of ghostly grasshoppers and the priest. It's the priest, usually a fine, good-natured man who nevertheless deems it blasphemy should a parishioner challenge him on his weather forecasts. Ireland is also the old farmer who had hand-picked the stones from his field only to be chased from this very field by an English landlord. And it's other honest folk who suffered a great deal, but who are incredibly proud of this suffering and can't speak of anything else. Ireland is the friendly Irish auntie, it's the romantic Nora who visits the old round tower day-dreaming as she waits for Larry for the past eighteen years. And it's Keegan, the gentle, melancholic visionary whose beliefs were too pure to remain a priest. Ireland is the whole island suspended in its own reverie. It's there, waiting. It needs fresh blood. A parliamentary seat has fallen vacant. Along come Larry Doyle, the new Irishman, and Tom Broadbent, the jovial Brit with his liberal sloganeering. Larry Doyle says to the Irish: don't be so Irish. First of all, help poor Patsy. It's a disgrace the way you exploit him! Have you people finally been able to buy the land you were once driven from by the unmerciful landlord? Well that won't help Patsy a whole lot, and it won't help you poor divils either, and least of all you, Matt Haffigan, former tenant farmer. 'Is Ireland never to have a chance? First she was given to the rich; and now that they have gorged on her flesh, her bones are to be flung to the poor, that can do nothing but suck the marrow out of her. If we can't have men of honour own the land, let's have men of ability. If we can't have men with ability, let us at least have men with capital. Anybody's better than Matt, who has neither honour, nor ability, nor capital, nor anything but mere brute labour and greed in him, Heaven help him!' This is what Larry Doyle says, and he continues: 'Anyhow, we Irishmen were never made to be farmers; and we'll never do any good at it. We're like the Jews: the Almighty gave us brains, and bid us farm them, and leave the clay and the worms alone.'

It's all so very true. The Irishman Larry Doyle puts forward such extremely clever arguments, and yet meanwhile the stupid Englishman Tom Broadbent wins the mandate. He never comes up with the idea of telling the voters things they don't want to hear. He talks about the great principles of the liberal party from the word go, saying that with their help 'an Irish legislator shall arise once more on the emerald pasture of College Green', and that then everything will be fine, that the priest need not worry as he won't be stripped of any of his power and that Rosscullen's local cricket club will receive funding. – What, no one plays cricket here? Well then, another sport. And if the esteemed constituent Haffigan wishes to have his pig transported home, it would be the candidate's honour to drive the pig home himself in his motor car.

Exit Broadbent. Murmurs of approval sound behind him. The priest comments indulgently: 'Well he hasn't much sense, God help him; but for the matter o' that, neether has our present member.'

That's just it: there is far too much sense in Ireland, though not enough energy. What does it matter that the pig in Tom's car is just as ludicrous as Tom in the electoral assembly, and that the car is falling asunder while everyone in Rosscullen is breaking their sides laughing? The Irish would laugh an Irish person to death; an Englishman would talk himself out of the embarrassing situation.

Aunt Judy waves her knitting in the air screaming 'hip nether hurrah', and Rosscullen has a new member of parliament, who is by no means Larry Doyle. It seems that this Anglicised Irishman hasn't become quite so capable and competent after all. For example, he constantly gets his wires crossed with Nora and she with him in their romantic affliction. She is an Irish woman – she cries. Tom Broadbent stands next to her while she does so, charmingly at ease as he tells her: 'Cry on my chest: the only really comfortable place for a woman to cry is a man's chest: a real man, a real friend. A good broad chest, eh? not less than forty-two inches —' What is Nora to do? She cries her eyes out on his chest. And right in the middle of their first flushes of engagement, Tom tells her she must canvass the wives of influential voters. This fine chap wins over everything he wants with calmness, confidence and cockiness. He's an Englishman. Larry Doyle may be anti-Irish, like George Bernard Shaw. He is, after all, an Irish dreamer, just like George Bernard Shaw.

But Larry Doyle will come good yet. He starts dreaming of real, smart things, while his father is still dreaming of ancient Irish kings. 'My father', Larry Doyle says, 'wants to make St George's Channel a frontier and hoist a green flag on College Green; and I want to bring Galway within 3 hours of Colchester and 24 of New York. I want Ireland to be the brains and imagination of a big Commonwealth, not a Robinson Crusoe island.'

He's still an Irishman, but now he's dreaming of action. But isn't Tom Broadbent his business partner? Broadbent knows very well what his plans are for Rosscullen: Money! He has already set up a syndicate and Larry Doyle joins in. A hotel is to be built in Rosscullen, with a golf course, of course. A motorboat will operate on the quiet river.

'Provided it does not drown out the Angelus!' stipulates Keegan, the old dreamer.

'Oh no', Broadbent reassures him, 'it won't do that: not the least danger. You know, a church bell can make a devil of a noise when it likes.' Indeed, the old church bells will even be mentioned in the hotel brochure. Tom Broadbent will also bring money into the county, set up a library, a school and a cricket club. And the ancient round tower will be carefully renovated. The Irish will play along because the syndicate will flood them with money. And if they don't want to play along then they can emigrate. Yes indeed, Tom Broadbent really has confidence in Ireland. But Keegan, the slightly insane priestly enthusiast, admonishes:

'And we have none: only empty enthusiasms and patriotisms, and emptier memories and regrets. . . . An island of dreamers who wake up in your jails, of critics and cowards whom you buy and tame for your own service.'

He continues: 'You will drive Haffigan to America very efficiently; you will find a use for Barney Doran's foul mouth and bullying temper by employing him to slave-drive your labourers very efficiently; and when at last this poor desolate countryside becomes a busy mint in which we shall all slave to make money for you, with our Polytechnic to teach us how to do it efficiently, and our library to fuddle the few imaginations your distilleries will spare, and our repaired Round Tower with admission sixpence, and refreshments and penny-in-the-slot *mutoscopes to make it interesting, then no doubt your English and American shareholders will spend all the money we make for them very efficiently in shooting and hunting, in operations for cancer and appendicitis, in gluttony and gambling; and you will devote what they save to fresh land development schemes. For four wicked centuries the world has dreamed this foolish dream of efficiency; and the end is not yet in sight. But the end will come.'

These words are spoken by an Irish dreamer. Larry Doyle, the efficient, Anglicised Irishman, is standing next to him and is furious. The good Englishman Broadbent, on the other hand, is genuinely moved, as he always is when he has heard a speech of morals. Wiping tears from his eyes, he says: 'I feel sincerely obliged to Keegan: he has made me feel a better man: distinctly better. I feel now as I never did before that I am right in devoting my life to the cause of Ireland. Come along and help me to choose the site for the hotel.'

Curtain. That is George Bernard Shaw's Irish play.

And there can hardly be anything better or more profound to be said about Ireland. Poetry is a marvellous thing! The very same George Bernard Shaw wrote a preface to his poetic piece. The preface might be just or unjust. It berates the English and the Catholic clerics, it soundly argues for Home Rule and against militarism. The very same George Bernard Shaw appends this passionately opinionated preface to a play in which all parties are right because they are all human. Which character is speaking from Shaw's heart? The efficient Englishman? The clever, Anglicised Irishman? The pious dreamer?

It is always the dreamer who speaks for the poet. Prefaces are another kettle of fish altogether. Larry Doyle wrote the preface to *John Bull's Other Island*, Keegan wrote the play itself. George Bernard Shaw is both characters. He is the Irishman of our times.

CHAPTER SEVENTEEN

The River Boyne

I f you want to get from Dublin to Belfast, from Irish Ireland to the Scottish puritanical Ireland of the north, you have to cross a small insignificant river. It is the River Boyne, and if you want to be all learned about it, you could call it the Irish *Rubicon, because this is where Ireland's fate was once decided.

Do I want to be diligent? I'm not quite sure. All I know is that I want to go to Belfast. But it's a short trip, and so it might be a good idea to dally the day away while getting there. It's simply dreadful to arrive in a strange city and still have a good deal of the day ahead of you. It's also dreadful to walk around a city you don't really know that well, constantly looking at your watch to see if it's time for the train. Leave early in the morning and arrive late evening, that's the only way to do it. But the trains travel too fast on this little island, even though they can also go pitifully slow.

Basically, I need to pass a day while on the road. And what could be more suitable than a historical site such as a battlefield. It shows extraordinary sophistication to disembark from an express train and visit a battlefield. It is praiseworthy. And perhaps the battlefield is resplendent with sunshine and green grass, enabling the traveller to take a break as he travels from one Irish city to another, from Home Rule to the Ulster Question. It is summer, after all. It only takes a bit of courage to do so in the middle of a very diligent trip.

And so I disembark in Drogheda, leaving my luggage at the train station. Straight away I notice a typical small Irish town at the mouth of a river, complete with a main street and plenty of history. I could walk through the town, but I could also walk around it, so I take the latter path. I walk along a country road with green hedges on either side, then along a footpath through the reeds. The river is beside me, while ahead of me is a pleasant valley. A spire beams in the background – the obelisk. There simply has to be an obelisk here between the fields and the meadows because it wouldn't be a proper historical site otherwise.

It's wonderful to walk along a small river in the sunshine, to take in a landscape that doesn't have any one particularly beautiful spot, but rather beautiful curves and vistas. That's Ireland all over: infinitely verdant countryside. A pleasant conversation would round off the experience, or if you are by yourself, reading a really good book while strolling along. This is important so you don't run the risk of constantly looking at the landscape, exclaiming: What a view! Behold the smoke billowing from the factory chimneystacks in Drogheda! The beautiful lupins!

Instead, you have to link all these curved points to surfaces by not paying too much attention to them. You have to set aside your tourist sensibilities and act as if you already know the landscape ad nauseam; you have to not act strangely towards the unfamiliar. In other words, take out a book.

I have the second volume of *Lord Macaulay's *History of England* in my bag. It's not a complete coincidence that I should fish it out of my bag at this precise moment, as I know there'll be something in there about the Boyne. I intentionally stopped reading when I reached the section about the Battle of the Boyne. And it pained me to do so because it's such an exciting historical work that you just want to devour it in one go. I spent almost an entire night by my electric lamp reading about how the *change from an old currency to a new one panned out. Quite an exciting topic, don't you think? Well, if one of the greatest human minds, *Sir Isaac Newton, thought it worthwhile to dedicate an important part of his life to monetary matters, then it must be equally worthwhile listening to an author such as Macaulay when he recounts the topic.

I pull out my *red Everyman edition from my bag. It's in very bad taste to be standing on a battlefield reading about its history in anything other than a guidebook. Therefore I decide not to treat Macaulay as a guidebook. Instead I pretend to walk along some random riverbank and happen to be reading the second volume of Macaulay's *History*. So, William of Orange's army marched down from the north towards the Stuart, *James, who had fled to Ireland after the *Glorious Revolution and was now standing alongside Irish Catholics at the River Boyne. (I'm not standing beside the River Boyne – the river beside me doesn't need any name, charming as it is.)

There was a bit of a hoo-ha as the Protestant army marched along in three columns: William's Dutchmen alongside English Whigs, Swedes, Huguenots, soldiers from Brandenburg, basically all those areas which the *Thirty Years' War had left Protestant. The volunteers from Ulster, the people from Londonderry, Enniskillen, Belfast, the puritanical colonists and the mortal enemies of Irishness form a separate group. They all stand along the banks of the River Boyne on 30 June 1691. I read the following in my book: *'Beneath lay a valley, now so rich and so cheerful that the Englishman who gazes on it may imagine himself to be in one of the most highly favoured parts of his own highly favoured country. Fields of wheat, woodlands, meadows bright with daisies and clover, slope gently down to the edge of the Boyne. That bright and tranquil stream, the boundary of Louth and Meath, having flowed many miles between green banks crowned by modern palaces, and by the ruined keeps of old Norman barons of the Pale, is here about to mingle with the sea. Five miles to the west of the place from which William looked down on the river now stands, on a verdant bank, amidst noble woods, Slane Castle, the mansion of the Marquess of Conyngham. Two miles to the east, a cloud of smoke from factories and steam vessels overhangs the busy town and port of Drogheda. On the Meath side of the Boyne, the ground, still all corn, grass, flowers and foliage, rises with a gentle swell to an eminence surmounted by a conspicuous tuft of ash trees which overshades the ruined church and desolate *graveyard of Donore.'

So over there was where the flags of the Stuarts and the *Bourbons fluttered in the wind, and the tents of Irish troops and the French auxiliaries were pitched. To the right – –

Oh yes, I am of course going for a walk along some random river. I am the one who thinks pilgrimages to 'sites' are in bad taste. I am simply here enjoying a summer's day.

Well, I'll be damned! You really go the distance in the literary profession: you feel ashamed of virtually every intellectual impulse, just as you are ashamed of every sincere emotion for fear of coming across as sentimental. Well not anymore, I am giving up this idiotic game of hide-and-seek. I can ceremoniously declare that this is not just any river, it is in fact the River Boyne, the Irish Rubicon. And I am interested in this great historical event, and I don't pay any heed to those who aren't interested in it.

I close the book and go straight over to the bridge and the stone obelisk. The obelisk was erected on the spot where William was shot at while having breakfast. He wasn't killed; it must therefore be a good place to have breakfast. I sit on the grass embankment and do just that. The red book is beside me. Every now and then I quickly read a page and then look around me to see if I can experience what I have read.

A charming little river. The Emerald Isle on one side, the Emerald Isle on the other side. People who bless themselves with the sign of the cross and are the descendants of ancient Irish kings live on the right bank of the river. The old English kings, on the other hand, were not kind to them, especially since they no longer cared to bless themselves, instead preferring the Book of Common Prayer to the Latin mass. Then along came another English king, one who again cared to bless himself and was good to the Irish, no matter what else he might have been. The English exiled him, not least of all for being friendly towards the Irish (but mainly because he was a bit of an idiot and an arrogant religious tyrant), and they acquired a new king from Holland. The deposed king travelled to Ireland, bringing a French Catholic army along with him. And all of a sudden, the Irish had exactly what they were looking for: a Catholic king of their own. Things hadn't been this good since the times of Brian Boroimhe. The parliament in Dublin was beside itself with delight. It abolished the laws of the oppressors and built a new Ireland.

The Boyne, however, has two banks. On the other side of the river, not right beside it but further north, are people who do not bless themselves and are actually not Irish at all, rather they are foreigners. They were against the old king but for the old laws. They were surrounded by a rebellious country. The powerful majority bore down on this isolated minority. But the minority consisted of Englishmen, of marvellous buccaneers who had in fact just started to conquer the world. The majority consisted of Irishmen who weren't capable of doing anything other than suffering and wallowing in self-pity. Tiny bands of troops were stationed in Enniskillen and Londonderry ready to take on an entire country and Louis XIV's army. But Ireland was unable to cope with these dispersed pockets of Englishness. And so a ship came and rammed the barricade that was meant to block off Londonderry's port. All of a sudden an entire army came along, headed up by the new king. This new king, a tenacious man from the House of Orange, had spent his life organising Protestant Europe against Rome and the French. Now, heading up Protestant Europeans of all nationalities, he was to decide the issue of whether Ireland would become a land ruled by

Protestant overlords, loot for the English, or whether it would become a Catholic satellite state of Louis XIV's, and thus an eternal threat for England and the work of the Reformation. Both armies took their positions.

And what about Ireland's dreamers? Did they draw strength from their ancient legends? Here on the Boyne *Bruga, the palace of the sorcerer Angus, towered over the land. Did they remember Finn's troop of heroes and how they once defended the ford to ward off foreign enemies? *Finn MacCool sat spellbound in the traitor Midac's palace. Defenceless, he and his loyal companions were held captive by evil magic, while the foreign army was already making its way across the river to slaughter the helpless heroes. But the Fianna, Finn's band of warriors, dispatched spies to find their leader. And one spy after another heard Finn's spellbound voice sound from the mystic palace. Upon hearing it, they rushed to the ford, guarding it with sword and shield in hand until the next warrior approached. However, *Dermot O'Dyna of the Love Spot slew the three foreign kings from across the sea and drizzled their blood in the spellbound hall. And so Finn and his followers were released from the spell, even though they were not immediately restored to their full strength. Dermot O'Dyna defended the ford until the morning; by that time Finn and the Fianna's weakness had subsided, ensuring that not one of the foreign warriors escaped with their life. Ireland was free. *(Later, though, Finn forgot that he owed Dermot gratitude when he chased him around the country looking for the king's daughter Gráinne, Finn's wife, with whom Dermot had run away.)

If the Irish dreamed of their old legends in 1691, then it was an empty dream. Dermot's descendants floundered when guarding the ford and protecting the helpless king, who really seemed to have been robbed of all his strength by a paralysing spell. James Stuart stood on the banks of the Boyne; on the other side foreign mercenaries surrounded the foreign king. Dermot O'Dyna of the Love Spot was dead. The Irish could only spout on about him, but they couldn't replicate his deeds.

King against king. Between them, languid and peaceful, the river. One king had to make his way across the Boyne to fight the other. William jumped into the river. Upon seeing this, James shamefully ran for it. The Irish army was a disorganised bunch of freed slaves facing the biggest warlord of the day. They ran too. All of them behaved like dreadful cowards. The military reputation of the country was ruined. Yet the very same cowards later went into exile, with each and every one of them entering foreign military service and admirably battling their way around the world as diligent mercenaries.

The French détachement could not prevent the catastrophe. An Irish soldier shouted to his English persecutor: 'Let's swap kings and fight it out once again.' When James arrived back in Dublin, he commented to *Lady Tyrconnel: 'Your countrymen, madam, can run well.' To which the countess replied: 'Not quite so well as your majesty, for I see that you have won the race.'

That was the Battle of the Boyne, the last decisive battle between an eminently capable and an eminently incapable nation. Never was a crucial battle over so quickly, and seldom was one so decisive.

I close the book and look around. To the right, Irish Ireland. The land that then and ever since could not become Irish, so that today the word 'Irish' only means something that the Irish, much to their despair, don't even embody themselves. To the left, but further inland, English Ireland – the people who won the battle and still can't talk about anything else even today. In between the two is the innocuous, nice, shallow river. William was able to wade through it; there was no Dermot O'Dyna to defend the ford, and the river did not protect his country. Of course, the river drank the blood of the German *general Schomberg, but what river on earth would not have guzzled the blood of a German who fell in the name of the English Empire? Now the river acts as if nothing ever happened – as if it was really just any old river. Standing there looking at the water flow past, I can arise unaffected and return to Drogheda, because it is, after all, time for lunch (something of a bothersome obligation in a provincial Irish town).

And yet I know that if the Boyne had been a deeper river, if King William had slipped up when crossing it, if King James had not been such a halfwit and if the Irish had been as capable as the English, then I would now be eating a different meal here in the restaurant in Drogheda, perhaps not any better, but it would be something Irish. Instead, Ireland is a country with no national cuisine, a country with foreign cuisine prepared by foreign cooks, a country where foreigners were able to wade through its borders. That's why Ireland is what it is – and always has been.

Two rivers signify Ireland. The Shannon and the Boyne. The real Irish are touched with emotion when they look upon the Shannon and tell themselves wonderful stories about Brian Boroimhe. The others, the un-Irish Irish, the people of Ulster to whom I am now travelling, spit into the

Shannon and love the River Boyne. It's all the same to this phlegmatic river as it peacefully flows between the righteous and the wicked. A historical site lies along its banks, but grass grows here just as it does everywhere else. The grass and the water have no sense of history. But there are other real things that do – thousands of actualities which the tourist won't understand unless he has studied the River Boyne.

By the way, the sun was pleasant as I enjoyed my break lying in the splendid grass.

Chapter Eighteen

The Lost Ticket

I had my ticket punched as I went through the barrier in Drogheda train station. I was busy thinking about the Battle of the Boyne or the terrible lunch or something else entirely, but I was not paying too much attention to my ticket. A friendly porter carried my luggage. The express train stopped at the platform and the porter stowed my luggage in one of the carriages. That's when I realised that I did not have my ticket on me and told that to the porter who, having already secured his tip, optimistically replied: 'Oh, I'm sure you'll find it among your things.' And before I knew it, he had steered me aboard and closed the carriage doors.

I sat in-between a broad, healthy Irishman and a dark-skinned young woman of French appearance. I checked the four pockets of my waistcoat for my ticket, but couldn't find it. It was an open ticket for the north of Ireland, and I had just bought it that day in Dublin. It was quite expensive, too. What a pity. But I have more pockets than these and I checked each of them. Still nothing.

I sit back and revel in a moment of horror. Five minutes ago, I was an honest and diligent tourist continuing his journey having just visited a battlefield. Now I am a criminal sitting on an express train without a ticket. Is this considered a capital offence under Irish law? It is in Prussia. At least theoretically. But I have yet to lose a train ticket there; I respect Prussia too much. In Ireland, on the other hand, I will suffer the punishment. But in the meantime, I will enjoy the view from the train because this is why I am in Ireland – to see the country and not to be beheaded.

Having observed my behaviour, the Irish gentleman sitting next to me suggests that I check my wallet. His train tickets always find their way into his wallet when they go astray, he explains. I know for sure that my train tickets do not have a habit of doing this, but I nonetheless thank him for his advice and check my wallet. The ticket is, of course, nowhere to be seen in the vast emptiness that is my wallet.

*'Peut-être dans votre portefeuille, monsieur!' suggests the dark-skinned French lady. I can tell by her accent that she is definitely not French.

I know that I haven't taken my portefeuille out of my jacket since leaving Dublin, but I am meek and polite, so I take it out. The entire carriage stares at my portefeuille. The Irish gentleman insists that I take out every single note and piece of paper and unfold them to check if the ticket has somehow slipped into the folds. The dark-skinned lady draws my attention to the fact that there is one section of my travel wallet that I did not check. Maybe she is hoping that there are some interesting photos hidden in there.

*'*Futsch*!' I exclaim (as well as I can express this in English).

'Check under the seat!' the Irish gentleman says, and so I have to crawl under the seat.

Dundalk station. A clerk pulls the doors open. In Ireland, it is not common practice for a conductor to travel on the train and check the tickets, rather in every station an employee boards the train and re-checks the tickets, something that brings a little bit of excitement into the otherwise boring stopover. Excitement is at an all-time high on this occasion. The entire carriage holds it breath. 'The gentleman has lost his ticket', the woman explains. She looks at the train station clerk in such a way that he might immediately understand how unfortunate such a situation is for a poor traveller like myself. 'You will have to ring Drogheda station straight away', the Irish gentleman says. 'Find the ticket', the clerk replies. 'Maybe it's in your wallet'. 'Time to go', the stationmaster announces.

Newry station. I am the talk of the train. 'Check your portefeuille', the station clerk tells me. 'I'm going to call Drogheda station', the Irish gentleman declares. 'Quick, give me three shillings.' He dashes off. I tell the clerk he might as well behead me and be done with it! Or I could pay for the ticket again. All I want is to look out the window in peace and quiet. I will never know what Newry in County Armagh looks like if people keep distracting me.

'Have you already checked under the seat?' the clerk asks mercilessly. The train starts moving and the Irish gentleman with my three shillings has not made a reappearance.

I really just want to look out the window. There seem to be better fields here in comparison to the other Ireland, and far nicer farmhouses. 'Perhaps they'll find your ticket in Drogheda after all', the dark-skinned lady says in an effort to console me. 'Or maybe it's slipped into the fold in your jacket? Are your pockets torn by any chance?'

She looks as if she would readily darn up the holes in the lining of my pockets.

Tanderagee station. The station clerk opens the doors wide and wants to know about my wallet and my portefeuille. I say I've had enough and want to pay the fine. He tells me I am to report to the stationmaster in Belfast. Until then, at every train station each clerk will triumphantly surmise that my ticket is in my wallet, my portefeuille or under the seat. This seems to be an Irish national superstition. And now, just before the train carries me away from Tanderagee forever, the Irish gentleman storms in, gasping for air. He had to dash onto the adjacent carriage at the last station. He almost missed the train as my three shillings afforded him a lengthy phone call. The whole of Drogheda has been mobilised, and everyone is looking for my ticket. I get the impression that if I were to give him another three shillings, the gentleman would ring the viceroy in Dublin, telling him to send the garrison to the battlefield on the Boyne and have them comb the area for my lost ticket.

*Lough Neagh, the huge lake of northern Ireland, is the next site that is supposed to materialise along the route in Moira. But how can it materialise when a train clerk is blocking the view on exactly that side of the train and when said train clerk simply cannot understand that my ticket is not under my seat. That's what train tickets do, after all!

In short, I cannot enjoy the countryside because I have lost my ticket. The only thing I become acquainted with are the people, and I get to know them for what they are: very friendly, extremely helpful, somewhat loquacious and of the opinion that every foreigner is an idiot who has to be prudently looked after. Prussian passengers wouldn't have given a damn about my ticket woes. Prussian railway officials would have treated me as a dangerous criminal, but only the once. After suffering my punishment, I would have been allowed to look out the window again – assuming that in Prussia leaning out the window is not deemed a punishable offence. Everyone is sympathetic here, if such sympathy makes for a bit of gossip, and it is not considered a matter of life and death when certain rules are not obeyed.

The train arrives in Belfast station and my co-passengers disappear. I alight from the carriage with the heavy heart of a poor sinner. I will now be interrogated in the station office. I will pay for the ticket again. But I notice that I don't have to go through any turnstile. Just like in London, the platform merges into the street without any further ado. The taxis are located just three feet from the train. All I have to do is wave at the coachman and I would escape a gruelling fate.

And now comes a tremendously moral ending to this true story. I say to myself: if the people are decent to me, then I will be decent in return. No one bit my head off or treated me like a criminal. And for that reason I will go to the station office and will voluntarily pay my fare so that I will learn my lesson and look after my ticket the next time.

And so I head to the stationmaster's office.

'Oh yeah', the stationmaster says, 'I know. I just got a call from Drogheda – your ticket was found on the platform. You can collect it tomorrow.'

Virtue triumphs! Since the beginning of time in Ireland, never has such a great virtue been rewarded in such a way. I was at peace with this kind, unbureaucratic Ireland and Ireland was at peace with me.

CHAPTER NINETEEN

A New Suit

I was in Belfast. Belfast is a city that fell on Ireland from the moon, and a very English moon at that. It's absurd, but it needs to be stated: the streets of Belfast are clean. There is also no connection between Belfast and ancient Irish kings; the city has been an English colony from time immemorial. A fortress of the Protestant garrison in Ireland, it looks as Irish as Cape Town or Sydney. (I have never been to these cities, but I can imagine what they are like; I can imagine what any British colonial city is like.)

Buildings of note include the Victorian city hall. Do I really care about Belfast city hall? For God's sake, am I travelling abroad or not? I wish foreign countries would kindly uphold their foreignness. We have city halls, too, as well as warehouses and trams – –

When I think about it, in all of these respects modern Germany bears much resemblance to England. If you want to obfuscate the matter, you say American. But that is inaccurate – the real assimilation machine rages in London. Urban life in all nations of the world has rapidly become English, so why should Belfast be any different? In essence, what's un-English about Dublin is the neglect and the backwardness, alongside the ancient Irish kings, of course. Belfast is doing splendidly, and so it is becoming ever more English, just as every German city is becoming more English the more prosperous it becomes. Unquestioning comfort – that is Englishness, or at least the kind of Englishness that is accessible to foreign races. And after all, this Englishness offers something very convenient. If English men's suits are pleasant and practical, is it then gratuitous imitation to wear them? Simply put: we foreigners would never think of inventing such a thing. It is at this point that the machine grabs hold of us, pulling us into its vortex.

As regards English suits, by the way: you should only buy them in Ireland. Since I really have no desire to look at Presbyterian churches, I walk the streets of Belfast looking in the shop windows. There are a huge number of clothes shops. I really don't understand where all the people are who are meant to wear these suits. And these suits are so wonderful and cost practically nothing. If you want a ready-made suit, you will get one for between twenty and thirty mark, and not just a suit made of any old material, rather of the finest English cloth – woven in Ireland. If you splash out and spend forty or fifty mark, you will get the most beautiful tailor-made suit and will look like a lord, or at least what we in Germany imagine a lord looks like. (Real lords are far too illustrious that we mere mortals could ever emulate their dress sense.) But seriously, English tailors are the only ones who understand how to dress men. Maybe this has a much deeper meaning, namely that all masculine forms of modern culture are English, dressed in English garb.

And Ireland?

Much of the fabric in which the English envelope the world is woven by Irish weavers. This is true in many respects. Irish soldiers conquered India, and then taught English overseas territories the breakfast gospel according to the British Empire, i.e. bacon and eggs. It's just that Ireland hasn't had even a whiff of it yet. Why are the suits made from Donegal homespun fabric so cheap in Belfast? Cheap prices like these always have two sides, one of which is less pleasant than the other. Perhaps the Donegal and Kerry weaver cannot sell off his homespun fabric for a better price because of the competition on the global market, English competition to be exact. Because following the Battle of the Boyne . . .

I need to point out that we have to talk about the Battle of the Boyne once again – there's no getting away from it in Ireland. If you start talking about trousers, the name William of Orange immediately comes up, because you simply cannot conscientiously wear a pair of trousers made out of homespun Irish cloth without thinking of him.

It goes back to even before the battle of 1690. English farmers thought that Irish livestock were competing with their livestock. That's why importing Irish livestock to England was forbidden. Exporting Irish livestock further afield was also made impossible through a series of *Navigation Acts.

When the aforementioned battle was fought, it had already been impossible for the Irish to send their sheep across the water for more than a decade, and so they started to spin wool themselves. The god of war did not favour the Irish weavers – everything Irish was loot to English legislation. Spurred on by every factory owner and cloth merchant in the kingdom, the House of Commons directed a *petition to King William in 1699 to 'discourage' the Irish textile industry. The king, who in general was not very adept in matters relating to Ireland, as indeed in other matters too, acquiesced. Without further ado, it was forbidden to export processed wool from Ireland and to sell raw wool to any country other than England. All of this just so the English factory owners could buy materials cheaply.

This was what English colonial policy looked like before America taught the motherland a bitter lesson by defecting.

Just as Irish agriculture was strangled out of pure fear of competition, so too was the Irish textile industry. Following on from this, a new industry emerged in Ireland, not in Irish Ireland, rather here in Belfast in Ulster. The Protestant colonialists started to produce linen, and Belfast still has splendid linen factories to this day. The people of Ulster are unrestrainedly proud of this, forgetting all too willingly that the rest of Ireland is not responsible for its own lack of industry. In 1708, when linen factories were also meant to be set up outside of Ulster, namely in Leinster, the English authorities immediately took action. And today Ulster declares: Look at our thriving industry! You Irish have nothing the likes of what we have. You are an inferior race. There is no way that we, an English minority, will allow ourselves to be ruled by a national parliament where you hold the majority.

The disastrous industrial laws and the restrictive taxes and duties have in the meantime been repealed. But it is almost impossible to make up for the advantage English industry has over Irish industry. The new Ireland has a great future as an agricultural country. It has this future because England has become an industrial nation with little remaining farmland but a huge proletariat that needs to be fed. For similar reasons, Ulster's industrial edge is also very unfavourable for Ulster's political aspirations. Belfast is, after all, located on the island of Ireland and it is hard to understand why the linen industry of Belfast should not supply Catholic households with tablecloths. The more Ireland prospers, the closer Ulster will be tied to Ireland, even if they organise a thousand rebellions against Home Rule.

Another fact is that in aristocratic colonies such as Ulster the industrial workers stem from the despised masses of the oppressed race, and they join forces with the former. It was the same in Bohemia where Czechification began in the factories. In ultra-Protestant Belfast, most factory workers are Irish Catholics. When the Dublin port workers went on strike, their Belfast counterparts showed great support. The Irish proletariat of today doesn't have much time for sterile nationalism, but even less for the reactionary *master race of Ulster.

But all of this won't stop me buying a new suit if it is cheap. I go into the shop. The shop assistant shows me mass-produced suits: 'Genuine German craftsmanship!' he says, telling me that Irish fabric is tailored in Ireland, sewn in Germany and then re-exported back to Ireland. Wages are cheaper in Germany, he explains. We have really come far: in Germany, we pay a hefty sum for an 'English suit', for attire that is actually made out of homespun Irish fabric. The same suits, produced in Germany, are so cheap in Ireland that the difference in price would almost cover the cost of travelling here. What are we paying so much for? The English brand, nothing else. It is a tax on assimilation to the English ways. Time and again, those English amenities have proven themselves – sport, breakfast, meals, pipes, furniture, clothes – and if we want a piece of them, we have to pay the English for it. That's why we, too, are a nation ruled by the English, if not in political and intellectual terms, then in practical matters. Everything that signifies comfort and lifestyle is rapidly becoming English and Anglo-American the world over. So we have to pay for this, and then we have to pay again when we attempt to prevent the political Anglicisation of the world by way of elaborate armaments. That's us indeed, a powerful, civilised race for centuries, copying English lifestyle and arming ourselves against them at the same time. And how are the Irish to defend themselves against Anglicisation? They do not have any *dreadnoughts or regiments, they are located just hours from London and have been under English rule for centuries. When they have gained political autonomy, they will inevitably and irretrievably become colonial Englishmen and women.

Given these circumstances, you can seriously question the point of Home Rule. Here in Belfast where the people have felt English since time immemorial they do not understand why they should all of a sudden send their parliamentarians to Dublin instead of London. It's simple really – so that the people of Belfast feel like Englishmen, i.e. like people who rule rather than are ruled. An English colony only becomes thoroughly English when it is no longer directly ruled by London. That is what history has taught us. To be English means to rule. That's why in Ireland only the Protestants are English, and only they have been the ruling overlords up until recently. Give the country an Irish government and see how long it can hold out against the logic of the English assimilation machine!

I step out of the clothes shop and take a look around Belfast. Why is this clean, lively city so different from bleak and gloomy Dublin? Why are there statues of English monarchs and not of Irish national heroes on the squares? Why aren't there any signs in Gaelic lettering as in Dublin, even though no one can actually read them down there either? The simple answer is that Belfast was never oppressed by England, that, although the Irish of Belfast dream exactly like Irish people do, they dream of the British Empire and not of ancient kings. This is what makes the antagonism between Ulster and Irish Ireland so bitter – that two quintessentially Irish dreams collide.

When all the great-great-grandchildren of Irish kings rule Ireland once again, they will have to dream of something else – whether they like it or not. And what better a thing to dream of than the British Empire? Today Irish soldiers are fighting for the Empire, as they did in the past, in all corners of the world. The Empire belongs to the Irish, but Ireland does not belong to the Irish just yet. As soon as Ireland becomes Irish once again, the Irish people will become the most fervent British imperialists, just as they already observe English customs at the breakfast table and wear English attire. Ireland's future is British – there should be no doubt about this. The only people who might hinder this are the ultra-British Ulstermen. They want to maintain an Irish Ireland because only that way do they feel able to retain their distinct Englishness; they alone want to remain in charge. It is an arrogant and grandiose desire. The Puritans of Ulster are old-school Englishmen who have not yet assimilated the world to their ways, rather they want to rule a world of black underlings – rule them with the whip. But the English assimilation machine will have its way with them, too.

Chapter Twenty

Ulster

For a long time, everyone knew that it was a kind of *daytime overcoat. Then the people of Europe heard that Ulster was also a place in Ireland and that Ulster and Ireland hate one another. This geographical knowledge was then given a face, the face of a powerful man. Those who think of Ulster today think of *Sir Edward Carson, leader of the Orange Order and the mortal enemy of Home Rule.

Perhaps Home Rule is not a major concern for us continentals, and whether a few counties in the north-east of Ulster are against Home Rule is of even less concern.

But it does concern each and every one of us, and we should all sit up and take note, when the figure of a man looms somewhere on the distant horizon, a man of exceptional stature. Whether an important popular leader is right or wrong, whether he entangles the people in baleful or beneficial politics – all of this does little to change the human interest we show in such a great player. Today in good old Europe there lives a man who can stir the emotions of thousands with just a single word. It is the most honourable Sir Edward Carson MP, the uncrowned king of Ulster, the general of the Belfast militia, the prime minister of the revolutionary government. What an abundance of honours, some of which are quite dubious! But there can be no doubt that he wears them all like a man.

I have been reading and hearing about this man since the day I set foot in Ireland. He is either the devil incarnate or an archangel, that is how much he is condemned and praised. One thing is for sure: what he is doing is nothing unusual. He travels around Ulster openly organising a revolutionary army to fight against England under the pretence that Ulster loves and wants to remain part of England. If the government remains resolute and Home Rule is passed into law in a few months, Edward Carson

130

says that Ulster will not allow itself be ruled by the new Irish parliament. Ulster will not pay any taxes, and Ulster will fight. Because, as Carson states, if Ulster acquiesces to the liberal majority in the House of Commons and meekly joins an autonomous Irish state, the Irish Jesuit minions will chase the remaining Protestants from the island if they have not already burnt them at the stake. And, he continues, just as our forefathers once fought at the Battle of the Boyne ...

The newspapers report of little else. They recount how Sir Edward Carson is equipping the Volunteers. In Belfast and the surrounding lowlands there are countless drill clubs for the fervent members of the Orange Order. Oh, by the way, they are called the 'Orange Order' because of the Battle of the Boyne and William of Orange, of course. One of Belfast's biggest factory owners announced in the newspaper that he stands alongside his workers as a common soldier in a battalion they formed. His steward, a former sergeant, commands the gracious men. Another gentleman informs the press that he is being drilled by his own gardener. The people of Ulster proudly draw attention to such details just to show how democratic their movement is, but of course if it were actually democratic, they wouldn't even need to mention such things.

The Ulster Volunteers hold big parades. Former officers, even retired generals, command these crowds of farmers and townspeople. Active royal officers send telegrams of approval. The government doesn't move an inch. They think that the Ulstermen are bluffing, and in any case it's not against the law to *organise* a rebellion in England. Only the act of uprising itself is outlawed.

The Irish nationalists also think the Ulstermen are bluffing, and they laugh their heads off at the drill clubs and the provisional government that Sir Edward wants to introduce. Indeed, they laugh at him and always have him wearing a little crown in their caricatures of him as the king of Ulster, which he is, and they laugh at his aide-de-camp Captain Craig, they laugh at Ulster, the Battle of the Boyne and the English Unionists. But time and again, Ulster replies: Laugh all you want, we will fight. God knows, maybe the factory owner will hesitate, while his sergeant and his steward are pretty certain to pull the trigger. Because bluff or no bluff, an unprecedented air of fanaticism has taken hold in Ulster. You can't even buy a decent postcard in the shops – the only thing you see is Carson's picture and Carson's quotes, as well as caricatures of the evil Redmond – head of the Irish nationalists –

driving Protestants from the island. There are images of the Battle of the Boyne, of brave Orangemen who never surrender, and of the *Mountjoy*, the ship that breached the blockade during the *Siege of Derry, emblazoned with the inscription: Ulster is now the good ship *Mountjoy* and will resist Home Rule. There are pictures of the Covenant, the solemn oath of allegiance against Home Rule, and posters depicting Irishmen shouting 'Hurrah' when English soldiers fell in their droves during the *Boer War. And yet more pictures of Sir Edward Carson, Ulster's first citizen.

In all of this, Sir Edward Carson isn't even an Ulsterman, just as Napoleon wasn't a Frenchman. Carson was born in Dublin, but as a Protestant he is of course an Anglo-Saxon. He is a barrister, and one of the best in the land. He began his career in Dublin before moving to London, where he made his money and attained many honourable positions in the *Conservative governments: he was appointed PC (member of the *Privy Council), and in Germany we would surely hail him as Your Excellency. He also obtained the 'Sir' appended to his name by virtue of his efficiency and competency. He is estimated to be worth quite a lot of money. He could well afford to peacefully live out the rest of his years in London as an honoured man. Trinity College in Dublin, where the Church of Ireland clergy still dominate, repeatedly send him to the House of Commons as the university representative. He could easily sit pretty in the House of Commons, sedately pursuing his conservative politics, and wait and see if the Unionists might come to power once again and make him minister. But Sir Edward Carson is not one to rest on his laurels. People like him need the frantic pace of running around the country campaigning, the thunderous acclamation of impassioned assemblies, the fervour of resounding speeches. And so this ageing man, radiant as youth, goes around organising revolutionary armies, has himself elected head of the provisional government at a rally, and tours the country ceaselessly and tirelessly. With his loyal Captain Craig by his side, he thunders down country roads all across northern Ireland, today appearing in Armagh followed by Conservative lords and dukes, tomorrow presiding over a public meeting in Portrush, while on Monday he is in the Orange Lodge in Londonderry telling the people to get ready to resist paying tax to an Irish government. Then on Tuesday he is at the historical Boyne ford near Drogheda, looking on as the signal corps of the future Ulster army manoeuvres at this important historical site, inspecting the troops like a prince, speaking words of praise like a prince and enjoying admiration like a prince. Everywhere he goes, he is received by a guard of honour, and has long rows of well-disciplined farmers march past him, repeating the same headstrong phrases: 'We are loyal Englishmen and we want to remain part of the Empire. If Ireland is separated from the Empire, we will not obey this government of our enemies. We will fight just as we did at the River Boyne. No Home Rule! Long live the king!'

Sir Edward Carson is, after all, a Royalist, only that he would shoot at the king's troops if the king sanctioned Home Rule.

And across the whole of Ulster, cries reverberate: No Home Rule! No surrender! Ulster will fight and Ulster will be right! The Puritans of Ulster are a defiant, tough and impassioned people.

One weekend, when Sir Edward Carson was taking a rest from the tremendous exertions of agitation in his friend Craig's country house near Belfast, I took up his friendly invitation to visit him. I asked a coachman driving one of those small horse carriages with the open sides if he would be so kind as to make himself available for the afternoon for a trip. A dubious look crossed his face: a Belfast coachman is always appalled if you want to avail of his services. I tell him that I'm going to Craigavon. All of a sudden his face lit up, the coachman was after all a good Orangeman, and was more than willing to drive the foreign tourist to see Carson in Craigavon.

We travel through the hustle and bustle across the port bridge. We make our way down long, dusty suburban roads, which look very Irish all of a sudden. Then we pass by green lawns and quaint detached houses amidst the mansions of factory owners. Somewhere behind the lowlands we can see blue mountains and we get a whiff of sea air. Then we turn into the elegant entrance of a huge park – mature, well-kept lawns and the elongated glass veranda of a mansion come into view. Two older gentlemen are sitting in the glorious sun on divinely comfortable garden chairs under red canopies in front of the veranda, enjoying their weekend off. Captain Craig, big and sturdy with a healthy glowing face, gets up to greet me as I alight from the coach. 'How do you do', he enquires in an interested tone. Then it is Sir Edward Carson's turn. 'How do you do', he asks. This is one of the less silly English customs – to ask somebody how they are when you first meet them. This shows the other person that from now on you are interested in what they have to say, and they in what you have to say.

Then the second part of the formalities – chitchat about the weather. It's a fine day, isn't it? Yesterday, on the other hand . . .

By now I know this small talk off by heart, and so I have time to observe the man who will perhaps decide the history of England and Ireland, the 'new Cromwell' as his followers call the rebellious Ulsterman.

I see a typical Englishman: tall, strong, clean-shaven, with an aquiline nose and a somewhat protruding lower lip. His dark but slightly thinning hair is parted to the side across his high, angular brow, while his sombre eyebrows frame his stony eyes, which have surely witnessed much. Sir Edward is over fifty years old. But age defies an Englishman of his stock. So there he is sitting in his chair, of course wearing his comfortable and yet so formal clothes and smoking his small pipe. He is tired following a week of racing around in the car from public meeting to public meeting. It is a bit cheeky of me to quiz him on his political views at precisely this moment in time. But he is pleasant and friendly, and when I ask him he answers, and when he answers he is full of warmth and I can see the deep passion pulsating through him, even as he relaxes in a comfortable deckchair on the sun-drenched terrace of this park on his weekend off.

We move on from talking about the weather to discussing the summer. Sir Edward Carson complains about how tired he is and how he longs to go to a sanatorium in Wiesbaden. Indeed, he is a great friend of Germany, is part of the committee that promotes German–English relations, and loves to spend time in Germany.

I think of how the men of Ulster have repeatedly threatened the government: if you surrender us to the Irish, we will throw ourselves into Kaiser Wilhelm's arms. Meanwhile, at home, chauvinistic blockheads dream of exploiting Irish nationalists' aversion to England by military means (and they dream of this in the cold light of day in the newspaper). Complete nonsense. Because when it comes down to it, Irish regiments are and have always been England's most loyal troops. Just read the magnificent story in *Kipling's work about how a man in India wanted to induce an Irish regiment to mutiny, how the regiment took advantage of the free-flowing beer he provided and how it then, fired up by Irish rebel songs, bravely descended on the enemy. That's what the Irish are like. The Ulstermen, on the other hand, are stubborn, and if *Lloyd George provokes them, they are capable of many things. Yet aligning themselves with the Germans might be one step too far – even for them.

Sir Edward Carson doesn't say a word about treasonous sympathies or a hypothetical German invasion. Instead, he cheerfully speaks about how he is going to rise up against Lloyd George if the chap will not concede and breaks the alliance with Ulster. With a deep glow emanating from his eyes, the demagogue tells me how diligently the drill clubs are at work and how the people have cheered him on these past few weeks all over Armagh and Derry.

'Are your men armed?' I enquire, not expecting a positive answer.

'I cannot comment on that', Sir Edward replies, smiling at me. That'll do, Sir Edward – I've already heard enough rumours about gun running. Maybe you don't have anything against rumours. You are incredibly candid about your conspiracies and plotting. At any rate, you would probably much prefer that the government runs scared of you and you don't have to mobilise your army in the first place.

I don't say this out loud, rather I enquire as to the estimated number of soldiers the provisional government of Ulster has at its disposal.

'A hundred thousand!' Edward Carson says slowly.

Hmm, a few babies will have to join the ranks at that rate. According to the census of 1911, around 1.6 million people lived in the northern-Irish counties, historically known as the province of Ulster, and even Sir Edward Carson himself doesn't claim that each and every one of these people are willing to rise up against Home Rule. First off, there are almost 700,000 Catholics in Ulster. Naturally enough, they would not be ideal recruits for the anti-Catholic army. In any case, there are also a few men in Ulster who do not support Carson. Only four of the nine counties of Ulster are Orange strongholds; the Orange Order hopes to be able to count on two others to some extent. Only sixteen of the thirty-three Ulster MPs are Unionists. Even in Belfast almost one third of the population are Catholic. The workers' party is against the Orange Order. There is also no shortage of liberal-minded people, many of whom are good solid Protestants. There's no denying that in the lowlands of Ulster, in Down, Antrim, Armagh and Londonderry, support for the Ulster party is unconditional. But it is still quite a leap from cheerful acclamations at public gatherings to a full-blown uprising against the legal government, and it is difficult to understand why this leap has to be made at all. Meanwhile in England, in that country admired by us continentals as a paragon of political order, political violence has always been part of how zealous minorities operate in the political arena. Just as the suffragettes are now throwing bombs about the place and insulting ministers because the cabinet does not agree with their particular point of view on suffrage, so too will Ulster fight if the cabinet does not come round to their particular point of view.

Sir Edward Carson eagerly tries to make it clear to me that Ulster is in a terrible state of emergency and will have to fight if it cannot assert its views by peaceful means. He says: We are rich, the rest of Ireland is poor. We are English, they are Celts. We are Protestant, they are puppets of Rome. We have always been loyal to the Empire, they have always rebelled. Now the English government wants to violently expel us from England, while we fervently want to remain English. They want to hand us, the descendants of Cromwellian Puritans and Scottish Presbyterians, over to an ultramontane parliament that, while it might not immediately pass a law against equal rights for Protestants, will probably nonetheless send policemen, teachers and tax collectors to Londonderry on a daily basis.

I reply that we all know what an ultramontane government is, but that the majority of the Irish will not always subscribe to *ultramontanism. Right now, the Catholic clergy are the champions of national liberation, and their power increases exactly because the unionists make the religious antithesis into a political and national one. The Home Rule bill also provides all the guarantees possible to ensure the parity of both denominations; that Ulster is powerful and rich is yet another guarantee. Ultimately, if the Irish unionists do not like this Home Rule bill, then why don't they propose something better?

Sir Edward Carson vehemently takes to his feet, saying: 'Never!' He does not believe that autonomy is the answer for Irish Ireland. If its impoverished population will be driven from the Union, it will no longer receive the British capital it requires. I take the liberty of airing my doubts. Sir Edward Carson states that in any case this matter does not concern Ulster. He says that he twice made the suggestion to the House of Commons that the Irish should be granted their Home Rule, but to leave Ulster – and all of Ulster, including the Catholic counties – out of the equation. He continues by saying that you cannot force a royalist area out of the historical union with England and surrender it to hostile forces. This is not what the majority of the British people want, he maintains.

My reply: the House of Commons has, however, voted for Home Rule twice in a row. If they vote in favour of the bill a third time, it becomes law, even if the Lords reject it again. What will you do then?

'Then we will fight!' Sir Edward Carson says. Captain Craig nods, waving at me to stand up. He slowly leads me to the middle of the terrace, where a bronze plaque is embedded into the stone. The inscription declares: This is where Sir Edward Carson read out the *Covenant to tens of thousands of citizens on 13 June 1912, and this is where the Covenant was signed and sworn in. Solemnly invoking God the Almighty, the Protestants of Ulster vowed to die rather than submit to the despised people their forefathers so gloriously defeated at the Battle of the Boyne.

It's all about oaths and manifestos, emotions and pathos. I observe the good Captain Craig from the side and all of a sudden realise that he actually looks like an Irishman. At this very moment I cannot tell whether I hear in him the defiant voice of English superiority or the political fantasies of the Irish. Maybe it is a mixture of the two. I am convinced of Edward Carson's solid Anglo-Saxon stock. But he also displays a number of traits peculiar to the Irish. Isn't this perpetual talk of William of Orange just the same as the talk of Brian Boroimhe? In Leinster and Munster everyone is a descendant of ancient Irish kings, in Ulster they are all descendants of those who triumphed over these kings, of the heroes from the Battle of the Boyne and the Siege of Londonderry. But woe betide the country where two dreams collide!

Sir Edward Carson continues talking to me, hoisting one argument upon another. He is either right or he is wrong, but he essentially cares little about political logic. The ultimate argument of the people of Ulster, an argument that reveals them as quintessentially English, is their obsession, their fixed ideas on denominational prejudice and their unshakable sense of superiority. They do not want Home Rule, firstly because they do not want it, secondly out of conviction and thirdly because they do not want it. This is the strong impression you get. To be sure: much of what Carson says might well be true. Conditions in Ulster are much better than in the rest of Ireland. People work in neat towns, while in the countryside stolid farmers live in splendid manors. You can probably understand why wealthier and more prosperous people don't want to tolerate poorer and dirtier neighbours. But shooting across the fence at them?

And you can probably even understand why devout Protestants do not hope for much from an autonomous parliament that will initially be dominated by the Catholic clergy. And yet it seems that religious intolerance and religious fanaticism is more prevalent in the North than the South of Ireland. Irish nationalists are gradually shedding their radical leanings, whereas in Ulster the people scream for shotguns, ready to march to the River Boyne – in short, to rehash the religious war of the seventeenth century all over again. These defiant, standoffish people would be well capable of acting out their convictions, but nothing will come of it in the end. A civilised person living in the year 1913 would not even entertain such a thought.

Unfortunately, though, we are dealing here with emotions and passions. There are moments when both of my amiable interlocutors look completely fanatical, unable to utter anything but 'No!' and 'Never!'

The question is whether the majority of the population of Ulster will actually follow these men to war against their fatherland, to committing treason. For the time being, and while they are still parading with sticks instead of guns, their enthusiasm continues to grow.

My coachman observed how friendly Sir Edward Carson was as he shook my hand. And even though my coachman is a standoffish and unfriendly guy, just like most of the inhabitants of Belfast, he is terribly kind to me on the journey back to the city. He smiles down at me from his seat, beaming as he tells me that Carson and Craig are fine chaps, the best Irish people in the whole of Ireland. Well, the coachman certainly takes himself for an Irishman, and perhaps someday he will see the Irish in the south and west as brothers and countrymen. But time will have to pass before this happens, that's for sure. Yet the question remains: can and will a religious war erupt in a European country in 1915?

* * *

The next day I was present as Sir Edward Carson addressed the crowds in west Belfast. An air of excitement pervaded the entire city. The poorer quarters in the west were decked out in flags, the emblem of the United Kingdom was to be seen everywhere – on triumphal arches, over doors and on flags with Carson's name and image. Sometimes ropes were stretched across the road with stuffed puppets hanging from them: effigies of Mr *Asquith, Mr Lloyd George and Mr *John Redmond. Platforms were set up on a large football pitch at the edge of the city, and well-dressed ladies and gentlemen decorated with the Orange Order's insignia took their seats. A lady served as the chair on each platform, since an important women's association was in charge of organising the meeting. Tens of thousands of people crowded onto the meadow below. They whiled the time away singing and cheering. All of a sudden, the crowd jolted. Just as an electric current pulls loose iron shavings to a magnet, these individuals were suddenly melded into one single cohesive unit – the leader made his entrance through rows of people frenziedly screaming and waving. He was escorted by young men who wore a Union Jack ribbon around their arm with the inscription: Guard of Honour. ◦

Sir Edward now makes his way up onto the platform, where I – a foreigner – was kindly given a prominent seat. The masses below surge as one towards this platform as almost everybody has abandoned the other platform where another unionist leader has started his speech. The whole crowd shouts, screams and chants as one. Sir Edward Carson gently waves his hand, and silence descends on the pitch. Edward Carson is hoarse, his vocal cords have had to endure superhuman endeavours in the last few weeks. But everyone can hear him, they guess what he is saying, because he is always saying the same thing: 'We want this and we don't want that!' A crowd does not seek arguments, rather they want persuasion and energy. And when he stops talking, those seated on stage jump to their feet, while the crowd surges forward like a wild, uncontrollable wave. Thousands of hands in the air, thousands of hatless heads. Bold, provocative pistol shots ring out.

'We are serious!' is what these shots exclaim. 'We have weapons and we will use them.'

Following this great outburst, all is quiet for a moment before everyone starts singing: 'For he is a jolly good fellow'. The sea of people now part ways: accompanied by his haughty guard of honour, Sir Edward Carson makes his way to the other platform to give the same speech all over again. New speakers take to our stage. All of them hail the great leader of Ulster, speaking more about him than about his ideas. But very few people are listening, as most of them have elbowed their way over to the other platform to hear Sir Edward say the same thing over again, and to scream and sing all over again.

And there are other voices joining this boisterous ovation. A festive hymn suddenly rises from one corner of the pitch. These Puritan sons and daughters are very pious, as are the big, strong Puritan men and the sturdy, somewhat angular Puritan women who crowd around the platform.

And over on the other platform Sir Edward Carson is once again declaring: 'We are English, we want to remain English, and we do not want Irish autonomy. If Home Rule is forced on us, we will fight just as at the Battle of the Boyne!' 'No Home Rule!' thousands shout. People wave hundreds of flags, all decorated with the symbol of the Union. And once again pistol shots are fired. And once again there is a moment's pause before the crowd fervently intones 'God Save the King'.

'God save the king! Our most gracious king – –'

And yet they are ready to fight against the king's troops if the king signs the despised bill.

Sir Edward Carson stands at the railing with the calmness of a victor, looking down on the raised hands and enthused faces. And yet there is an air of tiredness on his face, and yesterday, in Captain Craig's villa, he said to me again and again: 'I am exhausted!'

And he looked it, too. It's no small task to whip a peaceful country into a frenzy of outrage and disgust, to maintain rebellious passions over the long summer months and to forge mass hysteria into a threatening weapon.

The uncrowned king of Ulster will continue to race around the country in his car, holding the same unyielding speech. Ulster cannot rest for one moment so as to ensure that, when the Home Rule Bill is passed, the people will be at the zenith of their fervour.

Make of it what you will. A strong man is playing a great game, and it is phenomenal to witness. Is this demonic man a fanatic of his own conviction or one of the ambitious ones?

The book I am writing will still be sitting on bookshelves long after this issue has been resolved. Home Rule is definitely on the way, this book can safely predict that much. The question then is whether Carson will really and truly lead Ulster into a civil war. We will only find that out when this book has already been read and passively sits on a bookshelf, unable to re-write itself.

For Ireland's sake I would like to hope that I am wrong about Sir Edward Carson. We are living in a tame age but also in an age when people bluff a lot. Will Sir Edward Carson really go as far as civil war? His opponents sneer at him – of course he won't. But I am not so sure – – He is incredibly headstrong and his tongue can be dangerously rousing. The question is whether this man can gingerly acquiesce at the last moment and live with it afterwards.

I am not going to make any predictions. We are, after all, living in a peaceful age.

CHAPTER TWENTY-ONE

For Home Rule

Dear Sir Edward Carson,

From an aesthetic point of view, it would be a joy to be able to agree with you. Men such as yourself are iron pillars to which one might very well pin one's enthusiastic heart. Defiance is always more sublime than political reason, the arrogance of feeling superior is more beautiful than political progress. But the aesthetic point of view has no place in the political world. Furthermore, I do not just see demagogues and politicians on the other side of the conflict, but also a man who, for some time now, enjoys the affection of my excited heart – George Bernard Shaw, the poet. He is a rebel just like you, and from an aesthetic perspective, the choice is not easy. So it's probably a good idea to put affection aside for a moment and instead speak about Home Rule factually and logically.

Given our own political context, we continentals perhaps have a clearer understanding of what is currently happening in Ireland and England. What is Home Rule but the proposed reinstitution of a parliament that was dissolved over a hundred years ago? If the Home Rule Bill, as it has been passed by the majority of the House of Commons, is signed into law, then Ireland will be granted a regional constitution, similar to Bavaria in Germany. But no, the British government will meddle in Irish affairs more than the German national government does in Bavarian matters. And yet Ireland, no matter how Anglicised it may be, has a much more consistent and distinctive collective identity than Bavaria. If the Bavarians had been robbed of their autonomy following the *Napoleonic Wars or following *1866, they would without a doubt now want their state parliament back, they would hate all northerners with a vengeance and would be instigating conspiracies, not resting until they were given back their autonomy and government. The situation is basically the same in Ireland, the only difference being that political sentimentality is much stronger and that the local 'northeners', i.e. the English, are even less popular here.

Ireland has been in a union with England, Scotland and Wales for more than a century, which is as much to say that Ireland is outvoted by the English on all Irish matters and that Ireland contributes to English matters in the most impertinent manner. The recent history of the English parliament revolves around the Irish question and the Irish question alone; it is poisoned by the Irish question.

This doesn't really concern us foreigners too much, other than to serve as an analogy for domestic issues. But it is curious to observe how a great and splendid nation allows itself to become embittered by a question of secondary importance. Does England really have nothing else to worry about than a regional Irish parliament, which was insignificant when it existed and will soon be insignificant once again? The military policeman from Limerick springs to mind, who is not pleased with having to spend his life watching over Ireland. Shaw once wrote of *Drake, the Spaniards' eternal foe, that it was magnificent how he really annoyed the king of Spain and singed his beard. But had Drake seized the enemy, tied him to a rope and held that rope in his hand until he died, would Drake himself then not have been just as much a captive as the king?

In the end, the prisoners are the ones who pay the price. In 1911, every Englishman had to pay an annual rate of 3.5 mark for their police, each Scottish man 2.5 mark and the poor Irishman almost 7 mark. The apathetic and ineffective bureaucracy that is Dublin Castle costs a fortune. According to official statistics, the Irish taxpayer has to pay twice as much for the woeful administration he must endure as the English taxpayer, who has much reason to be satisfied with his government. In the thriving industrial state of Belgium, the administration costs half as much as the administration of the poor and less populated Ireland. Since Ireland has to pay so much tax, it would be prudent to give them self-government, even if that means that less stipends and pensions would find their way from the Irish exchequer into the pockets of English lords and their idle sons.

You really have to bear this in mind when you see just how opposed the House of Lords is to Home Rule: the upper echelons of the British aristocracy would lose out mightily if Home Rule were introduced. It is questionable whether an Irish regional parliament would give the lord lieutenant of Ireland a yearly salary of four hundred thousand mark, which is more than the powerful president of the not exactly poor United States of America receives.

British India has exactly the same woes: it has to go hungry so that huge pensions can be squandered in London.

Who knows, maybe the Irish themselves are not the most economically minded people either, and will not be any better at keeping their house in order in the future. But they will then only have themselves to blame, and responsibility will no longer lie with England.

Many people are racking their brains as to what Ireland will be like after Home Rule. The people of Ulster are expecting the crassest form of mismanagement and the reintroduction of the *Holy Inquisition. Mismanagement of the economy can hardly be any worse than it has been during the Union. And heretics will not be burned at the stake, either.

It cannot be denied that, in certain respects, Ireland is the most clerical country in the world. The Irish farmer is controlled by his priest like no farmer in Bavaria would tolerate. But this situation does not have to last forever when all other conditions change in Ireland. The Catholic Irish priest, no matter how ill-informed, superstitious and domineering he might be, incidentally is and for the last century has been the single living cultural coefficient of a downtrodden race. He has other qualities, too: he is Irish, and therefore good-natured. No matter how bloody Irish history has been, heretics have never been burned at the stake in Catholic Ireland. Nowadays, many Protestants praise the tolerant disposition of Irish clergy. In Ireland you hear the story of an Anglican priest with a hefty sinecure, a magnificently old church, a beautiful rectory, but unfortunately, as is so often the case in Ireland, no parishioners. One day the bishop was to pay a visit. But dear reverend, where are you going to get parishioners from at such short notice? And so the reverend went to the Catholic priest next door, who possessed neither sinecure nor church, but had a huge congregation. The priest was friendly and lent his colleague a congregation so that the service attended by the bishop went nice and smoothly. It is an anecdote, but don't all anecdotes have a grain of truth to them?

I have a green book in front of me, filled with testimonies proclaiming that the Irish Catholic does not devour Protestants. Even stubborn Ulstermen will admit to this. There is only one kind of religious intolerance in Ireland, and it stems from the Protestant hypocrites of Ulster. In every public toilet in Belfast you will find slogans such as 'To hell with the pope!' scrawled on the walls. There is nothing of the kind in Catholic Ireland, perhaps because the people of Ulster are, after all, English people with their fixations, whereas the Irish are Celts obsessed only with their dreams. It seems to me that Irish ultramontanism has a lot in common with the dreamy Irish nature: it resembles a state of mind more than a political force. Up until very recently, English Protestants wanted to exterminate Irish Catholicism. Consequently, it is alive and kicking. Up until Catholic Emancipation, Catholic priests were the only Irish people in any sort of public office, and for a long time the only ones with an advanced education. The Irish priest was the natural leader of his people. It was impossible for decent Irishmen and women to feel anticlerical sentiment because of the persecution of Catholics. As Shaw once again rightly points out, had the French church been suppressed by the *Huguenots in Voltaire's day, then it would have been simply impossible for Voltaire to be anticlerical without being a traitor of his people.

It is not surprising, then, that every single Irish man and woman depended on their priest for as long as the Catholic Church had no rights (the only religious majority in Europe that has been oppressed by a religious minority for centuries). Priests have dominated Irish life since Catholic Emancipation precisely because the English wanted it this way. Clerics of the Church of Ireland made common cause with Catholic ultramontanism. With the support of Irish Catholic votes, the *English Church Party established the *Education Act of 1902, which surrendered education into the hands of the churches. In Ireland, this meant the Catholic Church. There are a huge number of schools in Ireland because of course a Catholic child cannot grace the same school bench as a Church of Ireland child, or a Church of Ireland child the same school bench as a Methodist. In all of this, there are a ridiculous number of people who can neither read nor write because the teacher has more important things to do than actually teach – he has the fear of God in him as he must answer to the priest. The priest (of any denomination) can dismiss the teacher as he pleases, and if the teacher doesn't like it, then he can lodge a complaint – to the venerable bishop. What is a daring flight of fantasy for even the most powerful European clergy – in Ireland is a reality. Given these circumstances, why should Irish priests support Home Rule? Can they really have it any better than it already is, working alongside the dominant English Protestants?

The fact of the matter is that the Irish priest is only influential because he is the leader of a national struggle; if the struggle is over, then the priest would no longer be important, and the influence of the church would be greatly diminished. Oh no, Home Rule, self-government for the Irish, would not be Rome Rule. No one knows this better than the Vatican. Papal diplomacy has flirted with the Anglican Church for a long time now, doing it the odd favour here and there. Irish clerics were not allowed to be openly friendly towards the English because otherwise they would have been chased away by their congregations, but when the *Fenian conspiracies and the plotting of other secret revolutionary societies failed time and again in the last century, the oh-so patriotic and nationalist Irish clergy were responsible because they threatened to excommunicate the members of said secret societies. There actually could not be anything more disagreeable to the Roman Catholic Church than Ireland breaking away from England, and even mere regional autonomy for Ireland does not please the Vatican in any way. Right now, eighty Irish Catholics sit in the House of Commons; following the reform there will only be around thirty. Is that really an appealing prospect for the Vatican? Another revealing fact is that many English Catholics vehemently oppose Home Rule, for they fear the loss of Catholic influence in the House of Commons.

And above all else, you can be sure that as soon as the Irish have their own parliament, they will also have their own anticlerical movement. I can see the day coming when the conservative Protestant reactionaries of Ulster form a bloc with the ultramontanists from the Catholic party, and the rest of Ireland will oppose them. The Irish clergy is all-powerful today because it exploited the Irish people's fantasies of ancient regal glory. But the Irish are waking up from this dream, and they are waking up to Home Rule. No, Sir Edward Carson, it will not be Rome Rule. It is in fact you who has propped up Rome Rule, which now dominates in Ireland. There is one thing that almost makes us believe in the universal claims of the Catholic Church: when zealots of any denomination rise up, be it Protestants in Ulster, Greek-Orthodox Catholics in the *Holy Synod, or the *Jacobins in the Parisian Welfare Committee, they are always indirectly fighting for Rome.

If you are against Rome, Sir Edward, then you should be supporting Home Rule. Ireland simply cannot become any more clerical than it already is. Of course, there will initially be a parliament peopled by peasants where the priest will call all the shots. But don't forget about the workers in Dublin and Belfast. They are almost like brothers in how they flout Catholic nationalism and Protestant ultra-conservatism. Their leader *Jim Larkin is more important to them than John Redmond and than you, Sir Edward – they want to live, not dream. The huge strike of dock and transport workers last year shows how powerful Irish workers already are. Brian Boroimhe and the Battle of the Boyne will soon be relegated to the political scrapyard. Modern problems are catching up with backward Ireland. All the junk and the relics of the past must, however, first be tidied away, and that is what Home Rule will do. It will relegate all the old tales and superstitions to the annals of history – all the things that today make Ireland, and indeed Ulster, Irish.

For Ireland, the era of nationalist dreams is over because they are about to be fulfilled.

CHAPTER TWENTY-TWO

The Giant's Causeway

You will not be able to enjoy Belfast until you have gone on that one sightseeing trip that you simply have to have done: 'Have you visited the Giant's Causeway yet?' is what the people of Belfast ask me as a tourist, right after they get the 'How do you do?' formalities out of the way. The tourist might be inclined to avoid the Giant's Causeway for that very reason, but then he thinks that, on a beautiful summer's day, this clean, pious, hardworking, industrial and praiseworthy city of Belfast more than likely looks nicest when left behind. So, on Sunday I take the early train. I look out of the sympathetic window as Belfast disappears behind me, and then the magnificent country houses of the Ulster industrialists come into view, followed by the shimmering fjord where Belfast is located. Small children wade their way through the shallows of the bay. Then we pass through dainty seaside resorts and extremely green meadows and even tillage fields – I am, after all, travelling through Ulster, and not the desolate part of Ireland. After two hours on the train, I arrive in the lovely seaside town of Portrush, take a seat on the tramway and whiz my way along the cliff coast.

It is truly delightful here. A beach surrounded by wild cliffs. Dark basalt shot through with red streaks of ochre and everything cocooned in that infinitely green grass you only find in rainy Ireland. A narrow pathway winds its way along the coast. With every ledge and with every bay the area becomes more beautiful. You want to keep going, all the way around Ireland. Then a mighty amphitheatre opens up, waves thunder through a natural arch while seagulls squawk overhead. Here the land does not gently meet the sea but abruptly, dramatically, harrowingly, almost like an open wound. The ochre is blood-red. This is where the world imploded, this is where Atlantis is buried. Geologists say that at one time, a single, enormous basalt plateau stretched from here to Scotland and as far as Iceland. Geologists have plenty more to say, too, but my tour guide is an even better source of information.

He is extremely proud as he shows me the great sites in the area. In the middle of one particular bay, jagged rock formations protrude out into the sea. From a distance, it looks like a rocky promontory, the only difference being that a good few little souvenir stalls are dotted around the place. But when you draw closer, you see something quite remarkable. This basalt cliff consists of forty thousand individual columns, each one more or less the same height and shape. They are tightly packed together, and you can walk across them as you would a badly paved road. The peculiar thing is that each individual column is pentagonal or hexagonal, while there is only one rectangular column, one octagonal, one triangular and three nonagons. It looks like a completely pointless heap of ruins. There is only one other place in all of Europe with something similar: the famous *Fingal's Cave on Staffa, off the coast of Scotland. And now enter the respectable geologists who know exactly why the volcanic basalt took on these strange shapes as it cooled down.

My red-headed tour guide laughs a lot and is certainly a real Irishman, not one of those imported Ulstermen. He is only somewhat impressed by learned geologists. In Ireland, common volcanic eruptions and ice ages are not responsible for anything; here, ancient Irish kings and heroes are. Pat, my guide, takes me to the very edge to show me this maze of regular columns and broken pillars. Do I really believe that something like this could just randomly come into existence? Of course we know very well how this came about, even if it was quite some time ago.

First off, there was the magnificent Irish giant *Finn MacCool. The entire area here belonged to him. On the right, you can see the amphitheatre where he used to entertain his guests as well as the immense, petrified pipes of his organ. Finn MacCool wasn't just any run-of-the-mill giant like the ones that tend to roam around in other countries, rather he was a national hero, a splendid giant of whom the Irish simply cannot get enough, and of whom the Irish dream about as much as they dream of King Brian. Finn MacCool was the chief giant and the champion boxer of Ireland. Now it so happened that another giant lived across the water on the island of the Anglo-Saxons, but he was by no means a decent fellow like Finn MacCool. This chap stood on the Scottish coast all day long roaring insults across the water. He just didn't want to swim across the sea to give good old Finn a clout across the head as he might catch a cold.

Of course, Finn MacCool could not tolerate such provocative behaviour for long. One day he resolutely went to the king, who at that time ruled over Ulster. He said: 'Your Majesty, I'll show that big talker. May I build a causeway from Ireland to their island?' The king had no objections, and my guide thinks that he also probably did not have the guts to refuse a request from his tallest subject. And so off went Finn MacCool to build a magnificent causeway from carefully hewn pillars – the Giant's Causeway. In the true spirit of Irish hospitality, as soon as it was finished, Finn invited the foreign ruffian to try out the causeway and come over to Ireland. He did just that and when he reached the Emerald Isle, taking in the beautiful views, Finn showed up and beat the living daylights out of him. And then Finn allowed him to stay. Naturally, the Brit could see that Ireland was the most beautiful part of the world and didn't have to be asked twice. He settled in Ulster, doing so tremendously well that he didn't even want to go back to the other unpleasant island. As a result, the causeway fell into disrepair, but you can see traces of it not just here but also on Staffa and on the island of *Rathlin, located between the two.

My guide's eyes are ablaze as he recounts the story of the Irish champion's victory. He evidently enjoys telling the story, no matter how many times a day he tells it. And for that reason alone I decide not to contradict him.

Later on I lay down on the soft, luminous grass on the steep slope. The sea below crashes against ragged cliffs. I am alone, save for a cheerful couple sitting behind the next boulder. The breeze makes it quite difficult to light my dear old pipe, but in the end I get it lit. And now I can admit that I do not believe the tour guide's story. It wasn't quite as he told it. Everything I have seen and experienced in Ireland so far convinces me that the guide is fibbing to bolster his national pride. I don't think it was the Irish giant who clobbered the British giant back then, rather the other way around. The uncouth chap from across the water remained on the island as a conqueror and his descendants are still here today.

The River Boyne springs to mind, where Finn MacCool's reputation was ruined by the defeat of his descendants, where the people of Ulster, the offspring of the foreign giant, were stronger than Finn McCool's dynasty.

And I also think of that afternoon on the football field near Belfast, of the rebellious demonstration of Ulster's race of masters. Indeed, they came over here to see who was stronger – them or the good-natured Irish giant. These Anglo-Saxon colonialists came to the land of the Celts with swords in hand, or rather with clenched fists. They have cultivated their land better than the oppressed, anaemic peasants of the indigenous race. Their cities are neater, tidier and more industrious; they are just like the cities across the water, like numerous majestic cities filled with their race in hundreds of subjugated countries all over the world.

And now they are to submit to a population of Catholic Celts? Work together with them? Allow their political ties to the homeland to be severed, their spiritual home?

It is here in front of the dark columns of the Giant's Causeway that you understand the issue that is Ulster. Is this where Atlantis sunk, the bridge that joined two worlds? England built the new Atlantis, the empire on which the sun never sets. The Giant's Causeway has long since fallen asunder, but England doesn't need walkways anymore and is no longer afraid of getting its feet wet. The English now have tremendous steamboats and no longer need a bridge. It only takes two or three hours to get from Ireland to England, and each and every ship is part of the economic and cultural ties between the two, which can never be undone. The giant from across the water has grown even bigger and even stronger; even in their rage, Finn MacCool's progeny are no longer able to rise up against him. But they will at some stage be his good friends if he shows good will towards them. And finally, after a thousand years, he is showing signs of friendliness. In any case, how significant can a modest regional parliament in Dublin be in the face of England's overwhelming naval supremacy? But it will mean a lot to the Irish – the honourable end to a gloomy story, the respectable conclusion to the duels between Finn MacCool and the other troublesome giant, a measure of moral satisfaction for the underdog. The descendants of the uncouth invader can stay put – Finn MacCool is a hospitable kind of fellow. But he wants his self-respect back. And the people of Ulster, who have after all been cultivating Irish soil and breathing Irish air for centuries now, they should not stand in the way of honourable peace between the two nations. Perhaps there will be another bridge between Ireland and the other island after all.

*A Postcard from the Irish Coast

This is the place where all the world explodes,
The remnants of Atlantis – here they rise,
The Ocean city, praised in odes,
Grows through the waves, toward the skies.

Eyes feast on this intriguing prey,
Red ochre running through the cracks.
Rugged columns, ocean spray,
Cleft of Earth's distress.

A soft green coat flows from afar,
Wraps its folds 'round secret scars,
'Hail Ocean, hold your spoils forever'.

A yell of a thousand gulls endeavour
For perished world one last lament
'bout what the waves ashore don't send.

* * *

'Behold the deadly element'.

CHAPTER TWENTY-THREE

The Land of Poets

I once again explored Belfast on foot and was tired of Belfast. It is summer, after all, and as a tourist I would like to do something other than admire the advances in the linen industry of northern Ireland and see how well swept the streets are of this big industrial city. There are green mountains and the sea. So where should I go?

What else does a person do other than go to the next travel agent and pick up some brochures.

A helpful travel agent says to me: 'Why don't you visit the Isle of Man! It only takes four hours to get there.'

There are some great moments when travelling. You travel from place to place and discover that people have two legs and smoke the same kind of tobacco wherever you go. The only thing that tells you that you are making your way around the country is the diminishing size of your wallet. All of a sudden, someone says: only four hours to the Isle of Man! And you start to entertain notions. The Isle of Man – that is something distant and indeterminate, something from geography lessons in school. What a pity that the geography teacher has already been there, because otherwise I would be on the cusp of becoming a famous explorer . . . Anyhow, I will have licence to show off in front of others. What do people know about the Isle of Man? What do I know about it?

I suddenly realise that I already know every nook and cranny of the Isle of Man, that I already have a sharp and detailed image of this distant island in my mind. But up until now, I just didn't really believe that it actually existed. The Isle of Man is the island of poet *Hall Caine, and in Hall Caine's novels all of the Isle of Man comes alive. But it is hard to imagine that it is meant to be the same island I can travel to this afternoon in a real steamboat.

Now, I did entitle this summer trip 'Irish Travels'. Should I interrupt my Irish travels to go and discover some other island? For God's sake, the island is only four hours from Ireland; I don't have to be so hard on myself. And who knows, maybe I will learn something about Ireland on the Isle of Man.

While the steamer is making its way across the Irish Sea, I consider what I have read about the Isle of Man: a Nordic rocky island between England, Scotland and Ireland. A small, autonomous state under British rule. So, it's a country with Home Rule, just four hours from Ireland. We will be able to see how Home Rule works in this part of the world. I also read that the people speak *Manx, a mixture of Celtic and Norse languages (I hope they will understand my exquisite English in the hotel). The cats there have no tails. And there is supposed to be lots of heather, I still have this impression in my mind. The population consists of upright fishermen and hardy farmers, melancholic folk with an inclination towards tragedy. Two of them are called *Deemster, and preside over judicial proceedings, loving a bit of drama now and again. They all adhere to old customs, holding *Things – the assembly of the sovereign people – in accordance with the ancient tradition of their Germanic forefathers. Oh, it surely must be an interesting island, or rather an isle, no less.

You can see cliffs in the distance as darkness descends. They loom larger as we approach, like a lonely, giant rock in the sea. But then a bay unfolds before us; up in the middle of this primordial solitude of the Nordic cliffs you can see something crawling along. It is unbelievable but, if we weren't headed towards a very romantic island of herring fishermen, you would definitely think it was the brightly lit carriage of quite an ordinary electric tram. And then there is another shimmer to the right. Do the fishermen have electric lights these days? No they don't, rather it's a really long urban quay garishly illuminated. This must be the main town, Douglas, but I had imagined it somewhat differently. Now we have to cross a long, loud, teeming landing bridge to get to the seaside resort and into the town.

What exactly is going on here? The entire quay is giddy with people singing, screaming and shouting. A traditional festival? A fair? There's a brass band, newspaper boys screaming their heads off, a jingling horse car, automobiles, neon signs advertising variety shows, dance halls and cinemas. The name of an operetta by *Lehár is emblazoned over the entrance to a theatre, while in between all of this is a nondescript row of multi-storey buildings – all of them hotels and guesthouses – as well as tens of thousands of excited, cheerful and loud people loafing around on the path between the hotels and the sea. So it seems I have landed in a huge seaside resort of the most unpleasant kind.

The next morning, I strolled around the town, not exactly uplifted by what I saw in the streets the previous night. There's no denying that the sea is very blue. I have no bone to pick with the sea, nor with the numerous agreeable little children playing in the sand in front of me. But the rest of it behind me and beside me! There's a carousel. Hundreds of shops sell gaudy postcards ('printed in Germany'!), even more shops sell tacky souvenirs decorated with images of the Manx cat with no tail or the comical Isle of Man coat of arms depicting three boot-cladded legs, just like the *Sicilian coat of arms. I can also have my photo taken very cheaply, complete with some strange sort of headdress. The photographer provides this peculiar prop for free. What's more, everywhere you go you can buy cheap candy floss. And in the middle of this, nothing but screaming and shouting. Young lads decked out in red Turkish Fezzes (this must be the attire of gaiety in this part of the world) strut around in their droves singing and trying to turn heads. It looks as if all the shop assistants from Manchester and Liverpool have descended on Douglas.

The only thing you want to do is escape the promenade, but the streets are even busier, even louder, filled with even more uncouth and loutish merriment. But to the right of the harbour there are green hills. It is probably lovely over there. – – What? I'm supposed to board this overcrowded ferry complete with musical accompaniment if I want to go across the harbour to the hills? It's probably even worse over there than over here on the promenade. OK, what about the peninsula to the left? I am about to board a horse-drawn railcar but see the following scrawled on its side in garish writing:

> Enjoy a visit to the secluded cliffs along the sea with a marvellous theme park and a gigantic electric swing.

What's a man to do if he finds himself in such a distressed state? He buys himself a newspaper. And so I go into a bookshop and request one. Would you like the *Daily Mail*, Sir? *The Manchester Guardian*? No, Miss, I would like a newspaper from the Isle of Man, about the Isle of Man. Oh yes, we have one of those. I scan through it while standing there. I read about a magnificent Pierrot group in the *Marina Villa, and the new cinema programme in the Palace. Oh look, in the corner there is a less important article: they are debating all sorts of grievances in the *House of Keys, the ancient assembly of the Isle of Man's estates. The newspaper is of the opinion that they should give up this charade of sentimental historical pageantry once and for all, and simply turn the island into an English county.

So that's the end then of a thousand years of autonomy. There were once ancient sea kings of Man, Nordic Vikings who, apart from themselves, would not tolerate any authority other than the Thing of their people. A special system emerged from the fusion of the Celtic clan structure and Germanic kingship: *Regum Manniae et Insularum, as the inscription reads under the oldest coat of arms with the Viking ship. Right through the Middle Ages there was a king of Mann, the most recent one being from the *House of Stanley. But at some stage one of these Stanleys, an earl of Derby, thought it was more appropriate to be known as a great lord, rather than a small king, and relinquished the title. But even today, the Isle of Man is not merely an English province. The inhabitants govern their small homeland by themselves. The local community assembles every year at Tynwald Hill. Many have the political ideal of subsuming the noble autonomy of smaller polities under an all-encompassing imperial flag. And now the repeal of this autonomy is treated like an insignificant news item, squeezed in between cinema advertisements. The following is to be found on the current Isle of Man coat of arms with the three legs of Man: 'Quocunque jeceris, stabit'. It's more so a motto for Manx cats than for a country. It means: 'Whithersoever you throw it, it will stand' – it will always fall into the hotchpotch that is the British assimilation machine.

I am overcome by a sense of anger towards the writer Hall Caine. It was he who enticed me to this downtrodden, degenerate area. But now I will read his novels once again and publicly prove that they are utter fabrication. So please, Miss, give me *The Manxman by Hall Caine! This little miss, probably a Manxonian woman from Liverpool, searches high and low in the little bookshop on the beach. Would I not prefer the new penny novel? Finally, she lays her hands on Hall Caine's novel.

Back at the hotel, I open the book and establish that for the most part it is not set here in Douglas, rather in Ramsey north of Douglas. Very well, I can go to Ramsey, but I'm not quite sure whether I should take the train, the electric tramway or the steamboat. The entire promenade is full of posters from the three companies vying for the customers' attention. Each of them claim that with the other mode of transport you don't really get to see any of the countryside. It's a very lonely island.

I decide on the electric tramway and am very happy with my choice. The hullaballoo of Douglas fades away. One can see the sea, and above it green plateaus and splendid treeless mountains. Now and again a verdantly overgrown glen extends down to the sea. There is a restaurant at each of these spots, along with a notice stating that entry to the glen costs sixpence, but you are guaranteed that this is the most celebrated glen on the island, and that the waterfall of the neighbouring glen is not half as splendid. Tall fuchsia hedges in full bloom obscure the view of the sea. Purple heather carpets the slope of the cloud-covered mountain *Snaefell, which, thanks to the electric mountain funicular, I could now very easily ascend, if I were so inclined. We finally arrive in Ramsey. Just as in Douglas, there is a beach with the same grains of sand and the same guesthouses in which the same kinds of people from Manchester speak about the same things and eat the same food. But there's not quite as much noise here as in Douglas, and on my first reconnaissance mission around the town I see quaint harbour districts with fishing boats, while tree-covered hills form the backdrop to the town. Perhaps you don't even have to pay an entrance fee to the hills here. You could definitely spend a week's holidays here in the summer.

And so I read Hall Caine's novel *The Manxman* stretched out on a green slope surrounded by gorse bushes and heather. It's not a modern book; the characters are either angels, or they are transformed into such. The book is replete with coincidences, repetition and dripping sentimentality. But nevertheless, it is a hefty, fascinating book full of passion. It's the story of an ambitious young man striving for success who must therefore get over the temptress he has fallen for. When he actually becomes Deemster he destroys the woman and his dutiful friend Pete. One day he has to sit in judgement of his own sins, and throws everything away so as to become a good person once again. The story closes with him, the judge, clasping hands with the repentant woman he left behind, and disappearing from the government building into the night.

After the first ten pages, you know that it's actually not fabricated. A true Manx man has written a true-to-life story about his island. Hall Caine made a lot of money with this book. He immediately returned to Man from the great big world of Englishness, bought *Greeba Castle and now often lives in his homeland. His homeland? Can this sea-lapped theme park still be the homeland of a Manx man and a poet?

Thanks to this charming book, you eventually realise that the beauty of the island is not yet completely dead, and that the character of the people has not yet been completely washed away. Has the Isle of Man now become the Isle of Manchester, as Hall Caine himself laments? Of course the giant swings in the theme parks are not very Nordic, or Celtic, or romantic, but if you have read the poet's book and look around with your eyes wide open, you will still find traces of the old Manx: Fishermen with fully grown beards and heaps of silver herring at the Saturday market. Or in the interior of the island you will find narrow trails that suddenly take you into a different world, into an almost completely isolated world where sheep graze on mountainous meadows and picturesquely charming farmsteads are surrounded by colourful gardens with quite a Mediterranean flair. When you have finally found a secluded spot like this – and it takes some looking – you can actually believe that you are indeed on the quiet, phlegmatic island you set out in search of. And you realise, this is a poet's country. Of course, it is harsh having to pay entry to a glen (through a turnstile!), the same glen where the lovers Christian and Kate rendezvoused amidst the fern and the rushing water of the stream. It is an embarrassment to be drinking tea in a restaurant where you see the following recollection beside a carousel: 'This is Hall Caine's "Manx Fairy" guesthouse where one day the old sectarian Caesar...'

In fact, it is hideous. There are still beautiful ancient Nordic runic crosses in cemeteries that were once silent. But I will avoid runic crosses if they are just about good enough to grace souvenir spoons. The Manx cats with no tails are bred especially for aficionados and sold at a high price. The normal everyday cats have tails just like every other decent British cat. When out and about, you hear the interesting Manx language just about as often as you hear an Inuit idiom. But it's wonderful when the author of one of the tourist brochures quotes an old Manx saying.

In short, you might wish that the brave old wizard *Mannanan Mac y Leir (yes, that's his name) still existed. This somewhat difficult wizard once ruled over Man, long before *Orry, the Viking king, arrived. He had the truly commendable habit of hiding the island in dense fog so that no one could find it. But now the Manchester middle class has found it. Since then there is no more fog, and the island lies bathed in the sun, a delight to the eyes. The brochures bear testimony to this. Even the wizard's best efforts wouldn't have been able to do anything about that. If it's in black and white, it must be true.

It's exactly for this reason that poets are more powerful than wizards. The Isle of Man described by Hall Caine will continue to exist for some time to come. *If you want to understand a poet's country, and especially if the world is full of electric amusements, then you have to go to the poet himself for enlightenment.

CHAPTER TWENTY-FOUR

Souvenirs

The steamboat brings me back to Dublin from the Isle of Man. I disembark, convincing myself that Dublin is as grubby as ever, thank God. Not that it is really any of my business anymore. I will soon be gone again. There is a little wad of tickets in my breast pocket. It was once beautifully full and thick; now its best pages have been torn out, leaving the following on the tatty remnants: Return journey.

Am I sad? No, I'm not. Ireland is a wonderful country, but after a while it becomes a bit annoying. It's like one of those decent, respectable people with a melancholic disposition whose eyes well up with tears as often as rain falls from the sky. Ever since I set foot in this country, it has looked at me through welled-up eyes. And yet it doesn't actually rain quite as much, just as those tearful people don't cry as often as one would expect. But I've had enough of this damp mist over my head and being reminded of a battle whenever I come across a river I like. It's altogether a rather joyless island.

When a journey draws to a close, your money also usually runs out. Nevertheless, you spend the last few days of your trip diligently running from shop to shop buying all sorts of stuff that you certainly would not give a second thought to even if it was free at home. This is what we call souvenirs, and it is impossible to arrive home without bringing some with you.

I walked around cursing good old Dublin city – Ireland is such a backward country. I can buy genuine Venetian mosaic jewellery cheaply everywhere in Europe. Even in Venice it would cost at most one lira more than in Wertheim's department store in Berlin. But in Ireland – prohibitively expensive. One might ask why I would bring Venetian mosaic brooches as a souvenir from Ireland? Well, but what else can I bring? OK,

I will concede that there are also brooches decorated with shamrock leaves made of green Connemara marble. But they are awful-looking. Plus, you wouldn't dare give a German a three-leaved shamrock for he would take it as a sign of bad luck. That's exactly why Ireland has had so much bad luck: because its emblematic shamrock has three rather than four leaves. So, what should I bring home as a souvenir? There are oak wooden carvings, but the small ones are not that nice while the bigger ones wouldn't fit into the suitcase of a modest tourist like myself.

I wave down a coach driver so he can take me from shop to shop. It's part and parcel of the experience, and it has to be a coach so that I don't collapse under the weight of the packages I purchase. The coach pulls up. It is one of the strange Irish coaches with seats facing left and right. I get onboard and let my legs dangle out over the edge. It is splendid, favourably priced entertainment. And now, am I really supposed to travel through the main streets of this taxing provincial city? Ah, there's no hurry with the souvenirs. I will consider the matter carefully, perhaps the Phoenix Park will inspire me. It's all the same to the coach driver, and so he is already speeding down the long, extremely dusty and most unpleasant quay along the River Liffey. In the distance you can see the Waterloo obelisk, what a joy. Then the greenery of the park picks up where the grubbiness of the city ends. It's such a delight to see huge lawns! They are not empty, angular and fenced off, rather anyone can walk on them, play football or cricket, and can sit or lie on the grass. Impressive herds of cattle solemnly walk around between the people because there cannot be grassland in Ireland where cattle do not graze. Up further you can also see magnificent tame deer. My coach driver stops at the polo grounds for a moment intending to stay there a bit longer because, like all Irish people, he is crazy about all equestrian sports. And it is indeed quite a spectacle to see the riders dressed in white and blue. They chase after the ball as it flies about the pitch with their long wooden mallets. Elegant carriages line the pitch, while well-dressed people sit in the stands watching the game. In the inner city, you always see nothing but shabbily dressed people, but here you are reminded that there is also a splendid aristocratic scene. The *Viceroy's summer residence is located behind the trees.

The coach continues, passing through wonderful avenues. There's no end to this park. If Dublin were anything like its city park, then Dublin would be a metropolis. But that's how things are in Ireland – time and again filth and poverty is found right next to evidence of a great and ancient civilisation. Oh no, I'm getting all soppy again. Today the weather is exceptional, it's the perfect farewell. The cattle on the meadow look utterly astonished: the sun is actually shining. Irish cattle are not used to this. Year in, year out they live their life in a state of mild dampness, because it doesn't get cold even in winter and the meadows stay wet and green. This makes Irish cattle very placid and very forlorn – I think they are constantly dreaming of the ancient king of the bulls. Indeed, Shaw was right. Irish fantasising is caused by the moisture in the air.

But not today. Today the Wicklow Mountains appear blue and clear just because I have to leave soon. It's a beautiful day and a very pleasant drive.

I eventually realise that I am not in fact only here to enjoy myself, and that I have a serious duty to fulfil. Right now, I have to think about what I am going to bring my friends back from Ireland. I have a think about it. What kind of Irish specialities are there? Initially I come up with something that's not really suitable as a souvenir: Irish stew. Strange that that would come to mind – I have not once been served Irish stew during my time in Ireland. And that's the way it should be, because you should never eat national cuisine in its country of origin. One time I was travelling through Italy when the train stopped in Gorgonzola. As an inquisitive traveller, I immediately disembarked and went straight into the nearest inn. I had an excellent dinner and then, full of emotion, excitement and with joyful palpitations, I ordered Gorgonzola for dessert. But then – actually, no, it's possible that the reader has not yet dined, and I don't want to ruin your appetite. I'll leave the story unfinished, and I will not say what this Gorgonzola looked like.

So, what else does Ireland have to offer in the way of souvenirs? Should I bring a bottle of whiskey with me? Whiskey is without a doubt the most popular native Irish product. But when I am asked which kind of Irish whiskey I prefer with my soda water, I always opt for a random variety of Scottish whisky. The potent Irish whiskey is something for the Irish. This race must love hangovers because they certainly love their drinking sessions.

There are also the Irish walking sticks (shillelaghs). But I don't want to be importing banned weapons into Germany. These sticks are usually either studded with thorns or have the shape of an almighty club. These were the kind of weapons the ancient Irish did, after all, like to carry around with them in the days when they still beat each other to death over the ancient

Irish kings. Nowadays, if an Irishman walks around with a shillelagh, he is unspeakably proud in his belief that he is doing his country a great service. People jokingly call these shillelaghs 'Irish shotguns'. But the English shotguns proved themselves to be the better weapons, and the only real use for these fashionable sentimental sticks is that there are plenty of fisticuffs when the whiskey is flowing. It can only end badly when an Irishman starts gesticulating with his shillelagh, because a stick like this with all its welts and spikes – –

Suddenly I have an idea! Lace! That's something my female friends would like as a souvenir from Ireland – genuine Irish lace. Now I will have to pay very careful attention and strictly distinguish between nice and not-so-nice ladies of my acquaintance. The reason being that there is lace from Ireland and then there is Irish lace. Really pretty, crocheted collars and blouse inserts – both affordable and practical. That's a gift for aunties and the likes. As far as I know, a lot of this crocheted lace that the ladies at home call 'Eirisch' is actually produced in the *Erzgebirge Mountains in Thuringia and sent to Ireland so that it can be sold back to Germany for more money. At the end of the day, that's a matter for the women to worry about. But there are also delicate and artful fabrics from Donegal and Limerick. Embroidered *Carrickmacross lace as fragile as a spider's web. And those who think you can get this for free in Ireland should come over here and take a look. The most divine pieces of Genoese lace are to be had for next to nothing on the *Riviera di Levante, whereas in Ireland every single centimetre of the illustrious textile costs two centimetres of silver. And the Irish are right to charge this much. But this isn't something I can give to just any old auntie.

I keep racking my brains and I begin to realise that there are very few genuine Irish articles. This country has next to no industry. But it's not just down to that – this country has so little characteristic products because it no longer possesses a national character. It's an English province – the most beautiful, the most impoverished and the dirtiest English province. It's a downtrodden country. The Irishness of Ireland has been exterminated, while the best and noblest Englishness of England has not yet become fully established in Ireland. Sometimes you might hear an Irish melody. The people have an Irish look about them and they speak English with an Irish accent – but can these things be considered national characteristics? They are but provincial idiosyncrasies. The ancient Ireland of the druids has left behind some traces, but only traces. The Irish language is still spoken on the westernmost fringes of the island. But now Thomas Cook is organising package holidays around the westernmost fringes of Ireland, and the tour guide tells how splendidly unspoiled, how very archaic the lonely hills of Donegal and the ragged fjords of Connemara still are. Contrary to expectations, I made a conscious point of not visiting these regions simply because Cook promotes them so much. Having to travel with thirty Americans in an open-top motor vehicle and having to stick my neck out to see? Beautiful landscape alone just isn't worth the hassle. There's no denying that Thomas Cook is indeed a blessing for Ireland, but for the old Irish culture he surely only heralds the beginning of the end. Thomas Cook will achieve what Cromwell and William of Orange couldn't. Cook will complete the Anglicisation of Ireland in no time at all. Make no mistake – the times we live in do not favour ethnographic relics. The Scots very much hang on to their ancient traditions, wearing kilts instead of trousers where they can still get away with it. Yet it's only pageantry, a nod to the old traditions, an admirable and reverent masquerade. Ireland, on the other hand, no longer even has any national costumes. What still counts as Irish? The only thing that still counts as Irish is the national lamentation, the longing for a sense of nationhood that has long since disappeared. This is not an isolated case in the history of the races, and great national anguish can also be counted as a national characteristic; however, this sense of anguish alone does not make for a unique sense of nationhood. The Irish strive for the rebirth of their people with tremendous tenacity, but when they are granted Home Rule and can finally lay to rest their yearning, they will soon notice that they are no longer driven by any real goal. The new Irish nation will be a lively, colourful variety of Britishness – Britishness with a touch of musical flare. If you say this to an Irishman right now, he will scream his head off at you, full of hatred, but it's true. Despite the best efforts of the Gaelic League, a new, autonomous Ireland will in essence not be a Celtic land, rather an English one. Of course, there will be big differences – Irish Catholicism will see to that. But there will not be an Irish nation. And it is exactly for this reason that Home Rule is a good thing. The new Ireland will be independent to the extent that it is un-English, and yet it will remain a part of the huge British imperial realm – because Ireland at the end of a long, violent history must realise that she has, after all, been assimilated by her harsh and superior conquerors.

It's natural enough that Home Rule is often the topic of conversation in Ireland. But I am, after all, supposed to be talking about Irish souvenirs, and I want to bring some mementos home for myself, too. Perhaps a book full of ancient tales, full of druidic magic, dancing, sprightly elves and the heroic clashing of swords (never has such a mundane country been so poetic). Maybe a few pictures showing lots of noteworthy ruins or cities where this or that event took place, or secluded bogs that would now be a flourishing landscape had this or that not happened. All the things that are reminiscent of Irish history in some way or other. On the really steep seaside cliffs, at the peaks of Irish mountains, in the lush undergrowth of the densest forests, on the shore of the silver lakes of Killarney and the luminous Bay of Glengarriff – no matter where you are in Ireland, you never forget what you gladly forget elsewhere, namely that the world was not and is not as it should be. On any given day, how often do people in Germany think of the *Thirty Years' War? Any educated person in Ireland cannot go twelve hours without being reminded of events from the seventeenth century at least once. Forests of glowing fuchsia and mountain slopes carpeted in gorse and heather do nothing to mitigate this.

What keepsake will I take home with me from Ireland? I will take home the memory of an extremely beautiful and an extremely unhappy country. I will also take home the realisation that this country is still as beautiful as it ever was, but perhaps no longer as unhappy, that this downtrodden paradise is slowly recovering. If I ever make it to Ireland again, maybe the streets of Dublin will be clean and maybe there will be less whiskey around, maybe the Kerry farmer will have a house rather than a hole in the ground as his dwelling, maybe the schools will have improved and the lunatic asylums will not be as overflowing. When such a time comes, Ireland will surely be less picturesque. But there is nothing you can do about this – soap might not be very interesting, but it is extremely useful. That's the way things are headed these days – towards uniformity. And when you think about it, this is hardly objectionable. The universe is not here to provide pleasure and entertainment for the tourist. And Ireland will still be beautiful when Irish children are no longer dressed in rags and when the Irish no longer have to emigrate in their thousands.

Coachman, take me back to Dublin! And then to the train station – once again a trip and a summer have come to an end, and thus another chapter of life's story.

CHAPTER TWENTY-FIVE

A Keepsake: Connla of the Golden Hair
(Taken from *P.W. Joyce's collection of ancient Celtic tales)

Connla of the Golden Hair was the son of Conn the Hundred-fighter. One day as he stood with his father on the royal Hill of Usna, he saw a lady a little way off, very beautiful, and dressed in strange attire. She approached the spot where he stood; and when she was near, he spoke to her, and asked who she was, and from what place she had come.

The lady replied, 'I have come from the Land of the Living – a land where there is neither death nor old age, nor any breach of law. The inhabitants of earth call us Aes-shee, for we have our dwellings within large, pleasant green hills. We pass our time very pleasantly in feasting and harmless amusements, never growing old; and we have no quarrels or contentions.'

The king and his company marvelled very much; for though they heard this conversation, no one saw the lady except Connla alone.

'Who is this thou art talking to, my son?' said the king. And anon she answered for the youth, 'Connla is speaking with a lovely, noble-born young lady, who will never die, and who will never grow old. I love Connla of the Golden Hair, and I have come to bring him with me to Moymell, the plain of never ending pleasure. On the day that he comes with me he shall be made king; and he shall reign forever in Fairyland, without weeping and without sorrow. Come with me, O gentle Connla of the ruddy cheek, the fair, freckled neck, and the golden hair! Come with me, beloved Connla, and thou shalt retain the comeliness and dignity of thy form, free from the wrinkles of old age, till the awful day of judgement!'

King Conn the Hundred-fighter, being much troubled, called then on his druid Coran, to put forth his power against the witchery of the banshee.

165

'O Coran of the mystic arts and of the mighty incantations, here is a contest such as I have never been engaged in since I was made king at Tara – a contest with an invisible lady who is beguiling my son to Fairyland by her baleful charms. Her cunning is beyond my skill, and I am not able to withstand her power; and if thou, Coran, help not, my son will be taken away from me by the wiles and witchery of a woman from the fairy hills!'

Coran the druid then came forward, and began to chant against the voice of the lady. And his power was greater than hers for that time, so that she was forced to retire.

As she was going away she threw an apple to Connla, who straightaway lost sight of her; and the king and his people no longer heard her voice.

The king and the prince returned with their company to the palace, and Connla remained for a whole month without tasting food or drink, except the apple. And though he ate of it each day, it was never lessened, but was as whole and perfect in the end as at the beginning. Moreover, when they offered him aught else to eat or drink, he refused it; for while he had his apple he did not deem any other food worthy to be tasted. And he began to be very moody and sorrowful, thinking of the lovely fairy maiden.

At the end of the month, as Connla stood by his father's side among the nobles, on the Plain of Arcomin, he saw the lady approaching him from the west. And when she had come near, she addressed him in this manner: 'A glorious seat, indeed, has Connla among wretched, short-lived mortals, awaiting the dreadful stroke of death! But now, the ever-youthful people of Moymell, who never feel age, and who fear not death, seeing thee day by day among thy friends, in the assemblies of thy fatherland, love thee with a strange love, and they will make thee King over them if thou wilt come with me.'

When the king heard the words of the lady, he commanded his people to call the druid again to him, saying, 'Bring my druid Coran to me; for I see that the fairy lady has this day regained the power of her voice.'

At this the lady said: 'Valiant Conn, fighter of a hundred, the faith of the druids has come to little honour among the upright, mighty, numberless people of this land. When the righteous law shall be restored, it will seal up the lips of the false black demon; and his druids shall no longer have power to work their guileful spells.'

Now the king observed, and marvelled greatly, that whenever the lady was present his son never spoke one word to anyone, even though they addressed him many times. And when the lady had ceased to speak, the king said: 'Connla, my son, has thy mind been moved by the words of the lady?'

Connla spoke then, and replied, 'Father, I am very unhappy; for though I love my people beyond all, I am filled with sadness on account of this lady!'

When Connla had said this, the maiden again addressed him, and chanted these words in a very sweet voice:

The chant of the fairy maiden to Connla of the Golden Hair

I

A land of youth, a land of rest,
A land from sorrow free;
It lies far off in the golden west,
On the verge of the azure sea.
A swift canoe of crystal bright,
That never met mortal view – –
We shall reach the land ere fall of night,
In that strong and swift canoe;
We shall reach the strand
Of that sunny land,
From druids and demons free;
The land of rest
In the golden west,
On the verge of the azure sea!

II

A pleasant land of winding vales, bright streams, and verdurous plains,
Where summer all the live-long year, in changeless splendour reigns;
A peaceful land of calm delight, of everlasting bloom;
Old age and death we never know, no sickness, care, or gloom;
The land of youth,
Of love and truth,
From pain and sorrow free,
The land of rest,
In the golden west,
On the verge of the azure sea!

III

There are strange delights for mortal men in that island of the west;
The sun comes down each evening in its lovely vales to rest;
And though far and dim
On the ocean's rim
It seems to mortal view,
We shall reach its halls
Ere the evening falls,
In my strong and swift canoe;
And evermore
That verdant shore
Our happy home shall be;
The land of rest,
In the golden west,
On the verge of the azure sea!

IV

It will guard thee, gentle Connla of the flowing golden hair,
It will guard thee from the druids, from the demons of the air;
My crystal boat will guard thee, till we reach that western shore,
When thou and I in joy and love shall live for evermore:
From the druid's incantation,
From his black and deadly snare,
From the withering imprecation
Of the demon of the air,
It will guard thee, gentle Connla of the flowing golden hair;
My crystal boat shall guard thee, till we reach that silver strand
Where thou shalt reign in endless joy, the King of the Fairyland!'

When the maiden had ended her chant, Connla suddenly walked away from his father's side, and sprang into the curragh, the gleaming, straight-gliding, strong, crystal canoe. The king and his people saw them afar off, and dimly moving away over the bright sea towards the sunset. They gazed sadly after them, till they lost sight of the canoe over the utmost verge; and no one can tell whither they went, for Connla was never again seen in his native land.

CHAPTER TWENTY-SIX

Farewell

Chug...chug...chug...

The sky is overcast as a melancholic morning train takes me to the port, where a ship will await me. It will take me away from here and soon I will be breathing in the fresh summer's air of home.

Green landscape flies past me; it will soon have disappeared from my sight, fluttered away with the wind of change. Farewell to this strange green country! You have remained impenetrable to me. Even though I am still here, travelling through your meadows and fields, I feel as if it was all but a dream.

I do not know whether I love or hate this green country with the overcast sky damp from tears. You are too sad, your corpses are buried in very shallow graves. No matter how long I live, I will never be able to love those twisted fairytales, old piles of rubble and ruins, and damp bogs. Your youthfulness has become aged – yet what youth I have left longs for youthful strength and energy. You have wept for aeons and never acquired the strength and energy of youth. Your bogs are full of fairy phantoms, the sun does not smile down on them. And you will forever mourn the crowns of ancient kings.

Germany's destiny has been realised. The ravens no longer circle the mountain of national sorrow. But Ireland remains one giant *Kyffhäuser. Here, the ravens continue to circle. Thomas Cook is the only one who can scare them away. Not to worry, he certainly will.

I visited this foreign country in the dampness and greenness of summer. I saw ancient abbeys, cloisters, towers, looming castles and fortresses. I searched for life in them, but I found only sorrow. I saw silver lakes overcast by an old darkness, the waves of the sea drowned out by songs of lamentation, the roaring of rivers muffled by the echo of bloody battles.

The future might hold some comfort: the sadness of bygone days will become commonplace. A new voice announces a joyful message: the sadness of bygone days will become commonplace! Everyday life follows on from bleak dreams.

Chug...chug...chug...

A port, a boat. A coast disappears. A country becomes blurred.

Was I ever really there?

I long to breathe in the fresh summer air of the woodlands of home.

Notes

p. 25   Shaw's works] George Bernard Shaw (1856–1950), Irish playwright known for the political and social criticism in his work. He penned over sixty plays, including *Major Barbara* (1905), *The Doctor's Dilemma* (1906) and *Caesar and Cleopatra* (1899), and won the Nobel Prize for Literature in 1925.

—   Home Rule] The Irish Home Rule movement demanded self-governance, or Home Rule, for Ireland within the United Kingdom of Great Britain and Ireland. The Irish Parliamentary Party campaigned for Home Rule in the British House of Commons and, between 1886 and 1912, a total of three Home Rule bills were introduced, two of which were defeated. The Third Home Rule Bill of 1912 was passed but implementation was postponed on account of the outbreak of the First World War. It was ultimately superseded by the Fourth Home Rule Bill, or Government of Ireland Act 1920, which partitioned Ireland. A parliament was set up in Northern Ireland, while the other twenty-six counties established the Irish Free State.

—   Reichstag] Here, the term does not refer to the building erected between 1884 and 1894 in Berlin's Tiergarten district, but to the German Empire's national parliament of the same name that was housed in the building.

p. 26   Hottentots] Racial term historically used to describe non-Bantu indigenous people of South Africa (today the term Khoikhoi is used).

p. 27   Peter's pence] Donation or financial contribution paid directly to the Holy See of the Catholic Church.

—   Adrian IV] Nicholas Breakspear (*c.*1100–59) was pope from 1154–9. He was the only Briton ever to hold this office. In 1155, he is said to have issued the papal bull *Laudabiliter*, which granted King Henry II permission to invade and govern Ireland so as to enforce the Gregorian Reforms on the semi-autonomous church in Ireland. The Norman invasion of Ireland subsequently took place between 1169 and 1171.

—   King Henry II] (1133–89) was king of England, duke of Normandy and Aquitaine, count of Anjou, Maine and Nantes, and lord of Ireland, and also controlled parts of Scotland, Wales and the Duchy of Brittany at various times. His reign lasted from 1154 until his death in 1189. Throughout history, he has not been viewed as a particularly pious king, but rather as a power-hungry monarch wishing to exercise his authority over church and state (cf. Amanda Martinson, 'The Monastic Patronage of King Henry II in England, 1154–1189', PhD thesis, University of St Andrews, 2008).

p. 28   Kant] Immanuel Kant (1727–1804) was a German philosopher. His work on epistemology, ethics and aesthetics greatly influenced modern philosophy; he was one of the foremost thinkers of the Enlightenment, infamous for complex and complicated diction and anything but 'funny'.

—   The victory of the Japanese] Might refer to the Russo-Japanese war of 1904–5 which resulted in a decisive Japanese victory that paved the way for the annexation of Korea.

—   the commotion in the Muslim world] Might refer to the emergence of a 'Young Turkish' movement inside the Ottoman Empire around the turn of the nineteenth century. Within this, pro-German forces became dominant around 1908 and formed a governing junta that threatened British dominance in the eastern Mediterranean.

—   conspiratorial Hindus with their bombs] In the early 1900s, several Indian independence movements committed assaults on, or planned assassinations of, British colonial administrators and military personnel.

p. 29   Hekla] One of Iceland's most active volcanos, located on the south shore of the island.

p. 30   Bautzen] Town in Saxony in eastern Germany, capital of the region of Lusatia, which had a population of around 20,000 in the early twentieth century.

—   Chemnitz] City in Saxony in Germany, which had a population of around 340,000 in the early twentieth century.

p. 31   Negro prince] Like the expressions Hottentot or Kaffir, the word Negro did not necessarily carry a pejorative meaning in the early twentieth century, yet the implication here, insinuating how ridiculous such a radical transformation would be, illustrates the racist potential of the designation.

—   Haussa] A large ethnic group in Africa, mainly found in north-western Nigeria and southern Niger. Before conquest by the British in the early 1900s, the Haussa Sultanate of Sokoto in northern Nigeria was known as an independent, largely Muslim political entity.

p. 32   Thomas Cook] (1808–92) English businessman who founded the Thomas Cook & Son travel agency. Thomas Cook can be said to have invented modern mass tourism with his organised tours and travel handbooks.

—   bread and games] A metonymic phrase from the Latin *panem et circenses* which critiques appeasement by diverting people's attention from social conditions and using entertainment and handouts to distract them from political action.

p. 33   red monthly] Publications such as *The Lady's Realm* or *The Ludgate Monthly / The Ludgate Illustrated Monthly* often had red cover designs.

p. 35   whether the invasion is about to begin] Even though some military strategists in Germany contemplated plans for a possible invasion of Britain as early as the 1890s, these never became official German policy. The talk of an impending invasion in Britain, stirred by a sensationalist press, was propelled by the German navy's vast programme of expansion during the preceding years and by a new tone in German politics that manifested itself in imperialist muscle-flexing (gunboat diplomacy) and not avoiding standoffs, as exemplified by confrontational behaviour during the two Moroccan crises 1905/6 and 1911 that antagonised France. Here a sense of paranoia within the British public is ridiculed.

p. 37   big cathedrals] Probably referring to St Colman's Cathedral in Cobh.

p. 38   green-covered guidebook] Cook's guides, Baedekers and John Murray's famous *Handbook for Travellers in Ireland* (many editions after 1866) were traditionally bound in red; *Black's Guides to Ireland* (e.g. the 8th edn, 1912) were bound in dark green. There was also a *Black's Guide to Killarney and the South of Ireland* (22nd edn, 1909) and a *Black's Guide to Belfast and the North of Ireland* (26th edn, 1912).

—   The church was only built in 1879 (by W. Burgess)] St Fin Barre's Cathedral in Cork city is a Church of Ireland (not a Catholic) cathedral completed in 1879 by the

English architect William Burgess. It is Gothic Revival in style (not Romanesque, as Bermann states).

— Catholic Emancipation] Process of removing substantial restrictions on Irish and British Catholics stemming from the Penal Laws. Various Relief Acts were implemented in the late eighteenth century, allowing Catholics to purchase land, granting them the franchise and admission to most civil offices. Daniel O'Connell, however, led Irish Catholic demands for greater emancipation. His campaign led to British prime minister Sir Robert Peel's introduction of the Emancipation Act of 1829, which admitted Irish and English Catholics to parliament. The Universities Tests Act of 1871 opened universities to Catholics. Any remaining Penal Laws were finally removed by the Government of Ireland Act 1920.

— Irish apostles] Twelve students who studied under St Finian in the sixth century at his monastery Clonard Abbey and became known as the Twelve Apostles of Ireland.

p. 40 anti-Ascendancy majority is in power] In 1905, the Liberal party formed a government in Britain under Sir Henry Campbell-Bannerman and, from 1908, H.H. Asquith. Asquith revived Gladstone's policy on Ireland, in particular the process of granting Home Rule to Ireland. The Third Home Rule Bill was introduced in the House of Commons in 1912.

— dreadnought] A battleship, especially from the First World War era. The name is derived from 'dread' and 'nought', i.e. fearing nothing.

p. 41 Oliver Cromwell] (1599–1658) English military and political leader. He led parliamentary forces during the English Civil Wars and served as the Lord Protector of England, Scotland and Ireland from 1653 until 1658 during the republican Commonwealth. He headed the English campaign in Ireland, also known as the Cromwellian conquest of Ireland 1649–53, bringing an end to the Irish Confederate Wars by defeating the Royalist and Confederate coalition in Ireland. During this time, a number of Penal Laws were introduced against Roman Catholics, and vast tracts of their land were confiscated as part of the Cromwellian plantation. In addition, thousands of Irish were sold into indentured servitude in the West Indies.

— Macroom] Market town in County Cork.

— Tourist Development Co. Ltd] Probably refers to the Irish Tourist Development Association founded in 1891 by Frederick Crossley, a former employee of Thomas Cook. Crossley established a publishing company in 1894 and began publication of the monthly journal *Irish Tourist*, and he subsequently acquired the Irish Tourist Development Publishing Company. In 1896 he set up the Development Syndicate (Ireland) Ltd which offered coach and steamer services in places not served by railways. Such a service may be what Bermann refers to when he describes his journey around west Cork on a motor omnibus. Crossley was also responsible for establishing the Shannon Development Company in 1896, offering steamer services along the River Shannon. Killaloe to Banagher formed the inaugural route, the route Bermann travelled after visiting Killarney and Limerick.

p. 42 Lone Gouganebarra] A remote settlement west of Macroom in County Cork. The name is linked to St Finbarr (Irish: Fionnbharra, often abbreviated to Barra), who is believed to have founded a monastery on an island in Gouganebarra lake in the sixth century.

— St Finbar] Finbarr of Cork is the patron saint of Cork city. He was bishop of Cork and abbot in a monastery in the city in the sixth and seventh centuries. For a time, he is reported to have lived on an island in what is now called Gouganebarra lake.

p. 43   Arbutus] Also: strawberry tree, a small evergreen tree. In Ireland, it can grow up to heights of fifteen metres. It only grows naturally in the Mediterranean and specific parts of Ireland, mainly in County Kerry in and around Killarney, as well as in Glengarriff Wood, County Cork.

—   Riviera di Levante] Coastal stretch close to Genoa, Italy.

p. 44   between 1641 and 1649 around six hundred thousand people were killed or sold as slaves to the West Indies] Indentured servants were Irish people sent to British colonies in the Caribbean and North America to work on plantations or as domestic servants. Their contracts stipulated passage, food and board for seven years of service, after which their masters were legally obliged to grant them 'freedom dues' (land or capital). Apart from voluntary indentures, penal transportations of political prisoners, vagrants and other 'undesirables' were frequent; they reached a peak during the Cromwellian conquests and settlements.

—   Lord Protector] Oliver Cromwell (see note on p. 41).

p. 45   gothic lettering] Irish on public signs is normally not rendered in the so-called gothic font (German 'Fraktur'), but a unique form of lettering known as Gaelic type or Irish character (as opposed to Roman). Resembling italics because of its leaning posture, a standardised variety of the font is today widely used on public signs in Ireland for Gaelic names and expressions.

—   Thackeray] William Makepeace Thackeray (1811–63) was a British author. He was best known for his satirical works, especially *Vanity Fair* (1848) and *The Luck of Barry Lyndon* (1844). He visited Ireland for four months in the summer of 1842 and subsequently published his impressions of the country in *The Irish Sketch Book*.

p. 49   earl of Kenmare] The title earl of Kenmare was created in the Peerage of Ireland in 1801. The earls of Kenmare, namely the Browne family, were English settlers who first came to Ireland in the sixteenth century. The Browne family variously owned large estates in Cork, Kerry and Limerick, and by the early twentieth century, although their landholdings were considerably reduced, they were still in possession of land surrounding the Killarney Lakes. The family, in particular Sir Thomas Browne, 4th Viscount Kenmare (1726–95), was involved in developing tourism in Killarney town and the demesne landscape of the Kenmare Estate.

—   Hiking is the Miller's Delight] First line ('Das Wandern ist des Müllers Lust') of a famous poem by Wilhelm Müller (1821) that was set to music by Franz Schubert as part of his cycle *Die schöne Müllerin*. It was, however, in the version by Carl Friedrich Zöllner (1844) that the tune became one of the best-known German songs. The famous opening line, containing a reference both to the author and to journeymen of a specific profession, became a slogan that epitomises a presumed German proclivity for hiking.

p. 50   Gap of Dunloe] A narrow mountain pass in County Kerry. It separates the MacGillycuddy's Reeks mountain range from the Purple Mountain Group range, and is a popular tourist destination on account of its scenery.

p. 52   Lord Bandon] Might refer to Lord Brandon's cottage at the head of the Upper Lake, Killarney. This was located on land owned by the Herbert family, who were granted land in Kerry during the reign of Elizabeth I.

—   Ross Castle] Ross Castle is located on the edge of Killarney's Lough Leane. It is thought to have been built by one of the O'Donoghue Ross chieftains in the fifteenth century. It was among the last strongholds in Munster to surrender to Cromwell during the Irish Confederate Wars. The castle was later associated with the Brownes, whose ancestors became the earls of Kenmare.

— Innisfallen Abbey] Innisfallen Abbey is located on an island in Lake Leane. It was founded in 640 by St Finian the Leper and developed into a centre of scholarship in the early Christian period. The *Annals of Innisfallen* were produced there, chronicling the early history of Ireland. The abbey was occupied for around 950 years before Elizabeth I dispossessed the monks of the abbey in 1594. According to legend, King Brian Boru was educated in the abbey.

p. 53 Eoghan Rudhan O'Sullivan] Eoghan Rua Ó Súilleabháin (1748–82), Irish poet, is considered to be one of the last great Gaelic poets. He was born in County Kerry and is thought to have attended a classical school of Irish poetry where English, Latin and Greek were taught. He initially set up his own school before working as a farmhand, then joined the British military in the West Indies before returning home to Kerry to set up another school. It was during his time as a farmhand that he reportedly wrote a letter for his master in four languages – English, Irish, Greek and Latin.

— illiteracy rates] Average school attendance in Ireland in 1902 is estimated at 65 per cent of boys of primary school age as compared to 84 per cent in England (Maighread Tobin, *Literacy and Society in Ireland, 1900–1980*, PhD thesis, Maynooth University, 2018, p. 92).

p. 55 James I] (1566–1625) King of England and Ireland 1603–25, successor of Elizabeth I. He also ruled Scotland as James IV from 1567 until his death. The first monarch of England from the House of Stuart, he was also the first monarch to reign over both England and Scotland, as well as Ireland. The Plantation of Ulster by English and Scottish settlers took place during his reign, which proved to be the most large-scale British settlement in Ireland.

— Connaught] One of the four provinces of Ireland, located in the west of the country.

p. 56 packed others onto slave ships and sent them off to wild negro countries to work on Lord John's sugar plantations] Irish indentured servants (see note on p. 44).

— Siege of Drogheda] The Siege of Drogheda (September 1649) took place at the beginning of the Cromwellian conquest of Ireland. Drogheda was held by Irish Royalists under the command of Sir Arthur Aston. Aston refused an order to surrender and the town was stormed by Oliver Cromwell and his Parliamentarian forces. The majority of the garrison were executed and many civilians killed. The few remaining Royalist soldiers were shipped to Barbados.

— Cromwell concluded] An alternative commentary is cited in Robert Hassencamp: *Geschichte Irlands von der Reformation bis zu seiner Union mit England* (Leipzig, 1886), p. 76: 'I am convinced that this divine punishment of barbarian fools whose hands have spilled so much innocent blood is just.'

p. 57 Don't we know this practice all too well??!] Refers to contemporary German attempts to revile oppositional forces or minority communities as 'innere Feinde' (enemies within), namely, since the 1870s Poles and Catholics, and since the 1890s increasingly Jews and socialists.

p. 61 Brian Boru] (*c.*940–1014) High king of Ireland from 1002–14 and founder of the O'Brien dynasty. Brian Boru led a political and military struggle to undermine the Uí Néill dynasty, who had held the high-kingship of Ireland for centuries. Brian Boru was killed at the Battle of Clontarf in 1014 when some of the kings who had submitted to him rebelled, forming alliances with the Dublin Vikings, their allies and other Vikings from overseas. The figure of Brian Boru quickly became legendary in Irish folklore and he is viewed as medieval Ireland's most famous ruler.

— Norman cathedral and castle] St Mary's Cathedral in Limerick, founded in 1168 AD. It was built on what was originally the royal palace of the kings of Thomond on King's Island. The term 'Norman castle' refers to King John's Castle, also located on King's Island. It was built on the orders of King John in 1200. King John, also known as John Lackland, was king of England from 1199 until 1216. The castle is one of the best-preserved Norman castles in Europe, with the walls, towers and fortifications still intact today.

— Church of Ireland] Autonomous province of the Anglican community, founded in 1536. When Henry VIII, as head of the Anglican Church, assumed the title king of Ireland in 1541, the Church of Ireland became the 'established church' and remained so until 1871, when the Irish Church Act 1869 'disestablished' it, i.e. legally separated church and state.

— William de Burgh] (*c.*1160–1205/6) Ancestor of the Burke / Bourke dynasty in Ireland, arrived there in 1185. Henry II appointed him governor of Limerick and granted him vast estates in Leinster and Connaught.

p. 62   Victoria Cross] Most prestigious award in the British military honours system, introduced in 1856 by Queen Victoria to distinguish soldiers in the Crimean War.

p. 63   Irish war between the Jacobites and Williamites] James II (1650–1702), the last Catholic monarch on the English throne (1685–8), was deposed in the Glorious Revolution and William of Orange, together with his wife Mary, proclaimed sovereigns. The Irish Catholic Jacobite forces were heavily supported by the French. The decisive battle between the two sides was the Battle of the Boyne (1 July 1690); further Williamite victories (Aughrim, Siege of Limerick) secured the overall success of the Protestant side. Although the Treaty of Limerick (1691) granted legal rights to Catholics, the Irish parliament refused to ratify the relevant articles and instead updated the Penal Laws against Catholics.

— Penal Laws] Set of rules, enforced since the establishment of the Anglican Church of Ireland, against Catholics and Protestant dissenters, excluding them from voting and holding public office, from the legal professions and the judiciary, banning inter-marriage, restricting property rights, land ownership and Catholic education.

p. 64   Irish mile] 2.048 kilometres. During the Elizabethan era, four Irish miles were generally equated to five English ones.

p. 66   St Anmchadh] (d. 1043) Said to have been expelled from the monastic island of Inis Cealtra (Lough Derg, a freshwater basin of the River Shannon) and to have had himself walled in at the monastery of Fulda in Germany.

— The hill with a strange hole in the side] Probably refers to the Devil's Bit in County Tipperary, a 478-metre-high mountain.

— Cashel, County Tipperary] Small town in the south of Ireland best known for the medieval complex (cathedral, round tower and castle) that sits atop the Rock of Cashel.

p. 67   Banagher station] Terminus of a branch line connecting the town of Banagher on the River Shannon to the Midland Great Western line, the main railway between Galway and Dublin. Opened in 1884, it ceased operation in 1963.

p. 69   Heringsdorf] Resort on the island of Usedom in the Baltic Sea, today close to the Polish border. German Emperor William II visited several times and it became a popular destination for Berliners. Distance from Berlin-Wilmersdorf *c.*250 kilometres.

p. 70   Wilmersdorf] City outside Berlin; incorporated as a Berlin borough in 1920.

— det freue ihm] 'he were very pleased'. Berlin dialect, representing non-standard pronunciation and grammar, the correct German would be: 'Das freue ihn'.

— Rixdorf / Neukölln] Bohemian Rixdorf was founded in 1737 when Friedrich I invited a number of Moravian Protestant refugees to live on his lands after they had been exiled from Bohemia. The village became quite prosperous and by the turn of the twentieth century was Prussia's largest village. It was so well known for its parties and drinking that the authorities decided to rebrand it as Neukölln. The village later became part of Berlin city.

— Balkans] Two Balkan Wars took place in 1912 and 1913 when Bulgaria, Serbia, Greece and Montenegro fought against the Ottoman Empire.

— the thought of France] Tensions between France and Germany were particularly tense after the so-called second Moroccan crisis in 1911. After France had occupied Fez and Rabat, ostensibly to assist the Sultan against a rebellion, Germany had sent a gunboat and further warships to the Moroccan coast, resulting in a stand-off. The crisis was resolved through an exchange of colonial possessions in western Africa. The remark more generally refers to the spiralling arms race between the European alliances.

p. 71 German invasion] see note on p. 35.

— Mister Meschugge] Pseudonym of bandleader Robert Krüger, one of the 'eccentric conductors' all the rage before the First World War, who not only introduced Germans to new musical styles such as Ragtime and Dixieland, but also entertained their audiences with extravagant physical performances. The adjective 'meschugge' (crazy) derives from the Hebrew and entered the German language via Yiddish.

— Eckersberg] Christoffer Wilhelm Eckersberg (1783–1853), Danish painter renowned for maritime scenes that stylistically resemble British Marina Art of the era, and also known for (Norwegian) landscapes reminiscent of Scottish landscapes – hence Bermann's ironic designation as 'quintessentially British'.

— Wannsee] Lake resort in the south-west of Berlin popular for swimming and recreation.

p. 72 Swinemünde / Ahlbeck] seaside resorts on the Baltic Sea close to Heringsdorf.

p. 73 Gaelic League] The Gaelic League (Irish: Conradh na Gaeilge) was founded in 1893 by Eoin MacNeill and Douglas Hyde. It was set up as a non-political and non-sectarian association dedicated to the promotion of the vernacular form of the Irish language and modern literature in Irish. It started out as a small Dublin-based group, which by 1905 had over 100,000 members in 900 affiliated branches. The Gaelic League's activities included Irish classes for young and old, lectures, fairs, excursions, exhibitions, dancing, recitations, musical concerts and plays.

— Ancient Order of Hibernians] An Irish Catholic fraternal organisation. It was founded in the US in 1836, but had its roots in numerous secret organisations and Catholic agrarian societies in Ireland in the eighteenth and nineteenth centuries. In Ulster it emerged at the end of the nineteenth century in opposition to the Orange Order and was closely associated with the Irish Parliamentary Party.

— Sinn Féin] (English: 'Ourselves') A left-wing Irish republican party active in both the Republic of Ireland and Northern Ireland. Founded in 1905 by Arthur Griffith, support and membership was initially weak, but after the Easter Rising of 1916 republicans came together under the umbrella of Sinn Féin, and in 1917 the party committed itself to the establishment of an Irish Republic for the first time.

p. 74 Meistersinger] Singers organised in a guild analogous to other urban trade guilds. The institution was made famous by Richard Wagner's opera *Die Meistersinger von Nürnberg* (1868) and the term subsequently entered the German vernacular.

p. 75   Bavarian Schuhplattler] A traditional folk dance performed mainly in Bavaria and Tyrol. The name is derived from how the dance is performed: dancers clap and strike the soles of their shoes (Schuhe), thighs and knees with their hands flat (platt).

—   Nijinski] Vatslav Nijinsky (1889 or 1890–1950), Polish-Russian ballet dancer and choreographer, hailed by many as the greatest male dancer of the twentieth century.

—   hornpipe / jig or a reel] Styles of Irish traditional music, lively dance tunes in 4/4, 6/8 or 3/6 times; also popular in composed dance suites of the early modern and Baroque periods (Gigue, Giga).

—   Peter Altenberg] (1859–1919) Modernist Viennese writer, famous for his short impressionist prose sketches of everyday situations. One of Bermann's most revered literary heroes.

p. 76   A Nation Once Again] Song written by Thomas Osborne Davis in the mid-1840s. Davis was one of the founders of the Young Irelanders, which aimed for Irish independence. The song was first published in *The Nation* (Irish nationalist weekly newspaper) on 13 July 1844 and quickly became popular among the Irish nationalist movement.

—   Gaelic League] see note on p. 73.

p. 77   'Puppchen'] Musical farce / operetta by Jean Gilbert (1912). One of the songs from this piece, 'Puppchen, du bist mein Augenstern' [Dolly, you are the apple of my eye] (lyrics by Fritz Junkermann) remained one of the most popular German tunes for many decades.

p. 78   upper house of the Irish parliament] House of Lords of the Parliament of Ireland consisting of hereditary nobles and bishops, established in 1782. From 31 December 1800, the Parliament of Ireland was abolished entirely as the Acts of Union 1800 created the United Kingdom of Great Britain and Ireland. The British and Irish legislatures were merged into a single Parliament of the United Kingdom after 1 January 1801.

p. 79   O'Neill clan] Group of families of Irish Gaelic origin who claim descent from the second-century high king Conn Ceadcathach (Conn of the Hundred Battles), and the legendary Niall Noígiallach (Niall of the Nine Hostages), who was high king of Ireland from AD 377 to 404. The Uí Néill claimed to be descended from Niall of the Nine Hostages and formed two branches, the Uí Néills of Ulster and the southern Uí Néills.

—   Statutes of Kilkenny in 1361] The Statutes of Kilkenny were a series of thirty-five acts passed by the Parliament of Ireland at a sitting in Kilkenny on the behest of the duke of Clarence between 1361 and 1367, aiming to curb the decline of the Hiberno-Norman lordship of Ireland through measures such as forbidding intermarriage with native Irish families.

—   Zwing-Uri] Castle in the Swiss canton of Uri, now ruined; constructed in the twelfth and expanded in the early fourteenth centuries. One of the fortresses built by the Austrian Habsburgs to control the independently minded Swiss population. Immortalised in Friedrich Schiller's play *Wilhelm Tell* (1803).

p. 80   Sir Edward Carson] Irish unionist politician. A barrister by profession, he was born in Dublin in 1854 and studied at Trinity College. His political career began when he was elected as Unionist MP for Trinity College in the 1892 general election and remained as such until 1918. He was also solicitor-general for Ireland (1892) and for England (1900–5). By 1906 he was a prominent politician in the United Kingdom. In 1910 he became the leader of the Irish Unionist Parliamentary Party and the following year leader of the Ulster Unionists. His political objective was to maintain the union between Britain and Ireland, and he was known as a charismatic and inspiring orator. He was the first signatory of the Ulster Covenant, which bound almost half a million signatories to resist Home Rule. He established the Ulster Volunteers – the first loyalist paramilitary group – which in 1913 became the Ulster Volunteer Force, and opposed the Home Rule bill as well as the Anglo-Irish Treaty of 1921 which partitioned Ireland.

— Irish Unionist Party] Founded in 1891, also known as the Irish Unionist Alliance. The party's main purpose was to oppose Home Rule for Ireland.

— autonomous Irish parliament] Also known as Grattan's Parliament, named after Henry Grattan, the deputy whose activism ensured legislative independence for Ireland. The measures by which this was achieved, known as the Constitution of 1782, gave the parliament greater control over Irish affairs. However, this was short-lived, as the Parliament of Ireland was abolished following the Acts of Union in 1800.

— William of Orange] (1650–1702) Also William III, was Prince of Orange, Stadtholder of various regions in the Dutch Republic from 1672 and king of England, Ireland and Scotland from 1689 until his death. He was heralded as a champion of the Protestant faith by many of his followers. He married the daughter of his maternal uncle James, duke of York. In 1685, James, a Catholic, became king of England, Scotland and Ireland. Many Protestants in Britain were unhappy with this development and William, in conjunction with English Parliamentarians, invaded Britain (the Glorious Revolution [1688]). James meanwhile drew support from Irish Catholics and from the Scottish highlanders. William of Orange defeated James at the Battle of the Boyne in 1690, and the Irish Jacobites surrendered under the conditions of the Treaty of Limerick in 1691. Having deposed James, William (and his wife) reigned over England, Ireland and Scotland until William's death in 1702.

— Irish Volunteers] Here referring to the Volunteers of the eighteenth century, i.e. local militia groups organised in Ireland in 1778. These groups were formed in order to provide protection against invasion when British soldiers were withdrawn from Ireland and sent to fight in the American Revolutionary War. The Volunteers were able to exert pressure on the otherwise preoccupied government in Westminster, resulting in legislative independence for the parliament in Dublin.

— 1798 Rebellion] Uprising against British rule in Ireland from May to September 1798 led by Theobald Wolfe Tone and the United Irishmen, a republican revolutionary group influenced by the ideals of the French and American revolutions. The United Irishmen, comprising Protestant liberals and Catholics, sought military aid from the French revolutionary government. A French army landed in Mayo but was overwhelmed by British forces. The rebellion was eventually suppressed by British crown forces.

p. 81   *John Bull's Other Island*] Play commissioned by Yeats for the opening of the Abbey Theatre in Dublin (1904), but it was not staged there in the end and premiered in the same year in London (Royal Court Theatre). It satirises Anglo-Irish relationships and the apparent susceptibility of rural communities on 'the other island'. A German translation by Siegfried Trebitsch, *John Bulls andere Insel*, appeared in 1909 in the famous publishing house of S. Fischer in Berlin.

p. 84   Queen's Theatre] Constructed in 1829 as the Adelphi in Pearse Street; since 1844 known as The Queen's Royal Theatre. The establishment closed in 1969 and the building was demolished in 1975.

— Father Murphy – the Hero of Tullow] Play by Ira Allen (1879–1927), first performed in 1909 and thereafter often revived. The playwright also directed and played the title role. The 1913 run is known to have involved two performances during the week plus a matinee on Saturdays and Sundays.

p. 86   Battle of Oulart Hill] Battle that took place on 27 May 1798 during the 1798 Rebellion in the village of Oulart, County Wexford, in the south-east of Ireland. Initially, a group of about 100 gathered together around Father John Murphy on the evening of 26 May. A skirmish ensued between a patrol of about twenty yeomen and Father Murphy's group in which two patrol members were killed. The next day, a rebel gathering of up to 5,000 massacred a group of 110 soldiers of the North Cork militia under Colonel Foote at Oulart Hill, who had been sent to prevent the rebellion spreading any further in County Wexford.

p. 88   St Columba] (Irish: Colm Cille) Irish abbot and missionary accredited with spreading Christianity in Scotland at the beginning of the Hiberno-Scottish mission. Columba was born in Gartan, County Donegal, in AD 521 and died on the island of Iona in AD 597, where he founded an abbey. Today he is a Catholic saint and one of the Twelve Apostles of Ireland.

— Hy-Niall] Hy-Niall were sects or subdivisions of a clan descended from Niall of the Nine Hostages (see note on p. 79), an Irish king and ancestor of the Uí Néill dynasties that were prominent in the northern part of Ireland from the sixth to the tenth century.

— ard reagh] or ard-rí. Irish term for the high kings of Ireland chronicled in medieval and early modern Irish literature. The high kings ruled from the Hill of Tara in present-day County Meath.

p. 89   King Brian of the Tribute] Brian Boru (see note on p. 61) earned this name because he collected tributes from minor rulers and kings.

— Brodar the Viking] Bróðir of Man was a Dane who lived on the Isle of Man and fought against Brian Boru in the battle of Clontarf in 1014. He is mentioned in the Irish *Cogad Gáedel re Gallaib* ('The War of the Irish with the Foreigners') from the twelfth century and the Icelandic *Njáls saga* ('The Story of Burnt Njáll') from the thirteenth century. Both Bróðir and Brian Boru died in the Battle of Clontarf, although accounts differ on who killed whom.

— Sigurd the jarl of Orkney] Sigurd Hlodvirsson, also known as Sigurd the Stout, was an earl (jarl) of Orkney. His death at the Battle of Clontarf in 1014 is recorded in the Annals of Ulster. In the saga tales chronicling his life, Sigurd is said to have used a raven banner, a symbol of the Norse god Odin, despite his conversion to Christianity.

— Sitric, the sea king of Dublin] Sigtrygg II Silkbeard Olafsson of Norse and Irish ancestry was king of Dublin in the late tenth and early eleventh centuries. He was allied to the leaders of the Leinster revolt and when defeated had to submit to Brian Boru, king of Munster. He plays a significant role in the Irish *Cogad Gáedel re Gallaib* ('The War of the Irish with the Foreigners') from the twelfth century and the Icelandic *Njáls saga* ('The Story of Burnt Njáll') from the thirteenth century and is named the main Norse leader at the Battle of Clontarf. He died in 1042.

p. 90   Morogh] Morogh or Murchad mac Briain in Irish was Brian Boru's son and heir.

— Torlogh] Torlough or Toirdelbach mac Murchada meic Briain was Morogh's son and Brian Boru's grandson. Both died in the Battle of Clontarf.

— Hero of Sulcost] Battle fought at Sulcost near Limerick in 968 in which Brian Boru drove the Danes from Limerick. They had previously defeated his brother Mahon, the king of Munster.

— battle bugles] Bermann will have received this, and many other details of this account, from Emily Lawless: *The Story of Ireland* (1891), pp. 60–70.

p. 91 Valkyries] Female figures of Norse mythology who determined who may live and die in battle. They bring their chosen ones to Valhalla in Asgard, which is ruled by Odin.

— Asgard] One of the Nine Worlds in Norse mythology, ruled by Odin and his wife Frigg.

p. 94 William Makepeace Thackeray] See note on p. 45.

— Baron Mikosch] Title character of a series of books of jokes, anecdotes and hilarious adventures of a fictitious Hungarian nobleman. Appeared on the German book market, compiled by different editors, from 1890 and quickly became established as a brand similar to that of Baron Münchhausen.

— Redmond Barry-Lyndon] *The Luck of Barry Lyndon* (1844), later reissued as *The Memoirs of Barry Lyndon, Esq.*, is a novel by William Makepeace Thackeray. It is a fictional autobiography detailing the exploits of an adventurer born into the petty Irish gentry who tries to climb the social ladder and become a member of the English aristocracy.

— Becky Sharp in *Vanity Fair*] Rebecca or Becky Sharp is the main character of Thackeray's novel *Vanity Fair*, published in 1848. Like Redmond Barry-Lyndon, she tries to climb the social ladder, in her case through marriage.

— Quotation 'I presume that there is…'] William Makepeace Thackeray, *The Memoirs of Barry Lyndon, Esq.* (London: Bradbury & Evans, 1856), pp. 1–2. The German version (no translator identified) came out in 1851 under the title *Memoiren eines englischen Livreebedienten* [Memoirs of an English Liveried Manservant].

p. 95 Henry VII] (1447–1509) First king of England and lord of Ireland from the House of Tudor, ruled from 1485.

— the Pale] Name given to an area in the east of Ireland surrounding Dublin which was under direct control of the English government from the Late Middle Ages. The area stretched from Dundalk in County Louth to Bray in County Wicklow and inland to Naas and Leixlip in County Kildare, and Trim and Kells in County Meath.

— MacCarthy More] MacCarthy Mór, meaning Great MacCarthy, token head of all the MacCarthys. MacCarthy Mór was the central line of the MacCarthy clan from Munster.

p. 96 Hohenstaufens, Hohenzollerns, Capetians] Family names of the dynasties of medieval German emperors, Prussian kings and the oldest French royal house – similar to Bourbon and Windsor as French and British royal family names.

— Barbarossa] Frederick I (1122–90), also known as Frederick Barbarossa, Holy Roman Emperor from 1155 to 1190. He was also crowned king of Germany, king of Italy and king of Burgundy. Barbarossa means 'red beard' in Italian. He was a descendant of two of the leading families in Germany, namely the Hohenstaufen dynasty and the House of Welf. He is often considered one of the Holy Roman Empire's greatest emperors because of his battlefield and political abilities. Barbarossa developed into a national myth in nineteenth-century Germany, symbolising national unity for the German national movement.

p. 97 Lambert Simnel] (c.1477–c.1525) Was feted by an Oxford clergyman as an offspring of the House of York and claimant to the throne of England. He claimed that the young lad (whose actual origins are unknown) was the earl of Warwick, son of George Plantagenet, 1st duke of Clarence and brother of both Richard III and

Edward IV, who was of a similar age (b. 1475) and was at the time imprisoned in the Tower of London, where he had allegedly died. Plantagenet followers such as John de la Pole, 1st earl of Lincoln, Francis Lovell, 1st Viscount Lovell, Gerald Fitzgerald, 8th earl of Kildare and lord deputy of Ireland (i.e. de facto regent) used this opportunity to mount a challenge against the accession of the Tudors: 'In Ireland the various strands of the movement against Henry VII finally coalesced' (Michael Bennett, *Lambert Simnel and the Battle of Stoke* [Gloucester: Sutton, 1987], p. 63). However, historians believe that not even the mastermind of the affair, Gerald Fitzgerald, would have believed in Simnel's legitimacy (Mary T. Hayden, 'Lambert Simnel in Ireland', *Studies: An Irish Quarterly Review*, vol. IV, no. 16, 1915, pp. 622–38, esp. 624–5), and according to contemporary sources another Irish noble, Nicholas St Lawrence, 4th baron Howth, 'perceived all this but a mad dance' (Donough Bryan, *The Great Earl of Kildare, Gerald FitzGerald (1456–1513)* (Dublin: Phoenix, 1933), p. 104). An improvised coronation of Simnel as King Edward IV took place on 24 May 1487 in Christ Church Cathedral, Dublin, whereby 'A coronet was taken for the occasion from the head of a locally revered statue of the Virgin Mary' (Bennett, *Lambert Simnel and the Battle of Stoke*, p. 6). As the insurgents were decisively defeated in the Battle of Stoke Field on 16 June 1487, the whole interlude was over in less than a month.

— duke of Clarence] Here referring to George Plantagenet, 1st duke of Clarence (1449–78).

— duchess of Burgundy] Margaret of York or Margaret of Burgundy (1446–1503) was duchess of Burgundy. She was the sister of Richard III, Edward IV and George Plantagenet, 1st duke of Clarence.

— House of York] A branch of the House of Plantagenet which overthrew the House of Lancaster and produced three kings of England – Edward IV, Edward V and Richard III. The House of York was succeeded by the Tudor dynasty.

— earl of Howth] Title in the Peerage of Ireland, before the eighteenth century the baron of Howth. Here referring to Nicholas St Lawrence, 4th baron of Howth (*c.*1460–1526), who warned Henry VII of the Simnel plot.

p. 99 Fitzgerald Tom] Sir Thomas FitzGerald of Laccagh (*c.*1458–87), brother of Gerald Fitzgerald, 8th earl of Kildare. Thomas FitzGerald was killed in the Battle of Stoke.

— Lincoln the Earl] John de la Pole, 1st earl of Lincoln (1462–87) who organised a Yorkist rebellion and was one of the leading figures supporting Simnel. He was killed in the Battle of Stoke.

— Lord Lovell] Francis Lovell, 1st viscount Lovell (1456–*c.*1487). Accompanied John de la Pole and Lambert Simnel to Ireland and fought on Simnel's side at the Battle of Stoke. He is thought to have escaped the battle, but it is uncertain if he survived.

p. 104 Jewish jargon] Variety of the German language characterised by the infusion of Hebrew and Yiddish expressions and often by an inverted syntax (in the German original: 'Jüdeln'). Used for satirical purposes and later with fervently anti-Semitic intention; in Jewish writing often employed to signal authenticity.

— Heine and Schnitzler, Swift and Shaw] The achievements of German writers of Jewish descent Heinrich Heine (1797–1856) and Arthur Schnitzler (1862–1931), as well as Irish-English writers Jonathan Swift (1667–1745) and George Bernard Shaw (1856–1950), are proof for Bermann that the adoption of a literary register is to be preferred to writing in either the minority languages Hebrew or Gaelic, or indeed the (allegedly) corrupted, slang versions of the standard languages, i.e. Jewish jargon and Hiberno-English respectively. It could be argued, though, that the particular richness of the named authors' registers is actually due to their (partial) rootedness in their Jewish or Irish (linguistic) cultures.

— Brehon law] Ancient native Irish law that was used in Gaelic areas until it was supplanted by English common law in the seventeenth century. Brehon Law developed from customs passed on orally from one generation to the next, and the laws were first written down in the seventh century. Brehons (judges) administered the law and acted as arbitrators.

— Jewish Territorialists] Territorialism was a secular branch of Zionism that promoted the acquisition of territory for Jewish settlement even outside Israel / Palestine – an idea spurned by the British offer in 1903 to make land in Uganda available for this purpose. The Jewish Territorialist Organisation was set up in 1905 and dissolved in 1925.

— Re-Orientalisation] Reference probably to the movement of Cultural Zionism that, though largely secular in orientation, promoted a cultural revival including a renaissance of Jewish literature and spirituality, and that allocated a role to Hebrew in this vision as language of general communication, not merely of scripture and ritual.

p. 105 democratic movement of 1848] Nationalist demands voiced during the revolutionary activities of 1848–9 in various regions of the Habsburg Empire included emancipation of national languages from the dominance of German in areas such as administration and education.

p. 106 Daibhi O'Bruodair] Important Irish-language poet of the seventeenth century. His poem *D'Aithle na bhFileadh* [The High Poets are Gone] laments the death of a fellow poet and also the decline of old Irish culture with respect to the poetic classes.

— Goldsmith] Oliver Goldsmith (1728–74), Anglo-Irish novelist, poet and playwright. His most famous work is *The Vicar of Wakefield* from 1766.

— Aodh Buidh MacCurtain] Seventeenth-century Irish poet from Clare. He spent some time on the continent and in 1728 published the first Irish grammar in English in Louvain.

— Goethe, Schiller and Grillparzer] German authors Johann Wolfgang von Goethe (1749–1832) and Johann Christoph Friedrich von Schiller (1759–1805) and Austrian author Franz Grillparzer (1791–1872), the towering classics of German letters who exerted a dominant influence over German and Austrian literature during and beyond the nineteenth century.

— Parnell, O'Connell and Redmond] All three were Irish nationalist politicians. Daniel O'Connell (1775–1847) led Irish Catholic demands for emancipation; following the Emancipation Act of 1829, he founded the Repeal Movement to repeal the Act of Union between Great Britain and Ireland. Charles Stewart Parnell (1846–91), nationalist politician of Anglo-Irish descent, was a member of the Irish Parliamentary Party, which was formed by Isaac Butt in 1874 with the aim of gaining legislative independence for Ireland. Parnell was also leader of the Home Rule League from 1880–2. Born into a Catholic gentry family, John Edward Redmond (1856–1918) was leader of the Irish Parliamentary Party from 1900 until 1918 as well as of the Irish National Volunteers.

p. 107 Beethoven, Nietzsche, Dumas] The 'van' in Ludwig van Beethoven's name is suggestive of his Flemish ancestry. His grandfather of the same name had in fact moved to Bonn from Mechelen almost forty years before Beethoven's birth in 1770. Friedrich Nietzsche himself claimed his distant ancestry to be Polish aristocracy, probably because of the similarity of his family name to that of a Polish noble who had moved to Saxony around 1700, almost one and a half centuries before Nietzsche's birth. Novelist Alexandre Dumas' father Thomas-Alexandre was born on Saint-Dominique as a natural child of Marquis Alexandre Antoine Davy de la Pailleterie and Marie-Cessette Dumas, a slave of Afro-Caribbean ancestry.

— Duke of Wellington] Arthur Wellesley, 1st duke of Wellington, was born in Dublin into an aristocratic Anglo-Irish family. The ancestral home of the Wellesley family is Dangan Castle in County Meath.

— 'My extraction is the extraction of most Englishmen'] George Bernard Shaw, *John Bull's Other Island*, 'Preface for Politicians'.

— commercially imported North Spanish strain] One legend contained in the *Lebor Gabála* [Book of Invasions, probably originating in the eleventh century] tells of an invasion by the sons of Míl Espáine (hence: Milesians). A *History of the Britons* (ninth century, Wales) traces the history of the Gaels back to Spain. This assertion plays a role in Irish political and identity debates ever since the early seventeenth century, when historian Geoffrey Keating resurrected the story of the Milesians, and hence a close connection between Spain and Ireland, to promote the legitimacy of the Stuart claim to royal power over Ireland. The reference to 'commercial' imports might allude to a conflation of legend with the visits of Phoenician trading ships on Irish shores.

p. 108   German translation by S. Fischer] *John Bulls andere Insel: Komödie*, transl. by Siegfried Trebisch (Berlin: S. Fischer, 1909).

p. 112   mutoscope] Coin-operated early motion picture device, patented in 1894, that used cards like a flip book. Viewed through a single lens, the contraption became popular in the peep-show business.

p. 114   Rubicon] River in the north-east of Italy. During the event that became known as the crossing of the Rubicon in 49 BC, Julius Caesar led his army across the Rubicon, then a northern boundary of Italy, thus defying the explicit orders of the Roman Senate to disband his army and return to Rome. This event triggered the Roman Civil War.

p. 115   Lord Macaulay's 'History of England'] Thomas Babington Macaulay's *History of England from the Accession of James the Second* (1848) was published in Leipzig, Germany, as part of Tauchnitz' 'Collection of British Authors' in 1849 in the English original.

— change from an old currency to a new one] Reference to the Great Recoinage of 1696 during which old and battered hand-struck silver coins were replaced by (regulated) forged coins.

— Sir Isaac Newton] (1643–1727) Influential English scientist. He was given the post of Master of the Mint in 1699 following his help in carrying out the Great Recoinage of 1696. He remained in this position until his death in 1727.

— red Everyman edition] Everyman's Library was founded in 1906 by Joseph Dent. Not all dust jackets of the pocket-size volumes were red.

— Stuart, James] See note on p. 55.

— Glorious Revolution] Revolution of 1688 whereby King James II of England was overthrown by English parliamentarians in alliance with William of Orange. King James II was replaced by his daughter Mary II and William of Orange, her husband.

p. 116   Thirty Years' War] Long and brutal conflict fought mainly in Central Europe from 1618 to 1648. It started out as a battle between Catholic and Protestant states in the Holy Roman Empire. The conflict turned into a more general power struggle between the European states, with most of the major powers from Sweden to France partaking in the conflict. Large mercenary armies were employed by the various states and the Thirty Years' War is believed to have resulted in eight million fatalities. The so-called Peace of Westphalia (negotiated in the cities of Münster and Osnabrück) ended the war and created a new balance of power in Europe.

— Beneath lay a valley] English original here reproduced from: Thomas Babington Macaulay, *The History of England from the Accession of James II*, vol. III (New York: Harper, 1856), p. 492.

— graveyard of Donore] Old Donore cemetery is located on the Hill of Donore in the Boyne Valley in County Louth. It dates back to medieval times, and was used by King James' camp during the Battle of the Boyne as a viewing spot.

— Bourbons] The House of Bourbon is an important ruling house of Europe of French origin. Its members are descendants of the fourteenth-century Louis I, duc de Bourbon. Bourbon kings first ruled France and Navarre in the sixteenth century, while in the eighteenth century, Spanish Bourbon kings and queens held thrones in Spain, Naples, Sicily and Parma. Currently, Spain and Luxembourg have monarchs from the House of Bourbon.

p. 118 Bruga] In Irish folklore, Bruga of the Boyne was a palace of Angus, a De Danann magician. The Tuatha de Danann were an ancient people who were said to have inhabited Ireland and believed to have possessed the power of magic. On account of Angus' magical powers, the palace could not be burned down, flooded or overcome by enemies.

— Finn MacCool] (Irish: Fionn MacCumhaill) Leader of the Fianna warriors in Irish mythology. The stories of Finn/Fionn and the Fianna form the Fenian Cycle (an Fhiannaíocht) and are set in the second to fourth centuries and are mostly narrated in the voice of the poet Oisín, Fionn's son. Stories linked to Fionn include *The Salmon of Knowledge* and *The Pursuit of Diarmuid and Gráinne*.

— Dermot O'Dyna] (Irish: Diarmuid Ua Duibhne, also known as Diarmuid of the Love Spot) According to legend, Dermot O'Dyna was a skilled member of the Fianna who killed thousands of warriors in battle to save Fionn and the Fianna. He is best known as Gráinne's lover, who was actually the intended wife of Fionn MacCumhaill.

— Later, though, Finn forgot that he owed Dermot] According to the legend *The Pursuit of Diarmuid and Gráinne*, Gráinne – the daughter of the high king of Ireland Cormac Mac Art – was promised to the ageing Fionn MacCumhaill. However, at the wedding feast she falls in love with Dermot O'Dyna on account of his beauty, and the pair run away together. Fionn pursues them around the country and eventually makes peace with the couple. However, many years later Fionn invites Dermot on a hunting trip and Dermot dies after being attacked by a boar.

p. 119 Lady Tyrconnel] Frances Talbot, countess of Tyrconnell (*c*.1647–1730), was an important figure at the Restoration court. She was born into an English Protestant gentry family, but converted to Catholicism and was instrumental in the foundation of several monasteries and religious communities in Ireland (Gratia Dei in Dublin and the Poor Clare and Dominican communities on the north side of the Liffey, Dublin).

— general Schomberg] Friedrich Schomberg (1615–90), son of a German count (Graf Meinhard von Schönberg), served in the Dutch, Swedish, French and Brandenburg armies before joining William of Orange on his expedition to England in 1688. He was created 1st duke of Schomberg a year later and served in Ireland as commander-in-chief of the Williamite forces.

p. 122   'Peut-être dans votre portefeuille, monsieur!'] 'Perhaps it's in your travel wallet'.

—   '*Futsch!*'] gone, bust, vanished.

p. 123   Lough Neagh] The largest lake in the British Isles by area, located in Northern Ireland.

p. 126   Navigation Acts] Acts of Navigation and Trade were started in 1651 and restored and tightened by acts in 1660, 1663, 1673, 1696 and thereafter. They were protectionist measures to safeguard and regulate shipping and commerce between England and other countries, and between England and her colonies. The acts stipulated, for example, that such trade only be carried out by English vessels manned with majority English crews.

p. 127   petition to King William in 1699] The Irish Woollen Export Prohibition Act of 1699 prohibited exporting Irish wool to England.

p. 128   master race of Ulster] The German original uses 'Herrenpartei', designating a community or 'party' in a given region or jurisdiction that considers itself entitled to dominate or master (cf. German: 'Herr', 'beherrschen') the rest of the population.

—   dreadnought] see note on p. 40.

p. 130   daytime overcoat] Since the 1830s heavy, warm, hard-wearing and sporty double-breasted overcoats were known in German as 'Ulsters', perhaps because of the use of Donegal (tweed) fabric. In contrast to its English namesake, the German 'Ulster' did not sport a cape.

—   Sir Edward Carson] (1854–1935) see note on p. 80.

p. 132   Siege of Derry] Conflict during the Williamite War between William of Orange and James II. Jacobite forces besieged the town in 1688–9 and tried to starve it out following failed attempts to attack it. Three ships, *The Phoenix*, *The Mountjoy* and *The Jerusalem*, rammed the barricades on the River Foyle, providing provisions for the townspeople and ending the siege after 105 days.

—   Boer War] Here the second Boer War 1899–1902 is meant. This reference will have struck a particular chord with readers, since the German public enthusiastically and overwhelmingly supported the cause of the tiny African republics against the global superpower.

—   Conservative governments] Edward Carson entered parliament in 1892 when the Liberal Gladstone formed his fourth ministry. The marquess of Salisbury and thereafter Arthur Balfour led Conservative governments from 1895 to 1905, when the Liberals again formed a (minority) ministry that lasted until the outbreak of the First World War. Carson obtained his knighthood upon his appointment as solicitor-general for England in 1900. At the end of the Conservative government in 1905, he was rewarded with membership of the Privy Council, the college of advisers to the British monarch.

—   Privy Council] Body of advisers to the monarch of the United Kingdom, usually consisting of senior politicians.

p. 134   Kipling] Rudyard Kipling (1865–1936); probably refers to Kipling's short story 'The Mutiny of the Mavericks' (1891). The story tells how Mulcahy, an agent of an Irish-American republican association, is sent to instigate mutiny against the British among Irish soldiers in India. The Irish soldiers, however, are deeply loyal to their regiment and recognise Mulcahy's aims. They nevertheless also realise that he is a good source of alcohol and allow him to believe they are on his side. The regiment is called to active service and Mulcahy thinks the mutiny is about to happen; however, the Irish soldiers are delighted to go into battle and Mulcahy is sent off with them, subsequently dying in combat.

— Lloyd George] During the Asquith government (see note on p. 12), David Lloyd George (1863–1945) served as chancellor of the exchequer (1908–15).

p. 136 ultramontanism] Literally: beyond the mountains, originally used to identify non-Italian popes. From the eighteenth century onwards its increasingly polemical usage denounced political forces allegedly beholden to the prerogatives and authority of the pope, i.e. receiving their political orders from the other side of the Alps.

p. 137 Covenant] Ulster's Solemn League and Covenant, commonly known as the Ulster Covenant, was signed by nearly 500,000 people on and before 28 September 1912, in protest against the Third Home Rule Bill. Sir Edward Carson was the first person to sign the Covenant at Belfast City Hall, with a silver pen, followed by Lord Londonderry (the former viceroy of Ireland), representatives of the Protestant churches, and then by Sir James Craig.

p. 138 Asquith] Herbert Henry Asquith (1852–1928), Liberal politician, served as prime minister of the United Kingdom 1908–16.

— John Redmond] see note on p. 106.

p. 141 Napoleonic Wars] Here refers to the Congress of Vienna that took place after Napoleon's defeat in 1815. A post-war political order was decided that also changed the borders and sizes of several smaller territories inside the former Holy Roman Empire.

— 1866] The Austro-Prussian War of 1866 marked the penultimate step (before the Franco-Prussian War of 1870–1) on Germany's path towards unification. The result, an Austrian defeat, ensured Austria's exclusion from the prospective German Reich. The kingdom of Bavaria and several other German principalities were allied with Austria.

p. 142 Drake] Francis Drake (1540–96) was a captain and privateer. Appointed vice-admiral by Elizabeth I, he served as second-in-command of the British fleet in the battle against the Spanish Armada in 1588.

p. 143 Holy Inquisition] Generic term for a system of policing within the structures of the Catholic Church aimed at combating heresy by detecting and prosecuting heretics of all ilks, from Cathars in France to Hussites in Bohemia. Mostly led by Dominican friars, the Inquisition gained particular importance in the struggle against the Reformation, and it achieved notoriety for the cruelty of its methods (torture) and severity of its punishments (burning) on the Iberian peninsula – among other things in its persecution of converted Muslims and Jews.

p. 144 Huguenots] French Protestants. The Edict of Nantes (1598) granted the mainly Calvinist Protestants of France substantial rights (without enshrining complete equality with Catholics). The edict was revoked by Louis XIV in 1685, which led to mass emigration of Huguenots. The remaining Protestants had to suffer considerable discrimination. The French Enlightenment writer Voltaire (1694–1778) advocated freedom of religion.

— English Church Party / Education Act of 1902] The Education Act of 1902 provided funding for denominational religious instruction in elementary schools, thereby effectively handing over primary education in England, Wales and Ireland to the churches (Anglican and Catholic). The main movers within British conservatism behind this measure to stop the spread of secularism were known as the Church Party.

p. 145 Fenians] Umbrella term for Irish nationalists, originally those organised in secretive organisations such as the Irish Republican Brotherhood and its American branch the Fenian Brotherhood (both founded 1858). The term is derived from the name of the tales (Fenian Cycle) of Fionn MacCumhaill (see note on p. 118) and his warrior band, the Fianna.

— Holy Synod] Governing body (college of bishops) in Orthodox and Eastern Catholic churches. Here used more generally as assembly of Christian churches.

— Jacobins] Political faction during the French Revolution. Their ascendancy in the Revolutionary government (the Welfare Committee) is associated with the *Terreur*, the Reign of Terror, when the guillotine operated virtually non-stop.

p. 146   Jim Larkin] (1876–1947) Leading early organiser of the Irish labour movement (co-founder of the Irish Labour Party and two trade unions). He also founded the Irish Citizen Army, a militia that played a role in the Dublin Lockout of 1913 (an event that was unfolding while Bermann travelled in Ireland) and in the Easter Rising of 1916.

p. 148   Fingal's Cave on Staffa] Sea cave on the uninhabited island of Staffa, in the Inner Hebrides of Scotland. It became known as Fingal's Cave after the eponymous hero of an epic poem by eighteenth-century Scots poet James Macpherson.

— Finn MacCool] see note on p. 118.

p. 149   Rathlin] Island off the coast of County Antrim. It is the northernmost part of Northern Ireland and located just 25 kilometres from the southern tip of Scotland's Kintyre peninsula.

p. 151   Postcard] Though many songs and poems on the Giant's Causeway have been written (among the earliest a 200 pages-long ode by William Hamilton Drummond, *The Giants' Causeway: A poem* (Belfast, 1811), and a hymn by Letitia Elizabeth Landon, *Fisher's Drawing Room Scrap Book* (London, 1831), p. 43), the English original of Bermann's German verses, should it exist, could not be established.

p. 152   Hall Caine] Thomas Henry Hall Caine (1853–1931) was one of the best-selling authors of his time, author of fifteen novels and numerous plays, several of which were turned into films. Many of his novels appeared in English in Germany (in Tauchnitz' English Library), several others were translated into German: *The Bondman* (1891) as *Der Bürge* (1909), *Drink: A love story on a great question* (1901) as *Die Trunksüchtige* (1907), *The Eternal City* (1901) as *Die Ewige Stadt* (1904), *The Prodigal Son* (1904) as *Der verlorene Sohn* (1904). Many of the German versions enjoyed numerous print runs; most were published by Degener in Leipzig.

p. 153   Manx] Celtic language of the Indo-European language family that was spoken as a first language on the Isle of Man until the death of the last native speaker in 1974.

— Deemster] Title in the judicial system of the Isle of Man, chair of the High Court and co-chair of the Appeal division of that court.

— Thing] Governing assembly in early Germanic societies. The Manx form 'tyn' (or rather: Tynwald) is the name of the legislative bodies on the Isle of Man.

— Lehár] Ferenc/Franz Lehár (1870–1948) was an Austro-Hungarian composer, best known for his over forty operettas, among them *The Merry Widow* (1905), *Count Luxembourg* (1909), *Gipsy Love* (1910), *The Land of Smiles* (1929).

p. 154   Sicilian coat of arms] Known as a Triseklion or Trinacria, the Sicilian coat of arms shows the head of Medusa surrounded by three bent legs on a yellow and red surface. It was adopted in 1282 as the national emblem. On the Manx coat of arms, the legs are armoured and the background is red; there is no head. It also came into use in the late thirteenth century.

p. 155   Marina Villa] Located on the Harris Promenade, Douglas, the Villa Marina Kursaal, as it was known then, had in fact been reopened as an entertainment venue only days before Bermann visited the Isle of Man, namely on 19 July 1913.

— House of Keys] Lower House of the legislature (Tynwald) of the Isle of Man.

— Regum Manniae et Insularum] The medieval Kingdom of Mann and the Isles (or Kingdom of the Southern Isles) comprised the Hebrides, islands in the Firth of Clyde and the Isle of Man. Gaelic and Viking lords ruled over these lands either independently or as vassals of Viking overlords in various forms between the ninth and the twelfth century.

— House of Stanley] From the early fifteenth to the mid-eighteenth century, members of the Stanley family held the title king or lord of Mann. The latter was sold back to the crown in 1736, so that ever since, the English monarch has held the title. In 1485, Thomas Stanley was created 1st earl of Derby. He was the last to use the title king of Mann.

— *The Manxman*] Novel (1894) by Hall Caine (see note on p. 152). Published in English by Tauchnitz in Leipzig in the same year. A German translation appeared in 1901 under the title *Der Oberrichter* [The Chief Justice]. It was turned into a film of the same title in 1929 by Alfred Hitchcock.

p. 156   Snaefell] The Isle of Man's highest peak at 621 metres. The Snaefell Mountain Railway has been in operation since 1895, joining the village of Laxey with the summit of Snaefell on an 8-kilometre stretch of railway.

— Greeba Castle] Built in 1849 in neo-Gothic castellated style. Novelist Hall Caine rented it in 1894 and purchased the property two years later. It remained his residence until his death in 1931.

p. 157   Mannanan Mac y Leir] Sea god in Manx, Scottish and Irish legend ('son of the sea'), whose name might be derived from the island, or the island might have been named after him.

— Orry] Godred Crovan (d. 1095) was a Norse-Gaelic ruler of the Kingdom of the Isles (see note on p. 155), which he extended to also include Dublin. Founder of the Crovan dynasty that ruled in the Isles for almost two centuries until it was annexed by King Alexander III of Scotland in 1266. Godred may well be identical to the celebrated King Orry of Manx legend, a figure traditionally credited with instituting the Manx legal system.

p. 158   If you want to understand a poet's country] Bermann plays here with Goethe's well-known aphorism (*West-Östlicher Diwan*, 1819, p. 241) 'wer den Dichter will verstehn / muß in Dichters Lande gehn' [When you want to understand the poet, you have to visit his country] from a poem entitled 'Besserem Verständniß' [For Better Understanding].

p. 160   Viceroy's summer residence] Built in 1751 in the Phoenix Park near Dublin, the building was acquired in 1782 for the viceroys, the British crown's governors of Ireland, and served as their residence until 1922. In 1938 it became the official residence of the presidents of the Republic of Ireland (Áras an Uachtaráin).

p. 162   Erzgebirge Mountains] Literally 'Ore mountains', mountain range (highest peak 1,244 metres) in the east-westerly direction on the border between the German state of Saxony and the Czech Republic, formerly Bohemia.

— Carrickmacross lace] A decorative form of lace first introduced to Ireland in 1820 by Mrs Grey Porter. Following the Famine, a lace school was set up on the Carrickmacross estates in County Monaghan as a way of helping the starving tenants, and thereafter the lace became popular.

Riviera di Levante] see note on p. 43.

p. 164   Thirty Years' War] see note on p. 116.

p. 165   P.W. Joyce's collection of ancient Celtic tales] *Old Celtic Romances*, translated from
the Gaelic by Patrick Weston Joyce (London, 1879). The text reproduced here is on
pp. 106–11. The (very faithful) German translation given in the original must have
been Bermann's own, since in 1913 no German edition of Joyce's book was extant.

p. 169   Kyffhäuser] Small range of hills in central Germany (highest elevation Kufenberg
473 metres). In popular mythology, it is the resting place of Emperor Frederick
Barbarossa (see note on p. 96), who will emerge from his sleep in Germany's
greatest hour of need. Nationalist ideology promulgated that, by the unification of
Germany in 1871, Barbarossa was finally 'laid to rest'.

Further Reading

Modern Editions and English Titles

Bermann, Richard A., *The Mahdi of Allah: The story of the dervish Mohammed Ahmed*, transl. by Robin John (London: Putnam, 1931). Issued in the United States as *The Mahdi of Allah: A drama of the Sudan* (New York: Macmillan, 1932)

Höllriegel, Arnold, *Die Derwischtrommel: Das Leben des erwarteten Mahdi*, ed. by Florian Krobb (Berlin: Die Andere Bibliothek, 2019)

Bermann, Richard A., alias Arnold Höllriegel, *Die Fahrt auf dem Katarakt: Eine Autobiographie ohne einen Helden*, ed. by Hans-Harald Müller (Vienna: Picus, 1998) [first publication of Bermann's unfinished autobiography and selected other autobiographical pieces and sources]

Bermann, Richard A., alias Arnold Höllriegel, *Hollywood – Wien und zurück*, ed. by Hans-Harald Müller and Andreas Stuhlmann (Vienna: Picus, 1999) [a well-annotated representative selection of Bermann's journalistic work]

Bermann, Richard A., alias Arnold Höllriegel, *Zarzura: Die Oase der kleinen Vögel*, ed. by Michael Farin and Andreas Stuhlmann (Munich: belleville, 2003) [contains Hans Casparius' impressive photos as well as previously unpublished letters and documents]

Höllriegel, Arnold, *Amerika-Bilderbuch*, ed. by Michael Grisko for the Deutsches Exilarchiv (Göttingen: Wallstein, 2012)

Bermann, Richard A., alias Arnold Höllriegel, *Österreicher – Demokrat – Weltbürger: Eine Ausstellung des Deutschen Exilarchivs 1933–1945* (Frankfurt / Main: Die deutsche Bibliothek / Munich: Saur, 1995) [rich pictorial material and biographical sources]

Krobb, Florian, 'Exotik, Geschichtsrelativismus, Kolonialismuskritik: Arnold Höllriegels Epos *Die Derwischtrommel*', *Wirkendes Wort*, vol. 67, no. 2, 2017, pp. 247–67

Krobb, Florian, '"ein Kodak mit einer wilden Phantasie": Richard Arnold
    Bermann / Arnold Höllriegel', *Österreichische Kultur und Literatur der 20er
    Jahre – transdisziplinär: Ein Epochenprofil* (2018), http://litkult1920er.aau.
    at/?q=portraits/arnold-hoellriegel [contains an introduction to Bermann /
    Höllriegel's life and work plus a comprehensive bibliography]
Kucher, Primus-Heinz, 'Radio-Literatur und Medienromane im Zeichen der
    Medienrevolution der 1920er Jahre: Die Radiowelt-Diskussion. A. Höllriegels
    Hollywood-Feuilleton-Roman und F. Rosenfelds Filmroman *Die goldene
    Galeere*', in Primus-Heinz Kucher and Julia Bertschik (eds), *'baustelle kultur':
    Diskurslagen in der österreichischen Literatur, 1918–1933/38* (Bielefeld:
    Aisthesis, 2011), pp. 349–74
Müller, Hans-Harald, 'Ariel, Baptist, Belial, Merlin, Höllriegel – Richard
    A. Bermann: der Publizist und Schriftsteller', in Hartmut Binder (ed.),
    Brennpunkt Berlin: Prager Schriftsteller in der deutschen Metropole (Bonn:
    Kulturstiftung der Vertriebenen, 1995), pp. 145–75
Müller, Hans-Harald, 'Richard A. Bermann alias Arnold Höllriegel: Österreicher
    – Demokrat – Weltbürger', *Exil*, vol. 15, no. 2, 1995, pp. 5–16
Stuhlmann, Andreas, '"Das Jahrhundert der Technik hat seinen Dichter gefunden":
    Der österreichische Schriftsteller und Journalist R.A. Bermann (alias
    Arnold Höllriegel) als Anwalt und Kritiker des Kinos', *LiLi. Zeitschrift für
    Literaturwissenschaft und Linguistik*, vol. 27, no. 3, 1997, pp. 154–65

GERMAN TRAVEL WRITING ON IRELAND

Bourke, Eoin, '"Paddy and Pig": German travel writers in the "wild west", 1828–
    1858', *Journal of the Galway Archaeological and Historical Society*, vol. 53, 2001,
    pp. 145–55
Bourke, Eoin, 'England's backyard: Vormärz travel writers on the Irish question', in
    Detlev Kopp (ed.), *Wege in die Moderne: Reiseliteratur von Schriftstellerinnen
    und Schriftstellern des Vormärz* (Bielefeld: Aisthesis, 2009), pp. 217–28
    (Forum Vormärz Forschung, 14)
Bourke, Eoin, *Poor Green Erin: German travel writers' narratives on Ireland from
    before the 1798 Rising to after the Great Famine*, ed. and transl. by Eoin Bourke
    (Frankfurt / Main: Lang, 2011)
Dohmen, Doris, *Das deutsche Irlandbild: Imagologische Untersuchungen
    zur Darstellung Irlands und der Iren in der deutschsprachigen Literatur*
    (Amsterdam and Atlanta: Rodopi, 1994) (Studia Imagologica, 6)
Fischer, Joachim, *Das Deutschlandbild der Iren, 1890–1939: Geschichte, Form,
    Funktion* (Heidelberg: Winter, 2000) (Anglistische Forschungen, 284)

Fischer, Joachim, 'The Austrian who Stayed in the Lakeside Hotel in 1913, or, Why Richard Bermann Never Went to Killaloe', *Tipperary Historical Journal*, 2019, pp. 121–31

Holfter, Gisela, *Erlebnis Irland: Deutsche Reiseberichte über Irland im zwanzigsten Jahrhundert* (Trier: Wissenschaftlicher Verlag, 1996) (Grenzüberschreitungen: Studien zur europäischen Reiseliteratur, 5)

Holfter, Gisela and Hermann Rasche, 'German Travel Literature about Ireland: The saga continues', in Jane Conroy (ed.), *Cross-Cultural Travel: Papers from the Royal Irish Academy International Symposium on Literature and Travel* (New York: Lang, 2003), pp. 459–68 (Travel Writing Across the Disciplines: Theory and Pedagogy, 7)

Hünseler, Wolfgang, *Das deutsche Kaiserreich und die irische Frage, 1900–1914* (Frankfurt / Main: Lang, 1978) (Europäische Hochschulschriften III, 106)

Kabdebo, Thomas, *Ireland and Hungary: A study in parallels*, with an Arthur Griffith bibliography (Dublin: Four Courts Press, 2001)

Klieneberger, H.R., 'Ireland through German Eyes, 1844–1957: The travel-diaries of Jakob Venedey and Heinrich Böll', *An Irish Quarterly Review*, vol. 49, no. 196, 1960, pp. 373–88

Kluge, Hans-Dieter, *Irland in der deutschen Geschichtswissenschaft: Politik und Propaganda vor 1914 und im Ersten Weltkrieg* (Frankfurt / Main: Lang, 1985) (Europäische Hochschulschriften III, 268)

Ó Dochartaigh, Pól, *Julius Pokorny, 1887–1970: Germans, Celts and nationalism* (Dublin: Four Courts Press, 2004)

Oehlke, Andrea, *Irland und die Iren in deutschen Reisebeschreibungen des 18. und 19. Jahrhunderts* (Frankfurt / Main: Lang, 1991) (Münsteraner Monographien zur englischen Literatur, 10)

Prill, Felician, *Ireland, Britain and Germany, 1870–1914: Problems of nationalism and religion in nineteenth-century Europe* (Dublin: Gill & Macmillan, 1975)

Rasche, Hermann, '"…A Strange Spectacle…": German travellers to the west, 1828–1858', *Journal of the Galway Archaeological and Historical Society*, vol. 47, 1995, pp. 87–107

Wheatley, Leesa, *Forging Ireland: German travel writing, 1785–1850* (Trier: Wissenschaftlicher Verlag, 2018) (Irish-German Studies, 10)

Woods, Christopher J., 'Select Documents XLI: Johann Friedrich Hering's description of Connacht, 1806–7', *Irish Historical Studies*, vol. 25, no. 99, 1987, pp. 311–21

aan de Wiel, Jérôme, *The Irish Factor, 1899–1919: Ireland's strategic and diplomatic importance for foreign powers* (Dublin: Irish Academic Press, 2008)

aan de Wiel, Jérôme, 'What Will the British Do? The Irish Home Rule crisis in the July crisis', *International History Review*, vol. 37, no. 4, 2015, pp. 657–81

Index